THE FIRST 100 WOMEN LAWYERS IN MISSISSIPPI

A publication of
THE MISSISSIPPI BAR
WOMEN IN THE PROFESSION COMMITTEE

Melanie Henry, *Managing Editor*
Maggie Traxler, *Associate Editor*
Deanne Mosley, *Executive Director*

THE NAUTILUS PUBLISHING COMPANY
OXFORD, MISSISSIPPI

ON THE COVER

1. Mary Chapman Easterling
2. Betty Bartee Tucker
3. Edythe Evelyn Gandy
4. Evelyn Hunt Conner
5. Susie Blue Buchanan

6. Mary Sue Brannon
7. Nell Wilkinson Hunt
8. Clare Sekul Hornsby
9. Zelda Siegel Labovitz
10. Viola Lee James Hilbert

11. Ruth Leola Chrismond Franck
12. Martha Wilson Gerald
13. Vivian Cook
14. Linda Rives Brown Witherington
15. Lucy Somerville Howorth

The Mississippi Bar
Physical address: 643 North State Street, Jackson, MS 39202
Mailing address: P.O. Box 2168, Jackson, MS 39225-2168
Phone: 601-948-4471

Mission Statement: The Mississippi Bar shall serve the public good by promoting excellence in the profession and in our system of justice.
Vision: The Mississippi Bar is an invaluable partner in every attorney's practice and a trusted community leader that ensures the justice system is evolving to meet the needs of all Mississippi residents.
Goal 1: The Mississippi Bar promotes the highest standards of competence and professionalism, and fosters a legal profession equipped to serve the legal needs of clients and the larger community
Goal 2: The Mississippi Bar cultivates members' professional success with valuable practice resources and opportunities for meaningful member engagement
Goal 3: The Mississippi Bar fosters diversity and inclusion among members of the bar community
Goal 4: The Mississippi Bar strives to increase access to legal services and to promote and support a justice system that affords prompt and fair resolution
Goal 5: The Mississippi Bar builds public trust in the justice system through education about lawyers and the law
Goal 6: The Mississippi Bar sustains a responsive, flexible organization that advances its mission and the strategic plan

Published through a partnership with The Nautilus Publishing Company, 426 S. Lamar Blvd., Suite 16, Oxford, MS 38655. The publisher wishes to thank Kris Gilliland and the University of Mississippi Law School for references and sources cited from: "Dared to Enter a Man's World:" Mississippi Women Lawyers, 1914-1964, 85 *Miss. L.J.* 1479 (2016-2017) (with Bette Bradley & Ellie Campbell).

ISBN: 978-1-949455-24-3

...s dedicated to all Mississippi women lawyers

...the female Mississippi lawyer lives:
...or the cause that needs assistance;
...or the wrongs that lack resistance;
For the future in the distance
For the good that she can do.

Loosely adapted from the 1915 Mississippi Bar report
of the Welcome Address at the 1915 Annual Convention

DONORS

Pillars

Mississippi Bar Foundation
The Mississippi Bar

Trailblazers

Fellows of the Young Lawyers of The Mississippi Bar

Pioneers

Women in the Profession Committee of The Mississippi Bar
Young Lawyers Division of The Mississippi Bar

Champions

Susie Blue Buchanan Sponsorship Level

1st female lawyer licensed to practice before the Mississippi Supreme Court

Melanie Henry	Joy Lambert Phillips
Jessica E. Murray	Webb Sanders & Williams

Evelyn Gandy Sponsorship Level

1st female lawyer elected state representative, state treasurer, insurance commissioner, and lieutenant governor of Mississippi

Justice Dawn Beam	Kay B. Cobb	Joy Lambert Phillips
Dean Pat Bennett	Attorney General Lynn Fitch	Jennifer Hughes Scott
Jenifer Branning	Jennifer Ingram Johnson	Temperance and Christopher Steiskal
	Ann Odom	

Lucy Harrison Greaves Sponsorship Level

1st female member of The Mississippi Bar

Renee Harrison Berry	Melanie Henry	Amarette Speights
Meta S. Copeland	Joy Lambert Phillips	Maxey Wann PLLC
Meredith Gowan Le Goff	Jennifer McGuire Rogers	

Clare Sekul Hornsby Sponsorship Level

1st female Local Bar Association President

Capital Area Bar Association	Cynthia S. Joachim	Karen Sawyer
Dulin and Dulin, LTD	Jane Meynardie	Judge Rhea Hudson Sheldon
Chris Gouras	Joy Lambert Phillips	Margaret H. Williams

Mary Libby Payne Sponsorship Level

1st female Mississippi College Law School Dean

M.J. Alexander	Cecile C. Edwards	Judge Mary Libby Payne
Betty Arinder	Shannon Sojourner Elliott	Felecia Perkins
Judge Sharion Aycock	Patti and Johnny Gandy	Joy Lambert Phillips
Chief Judge Donna M. Barnes	Judge Veldore Young Graham	Rachelle S. Richardson
Dean Pat Bennett	Karen Noblitt Haarala	Ellen Robb
Tangi Carter	Rebecca Hawkins	Jim Rosenblatt
Beth Clay	Melanie Henry	Lindsey Tew Simmons
Kay B. Cobb	Jennifer Ingram Johnson	Emmy Harper Stone
Senator Sally Doty	Ammie Nguyen	Anne Porter Veazey

Joy Lambert Phillips Sponsorship Level

1st female Mississippi Bar President

Debbie Bell	Stephanie Jones	Adrian Smith
Dean Pat Bennett	Juanita P. Kuhner	Christine B. Tatum
Michele D. Biegel	Blythe K. Lollar	Linda A. Thompson
Lynda C. Carter, Wise Carter	Judge Jacqueline Mask	Amanda Jones Tollison
Child & Caraway	Nicole McLaughlin	Lynda Traxler
Kay B. Cobb	Lisa L. Meggs	Katie Ryan Van Camp
Michael T. Dawkins	Judge Robin Alfred Midcalf	Margaret H. Williams
Anna Furr Dexter	Cynthia Mitchell	Courtney P. Wilson
Leyser Q. Hayes	Nancy Morse Parkes	Allyson Lambert Winter
Melanie Henry	Frank Phillips	

Lenore Loving Prather Sponsorship Level

1st female Mississippi Supreme Court Chief Justice

Judge Sharion Aycock	Deborah S. Davis	Ellen Harvey McLean
Justice Dawn Beam	Cecile C. Edwards	Elise B. Munn
Dean Pat Bennett	Jan F. Gadow	Joy Lambert Phillips
Karen G. Clay	Bettie Ruth Johnson	Jennifer Skipper
Kay B. Cobb	Allison Pritchard Kizer	Anne L. Turner

Zelma Wells Price Sponsorship Level

1st female Judge in Mississippi

Martin and Annie Edwards	Joy Lambert Phillips
Judge Tiffany Grove	Kelly Hollingsworth Stringer

Constance Slaughter-Harvey Sponsorship Level

1st female African American Judge in Mississippi

Felicia C. Adams	Leyser Q. Hayes	Felecia Perkins
M.J. Alexander	Melanie Henry	Joy Lambert Phillips
Debbie Bell	Jennifer Ingram Johnson	Diane Pradat Pumphrey
Dean Pat Bennett	Susan Shands Jones	Kenya Key Rachal
Margaret Bretz	Catherine V. Kilgore	Judge Betty W. Sanders
Judge Debra Brown	Tara L. Lang	Judge W. M. Sanders
Melissa Thrash Carleton	Cynthia T. Lee	Susan M. Scaggs
Meta Cooper Danzey	Maron Marvel Bradley Anderson &	Janet R. Self
La'Verne Edney	Tardy LLC	Lillous A. Shoemaker
RaToya Gilmer	Judge Robin Alfred Midcalf	Vicki R. Slater
Judge Veldore Young Graham	Angela Miller	Constance Slaughter-Harvey
Tiffany M. Graves	Elise B. Munn	Nina Stubblefield Tollison
Kimberly McCray Hampton	Kimberly Nailor	Vangela Mechelle Wade
		Victoria V. Washington

Bessie Young Sponsorship Level

1st female University of Mississippi Law School graduate

Katherine Collier	Mary Margaret Kuhlmann	Ginger Weaver
Mary Kathryn Ford	Kathryn Kyle Moody	Thomas P. Welch, Jr.
	Joy Lambert Phillips	

First 100 Champion Sponsorship Level

Lilli A. Bass	Jennifer Hall	Wendy Mullins
Catherine B. Bell	Laurel Li Harris	Melissa Selman Scott
Carla J. Clark	Lindsey Herr	Catherine Servati
Jessica Carr Culpepper	Helen Maureen McDonald	Gina Bardwell Tompkins
Robert Galloway,	Mississippi Women Lawyers Association	Margaret H. Williams
in honor of Ann Bowden	Deanne M. Mosley	

CONTENTS

THE FIRST 100

1. Lucy Harrison Greaves	1914	
2. Mary Chapman Easterling	1915	
3. Bessie Young	1915	
4. Nettie Hood Bratton	1916	
5. Susie Blue Buchanan	1916	
6. Linda Rives Brown Witherington	1916	
7. Sara Lou Buchanan	1917	
8. Leota Angelina Taylor Kirkpatrick	1918	
9. Virginia Ruth Campbell	1919	
10. Abbede Sessions Peebles	1921	
11. Lucy Robinson Somerville Howorth	1922	
12. Vivian Cook	1922	
13. Ruth L. Bertrand	1922	
14. Eleanore Sophia Babendreer Moore	1922	
15. Lavonia Caradine Jiggitts Jones	1924	
16. Mary Gladys Hoover Williams	1925	
17. Nell Wilkinson Hunt	1926	
18. Evelyn Hunt Conner	1928	
19. Willie Yeates Rylee Pilcher	1928	
20. Margaret Hervey Jones Graham	1928	
21. Zelma Wells Price	1929	
22. Julia Ann Pollard Sheldon Griffin	1930	
23. Tommie Leverett Hays	1930	
24. Lyda Gordon Shivers	1930	
25. Lucille Brown	1931	
26. Pearl Marie McLellan	1931	
27. Anna Clara Melton Sims	1931	
28. Martha Louise Melton	1931	
29. Alice Lee "Allee" Dunn	1931	
30. Lena Carolina Zama	1931	
31. Ida Lou Simmons Lewis	1931	
32. Winifred (Winnie) Davis Greer	1931	
33. Ruth Leola Chrismond Franck	1932	
34. Elizabeth Gwin Kirschten	1933	
35. Helen Patricia Maltby Lumpkin	1934	
36. Elizabeth Watkins Hulen Grayson	1934	
37. Louise Mayo	1935	
38. Mary Sue Brannon	1935	
39. Matelyn Floyd Hines	1936	
40. Edna Loeb Friedman Fischer	1936	
41. Marguerite Ardella Williams	1936	
42. Josephine Louise Hood	1936	
43. Zelda Siegel Labovitz	1937	
44. Rhoda Catherine Bass	1937	
45. Betty Bartee Tucker	1938	
46. Lulie Reynolds Eddins Walker	1938	
47. Mary Caruthers Gholson Berger	1939	
48. Viola Lee James Hilbert	1939	
49. Doris Chastine Hartford	1939	
50. Sarah Adeline Chalk Tipping	1940	

51. Zulah Mayo Purvis	1941	
52. Genevieve Yonkers Schaffer	1941	
53. Mary Elizabeth West	1942	
54. Helen May Bloedorn	1942	
55. May Spencer Ringold	1942	
56. Alice Porter Nevels	1942	
57. Margaret Norman Yarborough McLean	1942	
58. Ivy Lee Buchanan	1942	
59. Sarah A. Charles	1942	
60. Martha Virginia Clarke Bunting	1942	
61. Edythe Evelyn Gandy	1943	
62. Hilda Howell	1943	
63. Lottie M. Steele	1943	
64. Ruth Rose Miller Deterly	1943	
65. Adeline N. Morris	1943	
66. Zelma Wells Price Schuetta	1943	
67. Dessie E. McManus	1943	
68. Martha Wilson Gerald	1944	
69. Allie D. Zeller	1944	
70. Bonnie Earline Smith	1944	
71. Marie Luter Upton	1944	
72. Cecile Cambre Alford	1944	
73. Lura Mae Womack	1944	
74. Dolsie Earlene Williams Doerr	1944	
75. Margaret E. Fisher	1945	
76. Virginia C. Searcy	1945	
77. Clare Sekul Hornsby	1945	
78. Walterrene Price Roderick	1945	
79. Mary Frances Ray Holloway	1945	
80. Ethel Ramsey Arrington	1945	
81. Maxine Brunn Crain	1946	
82. Elsie Cambre Parker Purser	1946	
83. Iva Lea Stringer Greer	1946	
84. Mary Emma Bullock McGee	1946	
85. Martha Rose Moffitt Parsons	1946	
86. Lottie Berniece Russell Pickard	1946	
87. Aline Jones Collum	1946	
88. Josephine Myrick Jameson	1946	
89. Claribel Hunt Moncure	1946	
90. Helen Daniel White	1947	
91. Mildred Wells Norris	1947	
92. Amy Burkett	1947	
93. Helen Jacobs McDade	1947	
94. Marguerite L. Williams	1947	
95. Nannie-Mayes Crump	1947	
96. Frances Porter Cunningham	1947	
97. Virginia I. Ferguson	1948	
98. Tillie Odom Nixon	1948	
99. Rose Price May	1948	
100. Rosalind Dottery Sanders	1949	

FROM THE WOMEN IN THE PROFESSION COMMITTEE OF THE MISSISSIPPI BAR

The roots of our women in the profession began with these 100 pioneers . . . these 100 trailblazers . . . these 100 women lawyers.

The *First 100 Women Lawyers in Mississippi* tells the stories of 100 women's lives spanning across the first four decades of the 20th century. The book follows these women as they broke ground, blazed trails and established themselves as members of the legal profession in Mississippi in the 1910s, 1920s, 1930s, and 1940s. From the first lawyer to the first judge, and every milestone in between, these women bravely built the foundation for future generations of women lawyers. Those of us who practice in Mississippi today are forever indebted to these pioneers. The significance of the challenges they faced—merely to practice within their chosen profession—can never be overstated.

One hundred years ago, Mississippi women gained the right to vote. One hundred years later, we recognize and celebrate these first 100 women lawyers in Mississippi and the 100 "firsts" - identifying the first female attorney in Mississippi to achieve a professional legal milestone. These diverse women broke the legal profession's glass ceiling and changed the modern legal landscape in Mississippi. These are women attorneys who, in courtrooms, classrooms, government agencies, and organizations, positively contributed to the legal profession.

It is our hope that the stories of these women will inspire future generations to protect the advances they made for women and continue their efforts to improve the status of women in the legal profession.

This has been a rewarding project for the Women in the Profession Committee. We owe a tremendous amount of gratitude to Melanie Henry, Maggie Traxler, and others who have labored tirelessly to bring the stories of these women to print.

While we celebrate the great accomplishments of Mississippi's first 100 women lawyers and the struggles they had to endure in their quest for professional equality, we invite you to renew your commitment to achieving true equality for all under the law. Their agenda is unfinished, so we must not become complacent. Our profession, our practices and our communities will be better for it and history will shine down on us for doing it.

The Mississippi Bar Women in the Profession Committee Chairs:

Tiffany Graves
Committee Chair 2014-2016

Judge Tiffany Grove
Committee Chair 2016-2018

Jennifer Hall
Committee Chair 2018-2021

FROM THE EDITOR

The beginning was November 2006, when I had just two more chapters to complete for The Mississippi Bar's *A Legacy of Service* book celebrating the Bar's Centennial. Everything had to be completed by December 24th to send off to the printers. I was at the Mississippi Department of Archives and History building in Jackson doing research for the final chapters. Governor William Winter was in the lobby autographing his latest book. At the copy machine was my friend, Carol West, a law professor at Mississippi College School of Law. She was an expert in women's history and belonged to the American Society of Legal History. She loved researching people, places, especially using the Census records. At that time, I had worked at The Mississippi Bar for 19 years. I told her I had files and files of information on Mississippi's women lawyers for the Centennial book — too much information to put in the centennial book. We looked at each other and stated that we ought to write a book on the first 100 women lawyers in Mississippi. Who else would want to write that book?! And the idea was born.

Carol and I spent the next few years gathering the names. This was no easy task: women lawyers' names changed with marriage; The Mississippi Bar was not mandatory until 1932; and the Bar's database was not started until 1970. All records before 1970 were kept on index cards in deceased members' files. Carol and I met monthly on our findings. We worked rigorously on the listing, but in December of 2011, Carol unexpectedly died. Mississippi College School of Law Professor Celie Edwards gathered all of Carol's files on the project and delivered them to me. I spent the next year combining our efforts.

Files were then made for the first 100 women lawyers and the research began. I will never be able to thank The Mississippi Bar's Communications Assistants who worked on this project over the years – Murry Ann Terry Penn, Ashley Sasser Gray, Stephanie Chace Kelly, and Maggie Traxler. Murry Ann worked on completing each woman's file, Ashley and Stephanie researched information and Maggie came to the project in the last few years with a gusto to get it finished. I informed Maggie every day that she had an "old soul," that she could have lived in the 1920s or 1930s. She laughed and agreed with me every time. Maggie's research skills are impeccable. She could find anything about these women lawyers – photos, newspaper articles, and obituaries. I cannot thank Maggie enough for helping me finish this project.

Two other people to thank are the Executive Directors of The Mississippi Bar. Larry Houchins was the Executive Director when we began this project and was 100 percent behind it. After he retired, Deanne Mosley became the Executive Director and supported the Women in the Profession Committee in finishing this publication. A special thanks goes to both of them.

This book was conceived as an idea at the Mississippi Department of Archives and History building. Now, 14 years later, it is being published by Neil White with Nautilus Publishing. Neil recognized that the stories in this book had to be told. These women's lives, their determination and will, need to be known. Neil's layout of each woman's section is strictly perfection. I am forever indebted to him.

The descriptions of these 100 women lawyers from the 1910s, 1920s, 1930s and 1940s – these 100 pioneers, these 100 trailblazers – are presented for you here. The definition of a trailblazer is someone who has to make that path for themselves . . . someone who blazes that trail, and doesn't look back. A trailblazer is someone who creates a pathway and marks it for others to follow.

These women lawyers are truly trailblazers.

Melanie Henry, *Editor*

A NOTE ABOUT THE SELECTION PROCESS

Compiling the *First 100 Women Lawyers in Mississippi* was a daunting task. The main criteria was that the women lawyers had to be admitted to the bar. To be frank, misinformation — especially among newspaper reports from the 1920s-1940s — was rampant. Reporters (often relying on information provided by family members) regularly misreported "firsts" by women lawyers, ranging from the first to practice law in the state to the first to argue before the Supreme Court. Case in point, the publisher of this book, Neil White, had always heard that his great aunt Viola James Hilbert (see pages 65-69) was the third female law student to graduate from the University of Mississippi Law School. When in fact, Viola was the 48th woman lawyer in Mississippi and the sixteenth to graduate from UM Law (she was the third woman to serve on the *Mississippi Law Journal*).

These inaccurate claims are understandable. First, most women who went to law school were the only females in their class — adding to the presumption that they were one of the few and first. Second, pride among family members for these trailblazers often lead to guesses and assumptions. In our research we discovered dozens of errant claims, some etched in marble.

For purposes of this book, we relied on The Mississippi Bar records. This was difficult as there was no list. Researching of names consisted of examining deceased members' files and reviewing the listing of members of the bar in the annual *Mississippi Law Journals*.

The listing of the first 100 women lawyers is accurate. If anyone locates another name of a woman lawyer admitted during this time, the Bar has no remaining record. We do apologize if anyone was inadvertently omitted from this publication.

Some women lawyers were admitted to the bar and never practiced law, practiced a short time, immediately left the state, or practiced for many years in Mississippi. They are all included in this publication as they had been admitted to The Mississippi Bar.

1910s

*I*n 1914, when Lucy Harrison Greaves was admitted to the practice of law in Gulfport, Mississippi, the very first paved road was being completed at the other end of the state in Lee County.

The nation was riveted by the prospects of prohibition and women's suffrage. And the world was on the verge of the war to end all wars. Mississippi politics were dominated by Governor Theodore Bilbo and U.S. Senator James K. Vardaman — both self-proclaimed white supremacists.

In 1915, Nellie Nugent Somerville (mother of Lucy Somerville Howorth) published her book *Who Takes Care of Mississippi Women?* The following year, the suffrage movement gained a foothold in the state. Members of the Daughters of the American Revolution, United Daughters of the Confederacy, and the Women's Christian Temperance Union joined forces to work on behalf of women's suffrage in Mississippi.

In 1917, Mississippi ratified President Woodrow Wilson's declaration of war against Germany. And the following year, Mississippi was the first state to ratify prohibition.

By the end of the decade, there were approximately 2,200 women attorneys in the United States. Nine of those were licensed to practice in Mississippi. None of these trailblazing women were allowed to vote, hold public office, or serve on a jury.

GAL STATUS OF WOMAN LAWYER IS DEBATE QUESTION

awyers and officials of the state
reme court have raised the question
o the legal status of Miss Sallie
Buchanan, the woman attorney
appeared before Mississippi's
est tribunal Monday and argued a

e point out that an attorney is an
er of the court and that in order
old an officer one must be a qua-
d elector. As Miss Buchanan con-
vote the humor of the situation
hat saves it. She was admitted to
bar in regular order and granted
ge to practice before the Supreme

MISSISSIPPI RATIFIES PROHIBITION AMENDMEN

Leads All States in the Union
Both Houses Act 15 Minute
After Governor Asks It.

Jackson, Miss., Jan. 8.—Mississip
was the first state in the union
ratify the proposed prohibition amen
ment to the federal constitution. Fi
teen minutes after Governor Bilbo ha

Lucy Harrison Greaves ❖ 1914

With the advent of World War I, many women were freed up from long-established social pressures. Lucy Greaves was one of those women to benefit from this freedom. She was the first female lawyer to pass a bar exam. She lived in Gulfport, and she did not attend law school. Lucy H. Greaves was admitted on July 28, 1914, in Harrison County. Chancery Judge J. M. Stevens of the Eighth Chancery Court District wrote, "I do hereby certify that the applicant to practice law, appeared before me at the June 1914 term of the Chancery Court of Harrison County, and in open Court, in conformity to Section 209 of the Code of 1906, to such examination for admission to practice law, she having been found otherwise, qualified. On application and request of the applicant, I permitted the examination to be written out on typewriter."

The Jackson *Clarion-Ledger* reported, "Gulfport has the distinction of having the only woman lawyer in the state, her name being Mrs. Lucy H. Greaves. She was admitted to the bar and formed a co-partnership with W. A. Phillips, the firm name being Phillips & Greaves and devoted its time to civil practice. Mrs. Greaves is an intelligent little lady, and worthy of the position she occupies."

Lucy was born on June 28, 1870, to Richard Benjamin Harrison and Virginia Emmaline Gee in Edwards. Dr. Walter Joseph Greaves married Lucy Harrison on December 23, 1885. Her husband's family home is near Pocahontas, Mississippi. Springdale Hills is what it is called today, but the Greaves family called it Boscobel. During the Civil War, the Greaves family reportedly could hear from their home the cannon fire of the fighting in the siege of Vicksburg, over thirty miles to the west of Boscobel. The family is said to have buried a treasure of gold there for fear that Grant and Sherman's approaching troops would loot the home. Legend has it that the worker who buried the treasure was blindfolded and made to walk in circles so that he could not remember where it was hidden. The treasure was never found. Later Boscobel was abandoned, and the property has since changed hands.

Lucy and Dr. Greaves were divorced in 1913. She lived at various times in Gulfport, Vicksburg, Biloxi, and Tampa, Florida. Lucy H. Greaves died on November 21, 1954, and is buried in the Biloxi Cemetery.

REPORT
OF THE
TENTH ANNUAL MEETING
OF THE
MISSISSIPPI STATE BAR
ASSOCIATION

HELD AT
VICKSBURG, MISSISSIPPI
MAY 4TH AND 5TH
1915

PRINTED BY HEDERMAN BROS.
JACKSON, MISSISSIPPI

HARRISON COUNTY

Goldman, Louis . . . . Biloxi
Griffith, V. A. . . . . Gulfport
Graham, D. M. . . . . Gulfport
Greaves, Mrs. Lucy H. . . . Gulfport
Guice, W. L. . . . . Biloxi
Hariston, J. M. . . . . . . Gulfport
Haydon, Charles . . . . . Gulfport
Heiss, J. L. . . . . Gulfport
Hickox, B. P. . . . . Gulfport
Hill, A. C. . . . . Gulfport
Langton, R. F. . . . . . . Gulfport
Leathers, J. A. . . . . . . Gulfport
Moore, W. T. . . . . Gulfport
McCoy, E. A. . . . . Gulfport
ize, J. H. . . . . Gulfport
ize, S. C. . . . . Gulfport

A WOMAN LAWYER

Jackson Clarion-Ledger.

Gulfport has the distinction of having the only woman lawyer in the state, her name being Mrs. Lucy H. Greaves. She was admitted to the bar, after a creditable examination by Chancellor Stevens. She formed a copartnership with W. A. Phillips, the firm name being Phillips & Greaves and devotes its time to civil practice.

Mrs. Greaves is a real Mississippian, native and to the manor born, Edwards being her birthplace. She is the daughter of R. B. Harrison of Edwards and was christened Lucy H. Harrison. After reaching mature womanhood she married Dr. W. J. Greaves.

Mrs. Greaves is an intelligent little lady, and worthy of the position she occupies.

Mary Chapman Easterling ❖ 1915

Mary Chapman Easterling was born on December 28, 1896, to E. B. and Irene Chapman in Claiborne County near Hermanville. She was educated in the Meridian public schools and attended the University of Berkeley California after high school. From there, she studied law at Cumberland Law School. She took the bar examination under Chancellor George C. Tann of the Second Chancery District. After receiving her law degree, Mary was admitted on May 24, 1915, and began to practice with the firm Wyatt Easterling & Thos. L. Bailey in Meridian. She married Wyatt C. Easterling in 1912 and was married until his death from a hunting accident in 1928. After nineteen years of practice, she became active with the FHA and six years later joined JAG Washington, the Judge Advocates Office of the United States Army, and was an adjudicator with the Veterans Administration. In 1944, the JA Japan Air Defense Force hired her as an administrative assistant, but she told her family that she was a "legislative analyst." She kept that position through the end of the occupation of Japan in 1954. She was admitted to practice before the Supreme Court of Japan and was instrumental in establishing the Women's Bar Association of Japan. When she returned to the U.S. from Japan, Mary made her office in Baton Rouge, then in Jackson. She was a former member of the American Bar Association, Hinds County Bar, the International Association of Women Lawyers, and an advisory member of the Japan Women's Bar. She was an active member of the Mississippi Genealogical Society, and of Galloway

Memorial United Methodist Church. Mary Chapman Easterling died on January 10, 1986, and is buried in Meridian.

Jackson Woman One of 10 Non-Shintos At Ancient Ceremony
Mrs. Easterling Describes Rites That Began In 4 B.C.

By JAY MILNER
Clarion-Ledger Staff Writer

A Jackson woman attorney, Mrs

"the liberator of Japanese women lawyers." She went to Japan in 1949 with the legal section of the

MRS. EASTERLING is shown here dining with the chief justice of the Japanese Supreme Court. An attorney with the Supreme Command of Allied Powers in Japan, Mrs. Easterling organized Japan's first bar association for women lawyers. She received many honors as the "liberator" of Japanese women lawyers. The chief justice is Kataro Tanaka.

In 1950, Mary Chapman Easterling organized the Japanese Women's Bar Association with five female attorneys. Within three years, seven Japanese women were serving as judges.

3

Bessie Young ❖ 1915

Bessie Young was born in Carroll County on November 29, 1879. When she was a child her family moved to Grenada. Her parents were John and Mollie McCain Young. She was the third daughter and lived with her mother, father, two brothers, and five sisters. She was educated in the Grenada public schools, and even as a child, she endeared herself to her family and friends on account of her sweet, unselfish nature. Once she completed high school, she studied art at Grenada College and graduated in 1896. She was an earnest worker in the Presbyterian church and sang in the choir.

In 1910, she was called to Lafayette, Louisiana to fill an un-expired term of one of the teachers in the high school. Before she realized it, she had learned to speak the French language. Later on in life, while she was in New York City, she took private lessons from a French instructor. After she returned to Grenada, she taught one year in the preparatory department of Grenada College.

A few years later in 1913, a college in Bloomington, Indiana accepted her for undergraduate work. Upon graduating, she immediately attended the University of Mississippi Law School and, in 1915, became the first woman law school graduate. She was one of twenty students. The Ole Miss yearbook quoted her as saying, "The countenance is the portrait of the soul, and the eyes mark its intention." It continued with the class historian as saying, "Proud? Why certainly

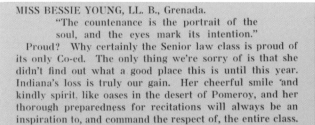

> MISS BESSIE YOUNG, LL. B., Grenada.
> "The countenance is the portrait of the soul, and the eyes mark its intention."
> Proud? Why certainly the Senior law class is proud of its only Co-ed. The only thing we're sorry of is that she didn't find out what a good place this is until this year. Indiana's loss is truly our gain. Her cheerful smile and kindly spirit, like oases in the desert of Pomeroy, and her thorough preparedness for recitations will always be an inspiration to, and command the respect of, the entire class.

(Above) Bessie Young's Ole Miss yearbook description. She transferred after annual photographs had been taken. (Below): The law building in which Young studied (1915)

LAW BUILDING

the senior law class is proud of its only co-ed. The only thing we're sorry of is that she didn't find out what a good place this is until this year. Indiana's loss is truly our gain. Her cheerful smile and kindly spirit, like oases in the desert of Pomeroy, and her thorough preparedness for recitations will always be an inspiration to, and command the respect of, the entire class."

Judge McGowen of the Grenada County Chancery Court admitted to practice in his court Bessie Young. Upon her admittance to the state bar in 1915, Bessie opened an office in Grenada and engaged in practice there. A Mississippi newspaper printed, "She is a most cultured, refined, and charming woman and can be relied upon to apply the rule of reason and good old fashioned common sense proposition she undertakes. She believes in old time Southern standards and Southern modesty. She has embarked in the law for the reason that she felt that it was her duty to help maintain herself and because, of course, she did not know what the future had in store for her."

She was elected as the Grenada County Bar Association secretary from 1917-1919. Bessie was practicing law when the United States entered the World War in 1917. She took charge of the sewing room where garments were being made for the soldiers and was then sent to Jackson to do war work for a year. The June 11, 1918, *Jackson Daily News* wrote, "In charge of the supplies department of the War Savings Stamp Bureau is Miss Bessie Young of Grenada who, having had charge of the office in Grenada brought to the work here an experience and a loyalty which has been invaluable."

After she practiced for two years in Mississippi, Bessie moved to Washington D.C. in 1917 and worked initially in the War Risk Department of the federal government and later in the Prohibition Enforcement Unit. Upon the repeal of the Eighteenth Amendment, the United States Attorney for the southern district of New York hired her to become an assistant attorney. From there, she was appointed to the U. S. Department of Justice in 1934 in Washington, where she served first as assistant and afterwards as an associate attorney in the Tax and Penalties Unit. She worked there until she died of cancer on March 1, 1938. Rev. C. A. Pharr, pastor of the Presbyterian Church, of which Bessie was a member, officiated, and she was buried in Odd Fellow Cemetery in Grenada. She was never married. "Miss Young's character, personality, brilliant mind, and legal ability marked her as one of Mississippi's outstanding daughters."

Lucy Somerville Howorth stated, "Bessie Young was brilliant, courageous, a person of character and grace."

The University of Mississippi Law School has joined forces with a dedicated group of alumnae to honor this trailblazer and her pioneer spirit by creating the Bessie Young Council and establishing a scholarship in her name. The goal of the Bessie Young Council is to assist those nontraditional students who bring diversity, fresh perspectives, and varied life experiences to the student body through scholarships and mentorship.

Advertisements for the opening of Bessie Young's law practice in Grenada, Mississippi, from Fall, 1915

Another Distinction for Grenada.

Grenada enjoys another distinction in having one of her daughters in the person of Miss Bessie Young to take the first diploma ever given a lady by the law department of the State University. Miss Young was one of the graduates of the 1914-15 class, she however, did not enter the University until after Christmas. She took her junior work in law at Indianapolis.

She is a most lovely character and possesses all the modesty and all the charm of the South's most honored womanhood. She has exceptional talent and will do well at whatever she undertakes. She has no matured plans as yet as to her profession.

Nettie Hood Bratton ❖ 1916

4

*N*ettie Hood Bratton was born on November 5, 1882, in Forest, Mississippi. She was the daughter of John J. Hood and Henrietta Clark Hood. The Mississippi Bar admitted her in 1916. Soon after, she went to practice with her husband, Thomas Stewart Bratton, at Bratton & Bratton in Jackson. In 1928, she was listed on the *Mississippi Law Journal* lawyer list and, in 1938, was in the *Bench and Bar of Mississippi*. She was a member of the Hinds County Bar Association. After forty years of practice in 1956, she retired to live on Greenwood Farm in Clinton. After her retirement, she resumed an earlier interest in painting. Her husband died in 1960. Nettie died on October 1, 1972, at the age of 89, after an extended illness.

HINDS COUNTY COURT HOUSE, JACKSON, MISS.

(Above) The Hinds County Courthouse where Nettie Hood Bratton would have spent many hours.

Nettie Hood Bratton and her husband, Thomas, were admitted to the bar in 1916 (left). Their firm, Bratton & Bratton, was often listed in the *Clarion-Ledger* as solicitors for property sale notices for the city of Jackson (bottom left).

Courts, Judges, and Lawyers of Mississippi 373

Bratton, Nettie H., Jackson
Bratton, Thos. S., Jackson

Witness my signature this the 6th day of February, 1934.
B. B. McCLENDON,
Commissioner.
BRATTON & BRATTON,
Solicitors   Feb. 10-17-24-Mar 3

Susie Blue Buchanan ❖ 1916

The newspaper headlines proclaimed "First Girl Lawyer is Admitted to Supreme Court of Mississippi." Susie Blue Buchanan was the first woman lawyer admitted to the Supreme Court of Mississippi in December of 1916. An article that appeared in a newspaper in December 1916 described her this way: "Miss Susie Blue Buchanan of Brandon appeared before the Supreme Court this morning and took the oath to practice before that high tribunal. This makes her the first woman ever qualified to practice before the highest court of Mississippi. A small and timid lady, she appeared at first to be entirely out of place among the lawyers and the judges, but as the oath was administered this feeling gave way to admiration for the brave little lady. She is a member of one of the foremost legal families of Mississippi, and is well known in Jackson where she spent several years of her girlhood. "

Susie was born on April 2, 1882, the eldest of ten children, to Judge William Buchanan and Maggie Gunn Buchanan. Susie Blue was called "Sissa" by the family. She was born in the Steven-Buchanan house, "The Magnolias," a Victorian house built by Richardson Stevens in 1860, which became the Buchanan family home in Brandon. She graduated from Brandon High School, then she attended the following colleges: Mississippi Synodical College, East Mississippi Female College, Harris College, and Millsaps College. After college, she taught school in Rankin County. She soon began reading law while serving as secretary to her father until his death in 1912. His partner, J.R. East, assisted in continuing her studies.

She became a member of the bar in 1916 and practiced in Brandon, Mississippi, where she lived with her sister Anna. In 1924, Rankin County hired her as their deputy chancery clerk, where she worked for the next fourteen

Susie Blue Buchanan (above) as depicted in *The Mississippi Bar's Centennial: A Legacy of Service.* (Left) The city of Brandon, Mississippi, featured Miss Buchanan in an advertising campaign celebrating 175 years of achievement.

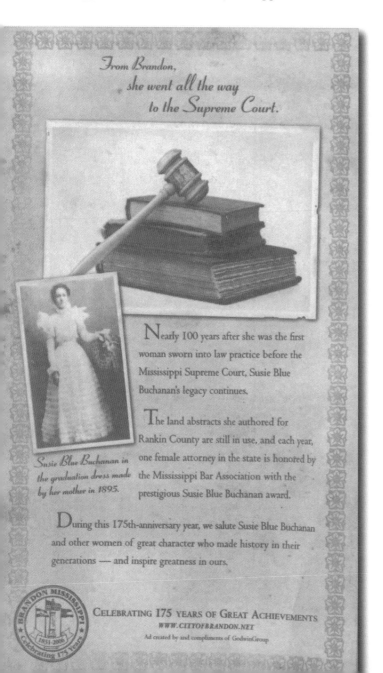

From Brandon, she went all the way to the Supreme Court.

Nearly 100 years after she was the first woman sworn into law practice before the Mississippi Supreme Court, Susie Blue Buchanan's legacy continues.

The land abstracts she authored for Rankin County are still in use, and each year, one female attorney in the state is honored by the Mississippi Bar Association with the prestigious Susie Blue Buchanan award.

During this 175th-anniversary year, we salute Susie Blue Buchanan and other women of great character who made history in their generations — and inspire greatness in ours.

Susie Blue Buchanan in the graduation dress made by her mother in 1895.

CELEBRATING 175 YEARS OF GREAT ACHIEVEMENTS
WWW.CITYOFBRANDON.NET
Ad created by and compliments of GodwinGroup

years. Her legal area was land abstracts, and she compiled a book of Rankin County plats called the *Susie Blue Book*. She also compiled a history of the Brandon Presbyterian Church and was a member of the Daughters of the American Revolution.

The *Mississippi Law Journal* added her on their lawyer list in 1928, and she was recognized in *Honor & Dignity of the Profession* for her outstanding work. The Buchanan House where she and her sister, Anna, shared in Brandon is still admired by many today. Susie Blue Buchanan died on April 11, 1938, of a heart attack at age 56. She was buried in the Brandon Cemetery with other members of her family.

Her name will forever be remembered as the Mississippi Bar's Women in the Profession Committee established the Susie Blue Buchanan Award in 1999 to annually honor a woman lawyer who has achieved professional excellence in her field and has actively paved the way to success for other women lawyers. This award is presented at the annual meeting of The Mississippi Bar.

Linda Rives Brown Witherington ❖ 1916

6

*L*inda Rives Brown was born in Macon and grew up in Meridian in the early 1900s. She was the Valedictorian of her senior class at Meridian High School. Linda attended the University of Mississippi as an undergraduate and the University of Mississippi Law School. She was Vice-President of her Junior Law Class in 1914-1915. Her senior year in law school, she was Poet of the class. She served as secretary and treasurer of the Blackstone Club in 1915 and was a member of the Y.W.C.A. Cabinet in 1915-1916. Linda graduated from law school with honors in 1916. She was the second female graduate of the University of Mississippi Law School. She married D. B. V. Witherington during law school. The yearbook quoted her as saying, "Marriage is a desperate thing." She was recognized in the *Honor & Dignity of the Profession*.

(Above) Linda Rives Brown's photo from the law school senior class of 1916.
(Right): Her quote and accomplishments listed in the 1916 -1917 Ole Miss yearbook.

MISS LINDA RIVES BROWN, LL. B. . . . . Meridian
"Marriage is a desperate thing."
Vice-President Junior Law Class 1914-15; Poet Senior Law Class 1915-16; Secretary and Treasurer Blackstone Club 1915; Member of Y. W. C. A. Cabinet 1915-16.

Sarah Lou Buchanan ❖ 1917

Sarah L. Buchanan of Booneville was admitted to practice in 1917. She was born on September 29, 1889, and received her early education in the local schools, graduating from Booneville High School. She attended Draughn's Business College in Nashville, Tennessee and received her law degree from Cumberland University Law School in Lebanon, Tennessee. Sarah also went by Sally. She was the first woman lawyer to argue before the Mississippi Supreme Court.

The *Hinds County Gazette* published on March 30, 1917, "For the first time in the history of Mississippi a woman lawyer appeared yesterday before the Supreme Court and argued a murder case. The woman was Miss Sally Lou Buchanan, of Booneville, and she appeared for the defense in the case of E. K. Brown, who was convicted of murder. Associated with her in the case was E. J. Kernaghan, senior member of the firm of which Miss Buchanan is a member and for which firm she was a stenographer before entering the practice. Opposed to her, in addition to the Assistant Attorney General, was J. E. Berry, the District Attorney, and who first employed Miss Buchanan as a stenographer in a law office. To the young lady's credit it can be said that she is a finished lawyer, and in a twenty-minute speech she demonstrated that she is thoroughly familiar with the principles of criminal law. She took up the record and analyzed it in a manner that was highly creditable, and wasted no time on superfluities."

In 1919, Sarah wrote an article about Mississippi for *The Women Lawyers' Journal* which stated, "I am ready to concede that we have great room for progress and improvement; both in the making of laws and their enforcement; so has every other State in the Union. It would not become me to say that we are the very pinnacle of perfection in legislation or administration, even if I could do so truthfully; therefore, I shall make no such claim. But I do believe firmly, basing that belief on such opportunity as I have had for comparison, that my State is certainly not the lowest in the scale when it comes to dispensing justice for women. Really, we're a bit above the average."

In 1920, she was a member of the Commercial Law League of America. On May 13, 1921, the *Jackson Daily News* reported, "Woman Lawyer Argues in West Point – A demurrer was argued in the case of J. D. Bell et al vs. J. K. Kaye. This case was brought here by consent of counsel from Prentiss County and argued before Chancellor McIntyre. Appearing in the case was J. O. Stovall of Okolona, Miss Sara Buchanan and E. C. Sharp of Booneville. Miss Buchanan is the first woman lawyer to appear at this local bar."

She was chosen in 1922 to be a member of The Mississippi Bar's Standing Committee on Legal Education and Admission. In 1930, Sarah began practicing law in Washington, D. C., working in real estate. In 1943, she was the Virginia state vice president of the National Association of Women Lawyers living in Springfield, Virginia. She was mentioned in a *Women Lawyers' Journal* article as "Associate in Legal Research with the Women's Bureau of the U. S. Department of Labor, giving her attention to state and national laws affecting the political and civil status of women in the United States. She prepared Women's Bureau Bulletins covering the legal status of women in the United States."

Sarah Lou Buchanan died on May 4, 1977, having lived in Lakeland, Florida.

Sarah Lou Buchanan, above right, at the Cumberland University Law School in Lebanon, Tennessee

FIRST WOMAN LAWYER BEFORE SUPREME COURT

JACKSON, Miss., March 26.—For the first time in the history of Mississippi a woman lawyer appeared

Leota Angelina Taylor Kirkpatrick ❖ 1918

The Jackson Daily News in 1918 stated, "Miss Leota Taylor received her diploma as bachelor of laws from Millsaps College. If the young student makes as rapid and as great a success of the practice of law as she has of the study thereof, the legal lights of the other sex will have a surprise coming."

Leota Angelina Taylor of Jackson was the first woman law student at Millsaps College in 1918 and president of the law class. She was first listed in the 1918 membership directory of the Mississippi Bar Association. For her services to the Jackson

---

School of Law—Second Year

OFFICERS

MANIER, MILLER	*President*
HIGGINS, JOSEPH	*Vice-President*
TAYLOR, LEOTA	*Secretary-Treasurer*
THOMPSON, ELMO	*Commodore Representative*

---

community, she was recognized in the *Honor & Dignity of the Profession*. She left Jackson to continue her studies at Vanderbilt University.

Leota was born on August 2, 1899, to William Brittain Taylor and Leota Bennett Taylor. She married Aubrey M. Kirkpatrick, and in 1924, they moved to Florida. Leota and Aubrey had three daughters. Leota continued practicing law in Florida until 1935, when she quit to become a housewife.

Leota Angelina Taylor Kirkpatrick died at age 75 on April 19, 1975. She is buried in Palm Beach, Florida.

(Top) Leota Taylor with her law school class. (Center) The Millsaps College yearbook listed her as the secretary-treasurer of the second year law school class. (Left) Leota Taylor listed last (and out of alphabetical order) in the 1918 annual meeting report.

REPORT

OF THE

THIRTEENTH ANNUAL MEETING

OF THE

MISSISSIPPI STATE BAR ASSOCIATION

HELD AT JACKSON, MISSISSIPPI
MAY 1 AND 2, 1918

— 196 —

Thompson, Harmon L.; City Police Justice.
Thompson, R. P. (Jack).
Trenholm, Ed. L.
Vardaman, James Money.
Vardaman, J. K., Jr.; in service.
Watkins, Wm. H.
Watkins, H. Vaughn.
Wells, Ben H.

Wells, W. Calvin.
West, F. M.
White, Dan; in the service.
Whitfield, A. H.
Whitfield, G. Q.
Williams, G. Edward.
Williamson, C. M.
Ward, E. C.; in the service.
Taylor, Miss Leota.

Virginia Ruth Campbell ❖ 1919

*B*orn on January 20, 1887, Virginia Ruth Campbell was the daughter of T. H. Campbell, Sr. Ruth was the secretary for Campbell & Campbell law firm in Yazoo City before she was educated at Ward's Seminary in Nashville. Ruth was admitted to the Bar in 1919. The *Yazoo Herald* stated, "She was the first Yazoo girl to take up the profession of law. There were very few women in the South who had then tackled the profession of law. She was warmly welcomed at the Bar and promised hearty co-operation."

The 1928 *Mississippi Law Journal* lawyer list acknowledged her as a practicing attorney and she was also listed in the *Bench and Bar of Mississippi* in 1938. Following her admittance, she became the election commissioner for Yazoo County. Ruth was a member of the Yazoo County Bar Association and the Commercial Law League of America.

The Yazoo Historical Association published a book, *The Yazoo County Story* in which Ruth authored a story entitled, "There's a Little Bottle." The article reads, "The writer of this article was in her law office early on the morning of August 29, 1939, expecting a client, W. G. McCauley of Chicago. When the client entered he informed me that oil had been discovered in Woodruff No. 1 in Tinsley. Both client and attorney forgot business and made for the McCauley car and soon were at the well site. Upon arrival, the two saw oil flowing over the derrick into the gullies surrounding the well. This writer became excited and ran up a hill to the Woodruff store and asked Mrs. Woodruff for a bottle. Mrs. Woodruff handed me a bottle and demanded a five-cent deposit, for which credit was asked until Mrs. Woodruff could call at my office and collect. This she never did, as she became too busy seeing people who wanted to buy mineral and royalty rights. Into the bottle was scooped some oil from a gully into which it was flowing and to this day the bottle of oil stands on a mantelpiece in the writer's law office, being actually the first oil discovered in Yazoo County."

Ruth Campbell died in March 1963.

(Above) Virginia Ruth Campbell at age 32, the year she received her law license. Photo courtesy of Ruth C. Williams. (Right) Campbell's photo from *Bench & Bar*. (Left) The May 12, 1960, edition of the *Yazoo Herald* covered Ms. Ruth Campbell's retirement.

The Yazoo City Herald

Bar Association Pays Miss Campbell Tribute

Resolution Adopted

1920s

In the 1920s, the world was introduced to Mickey Mouse, Charles Lindbergh flew solo across the Atlantic, the first Miss America was crowned, and John Scopes was arrested for teaching evolution.

The 20s were also a time of liberation for women. The decade started with a huge victory — ratification of the 19th Amendment. The "New Women" of the 20s embraced outrageous fashions, personal freedom, and new ideas that challenged the traditional role of women. The Traditionalists (and older generation of women) feared that the "New Morality" of the era would threaten family values and the conventional role of women in the home.

F. Scott Fitzgerald coined the phrase, "The Jazz Age," and free-spirited Flappers — the quintessential Roaring Twenties female icons — drank and smoked in public, wore short skirts, bobbed hairstyles, and make-up, and embraced unconventional attitudes.

The number of women working jumped 25% during the decade. And those who worked in the home enjoyed new labor saving devices and inventions that relied on newly available cheap electricity.

The decade also saw divorce made more accessible for unhappy couples, a woman preside over the U.S. House of Representatives, and Joan of Arc canonized.

Eleven women were admitted to The Mississippi Bar in the 1920s — including women who would become the first female judges in the state.

The Rise Of The Woman Lawyer

By Frederic J. Haskin

WASHINGTON, D. C., Dec. 19.

If you were in need of a lawyer, would you employ a woman? Thirty, twenty, or even ten years ago, you could not have hesitated. "I should say not!" would undoubtedly have been your answer.

Abbede Sessions Peebles ❖ 1921

The third female graduate of the University of Mississippi Law School, Abbede Sessions Peebles of Philadelphia, was born on October 19, 1883. Her parents were C. C. Sessions and Andoniram Louise Farmer Sessions. She was a graduate of Mississippi College and later graduated from the University of Mississippi Law School in 1921. While at the University of Mississippi Law School, Abbede was the senior law class secretary-treasurer. She married fellow law school classmate Ivey E. Peeples. The commencement program awarded bachelor of laws degrees to both husband and wife.

Abbede was admitted to practice on May 23, 1921. The *Daily Mississippian* dedicated an article about her and her fellow women classmates as these ladies endeavored to succeed in the law profession; she was also recorded in the Ole Miss yearbook.

Her husband was a charter member of the Philadelphia Rotary Club in 1926, serving as president. The *Jackson Daily News* reported on September 20, 1928, "Both Mr. and Mrs. Peebles graduated from the law school of the University with high honors. They taught school for a few years and then entered upon the practice of law in the city of Meridian. Shortly afterwards, Mr. Peebles was appointed assistant state superintendent of public education. After serving in this position for a year, Mr. Peebles and his wife moved to their old home in Philadelphia and bought an interest in the *Neshoba Democrat*.

As editor of this periodical, Mr. Peebles made it a dominant factor in the life of his county and state. Mr. Peebles recently sold his interest in the paper to his brother and with Mrs. Peebles as his partner, has entered upon the practice of law under the firm name of Peebles and Peebles. Jackson extends a cordial welcome to these young people and hopes that they may be very successful in the pursuit of their chosen profession."

Her husband died in 1977 when he was 88 years old. Abbede Peebles died on March 1, 1982, at the age of 98, with her last residence being in Bay St. Louis, Mississippi.

(Top Right) Peebles on the University of Mississippi co-ed basketball squad (her photo is top left). (Above Center) Abbede Sessions Peebles' junior law class photo from the Ole Miss annual. (Above Left) 1921-1922 Ole Miss graduation program. (Left) Peebles listed as secretary-treasurer of the junior law class. (Right) *Neshoba County Democrat* story about the Peebles' move to Jackson.

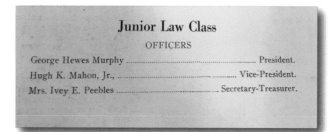

Junior Law Class

OFFICERS

George Hewes Murphy .... President.

Hugh K. Mahon, Jr., ... Vice-President.

Mrs. Ivey E. Peebles .... Secretary-Treasurer.

University of Mississippi

ISSUED QUARTERLY

SERIES XX   MARCH, 1922   NUMBER 1

ANNOUNCEMENTS *and* CATALOGUE

OF THE

UNIVERSITY OF MISSISSIPPI

UNIVERSITY P. O.

Freight and Express offices, Oxford

SEVENTIETH SESSION
SEVENTY-FOURTH YEAR
1921-1922

PUBLISHED BY THE UNIVERSITY

...ersity of Mississipp...

ISSUED QUARTERLY

MARCH, 1922   NUMBER

Ivey E. Peebles Locates In Jackson

The many friends of Mr. Ivey E. Peebles and his charming wife are happy to welcome them as permanent residents of our city. These young people lived here in 1925, when Mr. Peebles was assistant superintendent of public education and they made many friends, who will be glad to know they have returned to Jackson and purchased a home on Eastview street.

Mr. Peebles was educated at Mississippi College and at the University of Mississippi. Both Mr. and Mrs. Peebles graduated from the law school of the University with high honors. They taught school for a few years and then entered upon the practice of law in the city of Meridian. Shortly afterwards Mr. Peebles was appointed assistant state superintendent of public education. After serving in this capacity for a year Mr. Peebles and his wife moved to their old home in Philadelphia...

Lucy Robinson Somerville Howorth ❖ 1922

Lucy Somerville Howorth's remarkable life began July 1, 1895, in Greenville, Mississippi. Appropriately for a life devoted to social justice and the rights of women, suffrage was the first major historical movement with which Lucy was associated. Lucy's mother, Nellie Nugent Somerville, was actively involved in the early stages of the suffrage movement and took Lucy along to meetings.

After graduating from Randolph-Macon College in 1916 with the idea of perhaps becoming a psychiatrist, she went to New York City with a friend to study international law at Columbia University.

The advent of the Roaring Twenties found Lucy convinced that her calling was the law. Those who told her that law was no profession for a woman made her even more determined. Columbia University did not admit women to their law school in 1920, so Lucy returned to Mississippi to the University of Mississippi Law School. There, she was the secretary of the Blackstone Club. In the spring of 1922, Lucy Somerville graduated at the top of her law school class and delivered the commencement address. She was admitted to The Mississippi Bar in May 1922.

In September 1922, she joined the Cleveland law firm of Shands, Elmore, and Causey, where she argued cases in front of the Mississippi Supreme Court. Along with her law work, Lucy worked to begin a college in Cleveland, Mississippi, and drafted the bill creating the Delta State Teacher's College in 1924.

(Above) Photograph by Bachrach. Reprinted by permission of the Mississippi Department of Archives and History. (Below) Howorth's politcal ad for state representative.

Vote For
Mrs. Lucy Somerville Howorth

For Representative Hinds County

I sincerely appreciate the large vote given me in the first primary and thank my friends for their splendid work in my behalf.

As my qualifications for the office of Representative have been brought before you through the press, radio, public speeches and personal solicitation, I simply ask at this time for your vote and renewed activity, so that victory may be ours in the Second Primary, Tuesday, Aug. 25, and I again pledge the people of Hinds County that if elected I shall serve them unselfishly to the utmost of my ability.

LUCY SOMERVILLE HOWORTH,
Candidate for Representative Hinds County.

Lucy continued her involvement in women's organizations. "We are attempting in the United States, you and I, to do what has taken centuries for other people: that is, to build a unified community from great diversity of people. And we can succeed — with patience, kindness, tolerance, and understanding."

In 1924, she became the first female Bar member to formally address the association, reading a paper on "Laws about Lawyers." Bar President R. H. Thompson proclaimed at the 1924 annual meeting in Biloxi, "Gentlemen of the association, of the lawyer I am about to present to you, I can make three affirmations. First: The lawyer I present to you is a lawyer of eminence and an honor to the profession. Second: The lawyer I present to you is of the most sterling character, one of the cardinal virtues it loves. Third: The lawyer I present to you possesses every virtue and every grace. I take pleasure in presenting Miss Lucy R. Somerville, of the Cleveland Bar."

She was also elected as a delegate to the American Bar Association by acclamation in 1924. Three years later, Lucy was appointed United States Commissioner of the Southern District of Mississippi, an appointment from which her title "Judge" originates. Her political career began in 1931 when she ran for state legislature and won. That same year, she heavily supported President Roosevelt at the National Democratic

(Continued on next page)

LUCY R. SOMERVILLE
LAWYER
WEINBERG BUILDING
GREENVILLE, MISSISSIPPI

July 19
1 9 2 7

Judge W. C. Kimbrough
University, Mississippi

Dear Judge:

I have your letter of the 16th and will consider
it an honor to serve on your committee.

It seems to me that the Committee should concern
itself with the Law School of the University, and
its standards, with the standards required by law for
admission to the Bar, and with the conditions and
requirements of the State Board of Examiners.

I shall look forward to meeting with you and the
committee at sometime that may suit the convenience
of all.

With kindest regards to you and Mrs. Kimbrough, I am

Very truly yours,

Lucy Somerville

LRS:RES

Mrs. Lucy Howorth, Jackson's Woman Lawyer, Says Feminine Career Does Not Destroy Home

Editor's Note: This is the second of a series of stories on Jackson Business and Professional women who have won success.

By MARTHA HARRISON

Her definition of law is "mental gymnastics," for which she believes women have just as great a facility as men.

Being, as she terms herself, not the only woman lawyer in Jackson, but the only "noisy one," Mrs. Lucy Somerville Howorth ought to know.

A "noisy lawyer" in her definition, is one who appears in court, wrangling with judge and jury, and she is the only woman lawyer in Jackson who takes court cases.

Mrs. Howorth deplores the attitude of most southern women toward following careers, and, if an endorsement of the legal profession by her will encourage any of them to have greater confidence in their professional abilities, she is willing to submit to an interview.

"They consider law, medicine, and countless other vocations strictly the provinces of men," she scoffs. "They wail that they can't take part in the legal war of wits because they haven't logical minds, because their mental apparatus is a slower mechanism than that of men. When, if they would only admit it, women have always thought quicker than men. Not good in the war of wits! Why, that's what every courtship is, and the woman is usually the winner."

Mrs. Howorth didn't say that she was a better lawyer than her husband, but she did say, "Women take every quarrel, when the cause has been their own and soon trick the man into thinking he was to blame. He apologizes and she gets the decision. Now why wouldn't

women make good lawyers? If they employ the same mental tactics in cross-examination in the courtroom that they do every day on their friends and husbands, they'll be excellent. They'll have the witness contradicting himself and believing the contradiction."

Mrs. Howorth's cases include everything except criminal, although one of the first cases she ever had was a criminal case. Perhaps that is the reason she doesn't particularly care for criminal cases, because in this particular one, she was called upon to define a flatiron as a rather harmless weapon, a weapon whose use was by no means fatal. Her client was a negro who had wielded the flatiron, not with fatal, but with painful effect on another negro, and the case hung around the definition of the flatiron. If the flatiron was a deadly weapon, the charge would have to be "assault with intent to kill." If the flatiron was not deadly, the charge would be "assault and battery."

Commenting upon some of her experiences in the legal world, Mrs. Howorth revealed the wealth of interest her profession holds for her, the zest she draws from life and therefore the happiness.

"Women should have as much color, as much background in the pattern of their lives as men do," she vows, "If they have happy occupations outside the home, they bring something rich and new to the family relationship. They are fresh, always interesting in the minds of their husbands, because they are growing with the public life around them, with the progress of the universe."

Of course, she doesn't believe that every woman ought to have a profession. She agrees that the choice of a life occupation depends entirely on the individual.

(Continued on Page Five)

(Above Left) A letter to Judge Kimbrough accepting a committee appointment with the university. (Above Right) A groundbreaking 1931 *Clarion-Ledger* story about managing career and home. (Left) Lucy Somerville as an undergrad at Randolph-Macon. (Below) The cover of Howorth's biography: *New Deal Lawyer, Politician, and Feminist from the South.*

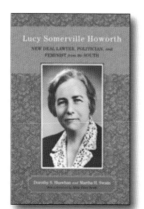

(Continued from previous page)

Convention, and he appointed her to the Board of Appeals of the Veteran's Administration in 1934. Lucy and her husband, Joseph Marion Howorth, moved to Washington, D.C., and continued to serve the public for the next twenty-five years. Eventually, she became the general counsel of the War Claims Commission and the first woman to hold the top "legal post in a federal agency."

Throughout her career, Lucy was involved in numerous women's organizations, including the YWCA, the American Association of University Women, the National Association of Women Lawyers, and the Business and Professional Women's Club. In 1983, Lucy was among nine women honored by Radcliffe College for lifetime achievements.

Lucy Somerville Howorth died on August 23, 1997, at the age of 102.

Vivian Cook ❖ 1922

The 1922 University of Mississippi Law School yearbook stated, "The opposing counsel will discover that Vivian combines with a gracious courtroom manner a ready wit and a thorough knowledge of law. Her individuality, enthusiasm, and sincerity have won for her a host of friends."

Born on October 9, 1902, in Ellisville, Jones County, Vivian Cook was the daughter of John Henry and Annie Griffith Cook. Her father was a wealthy planter and lawyer. She obtained her early education in the public schools of Pascagoula, Jackson County, and graduated from Lucedale High School in 1917. She took a business course in Laurel in 1917-1918. Vivian attended the University of Mississippi as an undergraduate and was a 1922 graduate from the University of Mississippi Law School. She was the junior law class secretary-treasurer.

Fellow law school classmate, Lucy Somerville Howorth, gave in an interview the following information regarding Vivian Cook: "Vivian's brother was a member of the Mississippi Supreme Court, and her father was an attorney. Vivian and her father had a great relationship, and [he] was partly responsible for her interest in law." According to Lucy, Lucy and Vivian watched out for each other in law school, as they were the only two women.

Vivian at once began the practice of law with her father, John Henry Cook, in Sumner. She initially practiced in Coahoma County as the first woman lawyer in that county. Then she moved to Clarksdale in 1923 and located her law office in the McWilliams building. In Dunbar Rowland's book *The Heart of the South*, he states, "She has acquired a number of most desirable clients and has a lucrative practice. She is a member of the Clarksdale Women's Chamber of Commerce, the Women Lawyers Association, and The Eastern Star. She organized the Division of the Chamber of Commerce in Clarksdale and served as its president the first year. She assisted in the organization of the Mississippi Federation of Business and Professional Women's Clubs in 1924."

Vivian Cook was also a member of the National Society of the Daughters of the American Revolution and the National Women's Party. The Women's Party had always interested her, and she took some affiliation with their movements.

Vivian married George W. Ascough and had two children; then she married Will Barber. Vivian Cook died on March 6, 1962.

(Top) Vivian Cook from the 1922 Ole Miss annual. (Above) Vivian's profile in the law school section of the annual. (Right) Vivian front and center in the Blackstone Club photograph from 1922.

13

Ruth L. Bertrand ❖ 1922

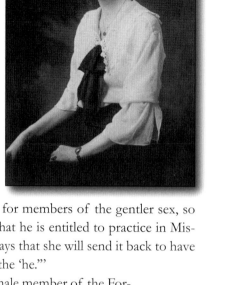

Hattiesburg's first female lawyer, Ruth L. Bertrand was born in October 1893 to John and Mary Bertrand. In 1911, she married Ben H. Waller. Ruth passed the bar exam in 1922 and began her practice in Hattiesburg.

On July 11, 1922, the *Jackson Daily News* reported the headline, "Hattiesburg Boasts of Woman Attorney." The article stated, "Ruth Waller, wife of Ben H. Waller, local contractor, is Hattiesburg's first woman lawyer. Mrs. Waller recently received her certificate to practice, and announced today that she will hang out her shingle and practice actively in this city. Mrs. Waller was born and reared in this city, and first commenced the study of law in the office of Mr. Pritchard, a Birmingham attorney. She did the last year of her study in this city under the tutelage of F. A. Zan Anderson and passed her bar examination on the first try. An amusing feature of Mrs. Waller's receiving a certificate is that the paper does not allow for members of the gentler sex, so her certificate reads that he is entitled to practice in Mississippi. Mrs. Waller says that she will send it back to have a 's' placed ahead of the 'he.'"

She was the first female member of the Forrest County Bar Association. In 1940, she divorced her husband, took her maiden name back and practiced as Ruth Bertrand.

Eleanore Sophia Babendreer Moore ❖ 1922

14

Jackson County gained its first female attorney with Eleanore Sophia Babendreer Moore. She was born in Covington, Kentucky, on November 27, 1900. Her parents were Charles Albert Irving Babendreer and Estelle Turner Babendreer. Her family moved to Ocean Springs in 1906 where both of her parents were physicians. She attended law school at Cumberland University and obtained her law degree in 1922. The Mississippi Bar admitted her on August 7, 1922.

Her first law practice was in Ocean Springs from 1922-1927. Eleanore's brother Eric also practiced law in Ocean Springs before relocating to Memphis. She moved from Ocean Springs to Biloxi where she lived from 1927-1931. She had offices in the Yerger building. She claimed Memphis as home, so in 1931 she moved to Memphis. In 1934, she moved back to Gulfport, and practiced law in the Hewes Annex. She was in the *Bench and Bar of Mississippi* in 1938. Eleanor presented seven cases before the Mississippi Supreme Court during her career. Eleanore Sophia Babendreer Moore retired in 1941.

During her career, Eleanor married Walter D. Moore, an accountant, from Florence, Alabama. They were married at her family home, Pinewood, in Ocean Springs.

Before she died on December 28, 1986, she was a regular Sunday school teacher at St. John's Episcopal Church in Memphis. She is buried at the Florence City Cemetery in Florence, Alabama.

At various times, her first name is spelled Elinor and her maiden name spelled Babendrier.

Lavonia Caradine Jiggitts Jones ❖ 1924

Lavonia Caradine was born on January 27, 1901, to the Honorable James Emmett and Olive Caradine of West Point, Mississippi. She was one of two children. Her father, an eminent lawyer, served in the Mississippi House of Representatives from 1904-1908. He was a prosecutor for Clay County and for the city of West Point. He also served as a Circuit Judge of the 16th District.

Lavonia attended the Mississippi University for Women where she graduated in 1922 with a Bachelor of Science in Physical Education. Lavonia "inherited her distinguished father's genus for the law" and entered the University of Mississippi School of Law in the fall of 1922. While a student at Ole Miss, she met Louis Meredith Jiggitts of Canton, a returning Rhodes Scholar (Jurisprudence St. John's College Oxford University). She and Louis were married on September 11, 1924, in West Point. Lavonia and Louis loved the arts - appearing together in a school play - and shared a passion for politics - she was voted Ole Miss Most Beautiful in 1923. They left Ole Miss upon Louis's graduation from the Law School with him becoming a member of The Mississippi Bar. Lavonia had to sit for the bar exam. Louis taught her the third year subjects and she was admitted on July 26, 1924. Louis went on to teach torts at the Jackson School of Law and encouraged women to pursue the study of law. Louis and Lavonia married on September 11,

Lavonia's 1924 Ole Miss yearbook photo. (Below) Louis Meredith Jiggitts was a football star, a member of the university orchestra, and a Rhodes Scholar. The couple met while students at Ole Miss.

1924, and moved to Jackson where they lived with Louis's grandfather, the Honorable Robert Powell, Circuit Judge of the 7th District. Louis became a partner in Powell, Harper and Jiggitts.

Lavonia and Louis began a very active life and became heavily involved with the Democratic Party. Louis served as Democratic National Committeeman from Mississippi, Vice-Chair of the Democratic National Committee, and Vice-Chair of the Democratic National Convention Philadelphia in 1936.

Louis served as the Reporter for the Mississippi State Supreme Court (Volumes 154 to 190) and Secretary-Treasurer of the Mississippi State Bar. Louis had served as the youngest commissioned officer in the American Army during World War I and afterwards served as a Captain commanding Company C in the Mississippi National Guard when it was inducted into the United States Army in autumn of 1940. He went on to serve at Headquarters of the Division as Intelligence Officer and served through many of the South Pacific engagements of the Seventh Army; however, after the Moratai invasion as a Lieutenant-Colonel he returned home fatally ill and passed away on March 22, 1945. Post No.110 of The American Legion was named in his honor.

Lavonia and Louis had two children Mary Anne Jiggitts Gowan Wells and Louis Meredith Jiggitts Jr. Lavonia worked for the Veterans Administration Regional Of-

(Continued on next page)

Lavonia Caradine Jiggitts Jones ❖ 1924

fice in Jackson as a lead claims examiner under Robert H. Dinsmore, Chief Attorney from 1945 until 1954.

In September of 1954, Lavonia married Dr. Edley Jones, Sr. of Vicksburg, the first chief of the otolaryngology division and one of the original faculty members of the University of Mississippi Medical School. They spent the next 25 years traveling extensively before his death in 1979. Lavonia became inactive status with the Bar in 1983. She passed away on March 6, 1988, and is buried at the Lakewood Memorial Park next to Louis.

Lavonia has two grandchildren who are members of The Mississippi Bar, step-grandson Edley H. Jones III and granddaughter Meredith A. Gowan Le Goff.

Story by Mississippi attorney Meredith A. Gowan Le Goff, granddaughter of Lavonia Caradine Jiggitts Jones.

L. M. JIGGITTS, Half-Back

Jiggitts, speed-merchant, broken field runner, student, and a Rhodes Scholar, was elected the best all-round athlete in school, and this was mainly on account of his prowess on the gridiron. Jiggitts is a product of the Canton High School and chose the University as the place for continuing his studies and athletic career. He actually does the 100 yds. in ten seconds flat, and during the past season his remarkable speed has brought sorrow upon the heads of his opponents. Jiggitts leaves in the summer for Oxford, England and he will be greatly missed at Ole Miss next year.

(Right) Lavonia was listed as "Most Beautiful Girl" in the Ole Miss yearbook's popularity contest. (Above) Lavonia's husband, Louis, was voted "Most Athletic" in the Ole Miss yearbook's popularity contest. In 1945, Louis returned home fatally ill after serving in the South Pacific in World War II. He died on March 22, 1945.

Mary Gladys Hoover Williams ❖ 1925

Holmes County was proud to have its first female lawyer. The mother of Parham H. Williams, Jr., Dean of the University of Mississippi Law School from 1971-1985, was attorney Mary Williams. Born in Pickens on October 8, 1897, and a lifetime resident of Holmes County, Mary Gladys Hoover Williams attended the Pickens schools. Her parents were Mr. and Mrs. J. R. Hoover. She graduated from Belhaven College. Mary met her husband, Parham Williams, in law school, and they were married on December 26, 1923. The couple remained in Pickens until 1924. They both graduated from the Cumberland University School of Law in Tennessee in 1925.

(Above) Parham Williams and Mary Gladys Hoover Williams. The couple met while in law school at Cumberland University School of Law. (Below left) Mary Williams, circa 1990. (Below Right) Mary's young son, Parham Williams, Jr., who would serve as dean of the Ole Miss Law School from 1971-1985.

After their graduation, they moved to Lexington. For the next two years, Mary taught school in Lexington.

She was a lifelong member of the First United Methodist Church where she taught the Friendship Sunday School class for many years. She was an active member of the Women's Missionary Society, an active member of the Magnolia Garden Club, and was an avid gardener. She was a certified flower show judge and judged flower shows throughout Mississippi for many years. She was a retired teacher and lawyer.

Mary died on August 20, 1992, at the age of 94 and is buried in Lexington.

Nell Wilkinson Hunt ❖ 1926

*P*ike County's first female lawyer was Nell Wilkinson Hunt. She was born in McComb on August 25, 1897, daughter of J. E. Wilkinson, one of the pioneer citizens of McComb. Her mother was Addie Edith Wilkinson. She graduated from McComb High School in 1918 and married Carlton Everett Hunt in 1921. Early in life, she entered the professional life of the city and became a stenographer to Edgar G. Williams, one of the vicinity's outstanding lawyers. She later became his office manager. While working with Mr. Williams, she studied law and passed the bar examination in 1926. She became a partner in the law firm of Williams and Hunt, specializing in chancery matters.

Upon admittance to the Bar, she practiced in McComb and became a member of the Pike County Bar Association. She later became Vice Chairman of the State Democratic Executive Committee. Being very active in the women's movement, she was vice president for Mississippi in the National Association of Women Lawyers as well as a member of the Daughters of the American Revolution (DAR). Nell had been named Good Citizenship Chairman of the State chapter of D. A. R.

Nell was president of the Mississippi Federation of Business & Professional Women's Clubs and District Chairman of the Mississippi Federation of Women's Clubs. She was president of the McComb Library Association.

Nell was selected for a national honor in *American Women.* The October 9, 1935, *Enterprise-Journal* reported that the current issue of the Illinois Central magazine comments on the selection of a well known McComb woman for an outstanding national honor: "Nell Wilkinson Hunt, lawyer and club-woman of McComb, Miss., has won a place in the 1935-1936 edition of American Women. The official who's who among the women in the nation. Her biography, with 1,214 others, was selected from 15,000 recommendations. Mrs. Hunt is with the law firm, Williams and Hunt, having been admitted in 1926. She was the first woman notary public in Mississippi."

During her work as an attorney, she presented two cases before the Mississippi Supreme Court.

Nell died at the age of 48 on April 8, 1946, after suffering a fall. All members of the Pike County Bar Association served as honorary pallbearers. She attended the First Baptist Church in McComb.

(Left) Nell Wilkinson Hunt sponsored mock trials in McComb through the Business and Professional Women's club. Women served on the jury, and as attorneys. The programs were wildly popular among McComb residents. (Top Right): Hunt's listing in 1928 Bar Association magazine. (Right) A story from the *Enterprise-Journal* announcing Hunt's inclusion in Illinois Central's magazine *American Women: The Official Whos' Who Among American Women.*

Marriage Before Judge and Jury Given

As Verdict In Damage-Heart Balm Suit

Mock Trial of Miss Quin Vs. Browder

Marriage then and there before judge and jury was the price a jury of 12 good men and women true made H. L. Browder pay in a damage breach of promise suit tried in a mock court Monday night at the McComb city hall before Chancery Judge R. W. Cutrer, of Magnolia. However, even that penalty was much cheaper than the $5,000 actual and $125,000 punitive damages sought by the plaintiff, Miss Lula Quin, in the original petition of complaint.

The mock trial, sponsored by the McComb Business and Professional Women's club, packed the auditorium of the city hall and kept the spectators and court attaches alike, including the judge in a riot of laugh-

der and a smattering of their testimony follows:

John Beard, straight-faced and without a twinkle of the eye, testified that the defendant bought Woolworth candy and came to his store and secured empty candy boxes in which he placed the cheap candy with the avowed purpose of tendering it to Miss Quin as a token of his love.

Roger Alford, of Alford's Jewelry store, told of the selection of the engagement diamond which later was fund on the finger of one Mrs. Harrilee Cook, named co-respondent by the plaintiff.

Dr. Elise Rutledge testified that following September 3, 1934, when Miss Quin was left waiting at the

PIKE COUNTY

Hutchinson, J. T., Summitt, Miss.
Parson, W. A., Summitt, Miss.
Cassidy, J. J., McComb, Miss.
Cutrer, L. W., McComb, Miss.
Davis, J. E., McComb, Miss.
Hewitt, F. D., McComb, Miss.
Hunt, Mrs. Nellie, McComb, Miss.
Jackson, W. F., McComb, Miss.
Jackson, F. V., McComb, Miss.
McGuire, J. S., McComb, Miss.
McGehee, L. H., McComb, Miss.
Mixon, W. B., McComb, Miss.
McLain, W. G., McComb, Miss.
Price, K. G., McComb, Miss.
Reeves, R. B., McComb, Miss.
Price, J. H. Sr., Magnolia, Miss.
Price, J. H. Jr., Magnolia, Miss.
Mitchell, Thos., Magnolia, Miss.
Wiltshire, J. A., Magnolia, Miss.
R. W., Magnolia,

Mrs. Nell W. Hunt In 'American Women

I. C. Magazine Comments Upon Selection of McComb Woman for Honor

The current issue of the Illinois Central Magazine comments as follows on the selection of a well known McComb woman for an outstanding National honor: "Nell Wilkinson Hunt, lawyer and club-woman of M

Evelyn Hunt Conner ❖ 1928

"Prominent Woman Admitted to Bar," was the headline in the *Clarion-Ledger* newspaper on February 17, 1928. It stated that two well-known citizens of the Gulf Coast were given license to practice in state Courts. "Mrs. Evelyn Hunt Conner has been admitted to the bar. Mrs. Conner was educated at the University of Mississippi in the literary department. She has been a stenographer for Walter J. Gex for nine years. Her practice in preparing his pleadings and her general education enabled her to take a successful examination before the state bar examiners. She will be one of the few lady lawyers in Mississippi."

PROMINENT WOMAN ADMITTED TO BAR

Two Well Known Citizens of Gulfcoast Given License to Practice in State Courts

Mrs. Evelyn Hunt Conner and Walter J. Gex, Jr., of Bay St. Louis have been admitted to the bar. Mr. Gex was educated at the University of Florida in the law school. He is son of Walter J. Gex, formerly a law partner of Senator Pat Harrison. He is one of the leading lawyers on the Mississippi coast.

Mrs. Conner was educated at the University of Mississippi in the literary department. She is a sister of Miss Melville Hunt, teacher in the Jackon High school. She has been stenographer for Mr. Gex for nine years. Her practice in preparing his pleadings and her general education enabled her to take a successful examination before the state bar examiners. She will be one of the few lady lawyers in Mississippi.

Evelyn H. Conner was born in Lee County in July 1896. Her parents were Will and Loula Hunt. She furthered her education at the University of Mississippi. Once admitted in 1928, she practiced in Bay St. Louis, becoming the first female lawyer in Hancock County. She became a member of the Hancock County, Mississippi State, and American Bar Associations. That same year she was listed in the *Mississippi Law Journal* as a member of the Bar. In 1938, she was listed in the *Bench and Bar* publication. In 1944, she was on the Subcommittee of War Finance of the Women Lawyers Association.

Evelyn had two sons. She was memorialized in 1972 at The Mississippi Bar's Memorial Service for attorneys who had passed away the previous year.

Willie Yeates Rylee Pilcher ❖ 1928

Born in August 1893, Willie Yeates Rylee Pilcher of Clarksdale was admitted to the bar in 1928. Her parents were Willie J. and Imogene Rylee. Willie was a member of The Mississippi Bar and the Tennessee Bar. The *Clarion Ledger* on March 16, 1928 reported, "Jacksonians Are Passed By Board - Miss Willie Rylee, who studied law in Mississippi, but whose home is reported to be in Holly Springs, and Thomas Allen Hartley, of Maben, tied for honors in making the highest grade, each attaining the 89 mark."

She authored "Enemy Aliens as Litigants" in the *George Washington Law Review* in 1943. Her brother, Robert Rylee, wrote a novel, *Deep Dark River*, based on his sister, depicting a young lady practicing law in Clarksdale going up against the establishment in a murder trial.

The George Washington Law Review

Combining, THE CONSTITUTIONAL REVIEW

Volume 11
1942-1943

The George Washington University Press
The George Washington University
Washington, D. C.

(Above) The George Washington Law Review, 1943, in which Pilcher's article "Enemy Aliens as Litigants" was published. (Right) A newspaper story detailing Pilcher's high marks on the bar exam.

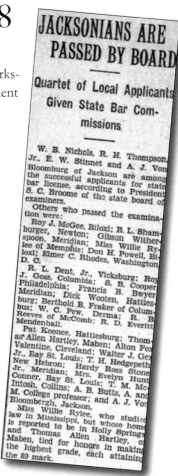

JACKSONIANS ARE PASSED BY BOARD

Quartet of Local Applicants Given State Bar Commissions

W. B. Nichols, R. H. Thompson, Jr., E. W. Stinnet and A. J. Von Bloomburg of Jackson are among the successful applicants for state bar license, according to President S. C. Broome of the state board of examiners.

Others who passed the examination were:

Roy J. McGee, Biloxi; B. L. Shamburger, Newton; Gibson Witherspoon, Meridian; Miss Willie Rylee of Memphis; Don H. Powell, Biloxi; Elmer C. Rhodes, Washington, D. C.

R. L. Dent, Jr., Vicksburg; Roy J. Goss, Columbia; S. B. Cooper, Philadelphia; Francis B. Bwyer, Meridian; Dick Wooten, Hattiesburg; Berthold B. Fraker of Columbus; W. C. Few, Derma; R. B. Reeves of McComb; R. D. Everitt, Mendenhall.

Pat Koonce, Hattiesburg; Thomas Allen Hartley, Maben; Alton Fox Valentine, Cleveland; Walter J. Gex, Jr., Bay St. Louis; T. H. Hedgepeth, New Hebron; Hardy Ross Stone, Jr., Meridian; Mrs. Evelyn Hunt Conner, Bay St. Louis; T. M. McIntosh, Collins; A. B. Butts, A. and M. College professor; and A. J. Von Bloombergh, Jackson.

Miss Willie Rylee, who studied law in Mississippi, but whose home is reported to be in Holly Springs, and Thomas Allen Hartley, of Maben, tied for honors in making the highest grade, each attaining the 89 mark.

Margaret Hervey Jones Graham ❖ 1928

Born on July 12, 1906, in Memphis, Margaret Hervey Jones was reared in Water Valley. Her parents were Charles Thomas Jones and Ida Hervey. She attended the University of Tennessee and the University of Alabama as an undergraduate. In 1928, she graduated from the University of Mississippi Law School and was featured in the Ole Miss yearbook. Margaret was the 7th female University of Mississippi Law School graduate.

Margaret married Robert Miller Graham. She was a practicing attorney in Jackson from 1936-1946 and was a medical secretary for Dr. T. E. Wilson, Jr. She also worked with the Mississippi State Archives.

Active in the Jackson Little Theatre and the Children's Community Theatre, she was called the "First Lady of Jackson Little Theatre." The May 31, 1956, *Clarion Ledger* stated, "Erstwhile attorney and present homemaker, Margaret has a Golden Touch all her own,

for whatever she tackles just seems to succeed for the sake of success. Born in Memphis, Margaret Jones grew up in Water Valley where she was valedictorian of her high school graduating class. Entering college on a scholarship, she graduated from the University of Mississippi with degree of bachelor of laws and forthwith came to Jackson to hang out her shingle as a lady lawyer. Being a practicing attorney was fine work, but along came the opportunity for a bright young woman to take an even finer position with the state in the Department of Archives and History. At college, she was a member of Alpha Psi Omega, national dramatic fraternity. In addition to Delta Gamma, social fraternity, and after coming to Jackson, she became active in the Little Theatre. She was a charter member and once president of the Community Children's Theatre. She has been active in PTA work and was senior president of Dancing Rabbit Creek society, Children of the American Revolution. She was a willing worker during World War II and served on the Woman's War Bond Board. From attorney to actress, from historian to housewife, from joiner to doer, Margaret Jones Graham has managed to accomplish everything she has set out to do with minimum fuss and maximum efficiency."

She was a member of First Presbyterian Church and a member of the Casual Club and La Finesse bridge club.

Margaret died on October 18, 1977, after a short illness and is buried in Lakewood Memorial Cemetery in Jackson.

Million-Dollar Ride Puts Graham in Driver' sSeat

By MARY ALICE BOOKHART

Hitch your Solid Gold Cadillac to a star and what've you got? — A 24-carat success!

Especially if the star happens to be Margaret Graham, long-time favorite of the Jackson Little Theatre and leading lady of its fifth and final production of the season, "The Solid Gold Cadillac," which opens tonight at the Playhouse for an eight-night run.

Erstwhile attorney and present homemaker (for a number of years now) for Husband Bob and Daughter, Hervey, our Margaret has a Golden Touch all her own, for whatever she tackles just seems to succeed for the sake of success.

Born in Memphis ("circa 1800," she teases) Mrs. Graham, then Margaret Jones, grew up in Water Valley where she was valedictorian of her high school graduating class.

Entering college on a scholarship, she graduated from the University of Mississippi with

tion. On the purely social side, she belongs to the Casual Club (is a former president of same), La Finesse Bridge Luncheon club, and the Lazy Daisies bridge club.

A member of the Presbyterian church, she has also taken an active part in community affairs. She was a willing worker during World War II and served on the Woman's War Bond Board.

From attorney to actress, from historian to housewife, from joiner to doer, Margaret Jones Graham has managed to accomplish everything she has set out to do with minimum fuss and maximum efficiency.

"You've gotta have heart," she quips. And she does have heart — yep, you guessed it — a heart of gold.

———

Add chopped raisins and walnuts to part of that 7-minute frosting (homemade or packaged) and use as a filling for layer cake. The rest of the frosting goes over the top and sides of the cake.

(Top) Margaret Hervey Jones Graham's photograph from the Ole Miss yearbook. (Left) A story from the *Clarion-Ledger* in 1956 that covers her career in theatre. In addition to staples like "Harvey", "Arsenic and Old Lace", and "The Man Who Came to Dinner", Graham also wrote, directed, and starred in her own original stage plays.

Zelma W. Price
ATTORNEY AT LAW
CITIZENS BANK BUILDING
Greenville, Mississippi

Zelma Wells Price ❖ 1929

*M*ississippi's first woman judge, Zelma Wells Price, was born on October 6, 1898. She was also the first female lawyer to practice in Washington County. In 1919, her father Walter Bunyan Wells, a deputy sheriff, was shot and killed by a man who refused to pay his gambling debt. Her mother, Mattie Lou Rish Wells, also died an early death at 43 from unknown causes.

Zelma graduated from Houston High School in 1916. She became manager for the Western Union Telegraph Company, then married Robert Lorenzo Price on May 6, 1917. Price never went to law school, but instead studied under W. Scott Watson in Greenville. On her way to take the bar exam, the vehicle she was traveling in was hit by another car, and her vehicle rolled down a hill. Injuries were minimal, but she was bandaged and bruised while taking the examination in Jackson. She was admitted to the bar in 1929, and her political career began in 1943. She ran for and won the state legislature three times. While in the legislature, she introduced and passed several significant bills, one of which was the Youth Court Act. Not long after, Price was involved in another automobile accident, this time breaking her back. To cast the deciding vote for the establishment of the University Medical Center in Jackson, she was wheeled to the House floor on a stretcher.

Zelma was the first woman appointed to be Chairman of the House Temperance Committee and later appointed to the Appropriations Committee. Due to her work with youth, she was Chairman of the Juvenile Delinquency Committee. Governor Hugh White appointed her to the County Court as the youth judge in Washington County, automatically instating her "Judge" title and status and making her the first woman judge in Mississippi.

During a speech to the Altrusa club in Memphis, Price told audiences she believed women had been "delayed pilgrims" in their journey towards recognition in the business world and

the professions. She also predicted women would never "make the grade, unless they stop their imitation of men." She expounded on this sentiment by going on, "Women complain that they are set apart. Well, they are. And they were set apart by God. Our anatomies and our minds are different. Neither superior or inferior, just different."

She was a member of the American Bar Association, National Association of Women Lawyers, Mississippi Economic Council and Chamber of Commerce, the American Judicature Society, National Democratic Advisory Committee, and the Business and Professional Women's Club, where she was president. She was also the legal advisor to the Girl Scouts Council. When Zelma retired in 1970, she was able to indulge her love for genealogy, completing 10 books on her family's history.

Mississippi Court of Appeals Judge Virginia C. Carlton is a relative of Judge Zelma Wells Price. Judge Carlton stated, "She was an inspiration to

(Continued on next page)

Mrs. Zelma Price New County Judge

Mrs. Zelma W. Price, member of the lower house of the state legislature from Washington county, was Thursday named county judge, succeeding S. B. (Bun), Thomas, resigned.

Gov. Hugh L. White made the appointment and Mrs. Price immediately announced she is resigning from her seat in the legislature.

A special election will be called in Washington county by the governor in the near future, to replace Mrs. Price in the law-making body.

A vacancy in the county judgeship was created when Judge Thomas resigned to accept a gubernatorial appointment as chancellor of the ninth district, succeeding the late Chancellor Frank E. Everett, of Indianola, who died there Tuesday of this week.

Mrs. Price is a prominent Greenville attorney, and has served in the late Chancellor Frank E. Ev-1944. She is a widow, 49 years of age, and a native of Calhoun coun-

(Continued on next page)

Zelma Wells Price ❖ 1929

us all to pursue excellence and to pursue justice!"

Judge Zelma Wells Price died on February 24, 1974, after a long illness at the age of 75 and is buried in Greenville. Upon her death, the *Delta Democrat-Times* reported on March 1, 1974, "The Judge was ever-mindful of the fact that she was a woman, succeeding in what was largely a man's world, and that other women who were not as fortunate or as gifted were held in second-class bondage strictly because of their sex. Her rulings from the county court bench toward the end of her ju-

dicial career were often pointedly precedent-shattering. She put women on county court juries when Mississippi still officially kept them off. She ruled at least one law unconstitutional because it discriminated against women, a mind-boggling step for a county court judge."

To honor her memory, The Mississippi Bar Women in the Profession Committee created the Price-Prather Luncheon at the Bar's Annual Meeting each year. It was first established in 1999 and was named to honor Zelma Price, first female judge in Mississippi, and Lenore Prather, first female Mississippi Supreme Court Chief Justice.

(Left and Top Left): Price was instrumental in getting women on juries (Top Right) Price enters the Capitol on a stretcher to cast a crucial vote. (Below) The *Greenwood Commonwealth* features the versatile Price.

1930s

The Wall Street Crash of 1929 plunged the nation into a depression. To make matters worse, Mississippi had never fully recovered from the Great Flood of 1927. Mississippi's average income — already the lowest in the nation at $287 per year — plunged to a paltry $117. On a single day in 1932, one quarter of all Mississippi's farmland was sold for back taxes. Women in the workforce faced a particular bias in the 1930s. With unemployment hovering at 25%, many thought a working woman was taking a man's job. In 1930, eleven million women were in the workforce in the United States. Seventy-five percent were teachers or nurses. The balance were almost exclusively domestic or clerical jobs. By the end of the decade, women lawyers would make up only 2.7% of all working attorneys in the United States. Despite the grim outlook, and the growing disdain for working females, Mississippi's women lawyers continued to push the gender boundary. In 1931, Lucy Somerville Howorth was elected to the House of Representatives; Mississippi native Burnita Shelton Matthews was elected president of the National Association of Women Lawyers; Helen Carloss and Bessie Young were rising stars in the U.S. Justice Department; and Zelma Price initiated her efforts to get women on juries in Mississippi.

In a decade that embraced Shirley Temple, Margaret Mitchell, Betty Davis, and an emerging Mississippian named Eudora Welty, The Mississippi Bar welcomed twenty-seven new women lawyers.

THREE WOMEN ARE LATEST ADDITIONS TO MISSISSIPPI BAR

Miss Allee Dunn, Formerly of Greenville, is Among Those Received as Newest Member – Two Other Ladies Are Included

(by The Associated Press)

Jackson, Miss. Sept. 22, 1931 – Three women are latest additions to membership in the state Bar Association with the right to practice before the state supreme court.

22 Julia Ann Pollard Sheldon Griffin ❖ 1930

On the day Julia Sheldon Griffin died at the age of 49, her good friend said, "She was a good lawyer." Julia Ann Pollard Sheldon Griffin was born on October 9, 1903, in Nehawka, Nebraska, to Rose Olive Higgins and George Lawson Sheldon. Her father was governor of Nebraska from 1907-1908. He moved the family to Avon, Mississippi in 1911 where he became a farmer and was later named State Collector of Internal Revenue.

Julia graduated from Greenville High School in 1919 and received her B.A. from the University of Nebraska in 1924, where she was the chairman of the Class Debate Committee. Julia paid her own way through college by part-time teaching. She taught for several years in Greenville. The *Delta Democrat Times* stated, "All this time, she had set her sights on being a lawyer. She studied law at the University of Nebraska, the University of Mississippi and the University of Alabama. She passed the bar examination in 1930 and hung out her shingle in Jackson in 1932. She had desk space in the offices of Hallam and Lyell. Those gentlemen were most kind, but there wasn't enough clients to go around in 1932, so Julia went back to teaching."

Julia Ann Sheldon married George Urquhart Griffin in August of 1935. They lived in Rolling Fork, then Tupelo. He died in 1944, leaving her a widow with two small children. The *Delta Democrat* article continues, "Once again she forsook teaching for the law. Julia Griffin was a valued associate of one of the oldest, and best-established law firms in Mississippi, Green, Green & Cheney."

Julia was named vice-president and program chairman of the League of Women Voters in Greenville. In May of 1947, she was the featured speaker at the YMCA Luncheon on Public Affairs – "Women's Responsibility to Her Government" held in Jackson.

Julia died on March 31, 1953, and is buried in Greenville Cemetery next to her husband.

(Left) Julia Ann Pollard Sheldon as a student.
(Below Left): *Clarion-Ledger* story about her YWCA speech.

Mrs. Griffin to Address YWCA Luncheon Group

Mrs. Julia Sheldon Griffin will be the guest speaker at the public affairs luncheon at the YWCA on Tuesday, May 20. She will speak on "Woman's Responsibility to Her Government." Mrs. Griffin is well qualified to speak on this subject, as she has been interested in government since her early childhood. Before moving to Mississippi, her father, George L. Sheldon, was governor of Nebraska.

Mrs. Griffin received her B. A. degree from the University of Nebraska and studied at the University of Alabama and the University of Mississippi. She is a member of the Mississippi Bar association and associated with the firm of Green and Green in the practice of law.

Mrs. Jesse L. White, president of the board of directors, stated that this would be the last of this series of public affairs luncheons. The fall and winter series will start in October. There will be a short business session of the membership at which time new members to the

Mrs. Ralph Hester, chairman of the membership committee which sponsors these luncheons, urges all members to get their reservations in early by calling the YWCA office by Monday, May 19.

Opti-Mrs. Camp For Girls To Open July 7

Seventy two girls of seven thru fourteen years of age can be accommodated at the Jackson Opti-Mrs club camp this summer, according to Mrs. O. H. Purser, camp committee chairman.

The camp will be held for two weeks beginning July 7 at the Optimist club grounds on Lake Phil Armitage at Raymond.

Girls may be enrolled for one or both weeks at a fee of $15 per week. Reservations may be made

PUBLIC Affairs Speaker: Mrs. Julia Sheldon Griffin, well-known Jackson attorney, who will be the featured speaker at last of the Public Affairs luncheon series this season at the YWCA Tuesday, May 26, at 12 o'clock.

Father was a Founder of Mississippi Republican Party

In 1898, during the Spanish-American war, Nebraska native George L. Sheldon was en route to Cuba when his train passed through the Mississippi Delta. Four years later, he returned to purchase a 1700 acre plantation south of Greenville. He served as governor of Nebraska from 1907-1908. Sheldon moved to Mississippi in 1909 to raise cattle and grow cotton.

George L. Sheldon

Sheldon fought for a two-party system in Mississippi. He appeared on the ballot as a republican candidtate for governor during several elections. He also ran for Senate as a republican candidate. He never captured more than a tiny percentage of the vote, as he knew would be the case.

George L. Sheldon is considered by many to the man who forged a path for the modern republican party in Mississippi.

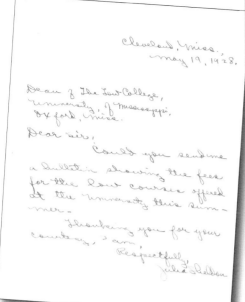

(Top Left and Right): Letters to the University of Mississippi Law School from Julia Sheldon; (Center): Julia Ann Pollard Sheldon Griffin's obituary.

Tommie Leverett Hays ❖ 1930

Hattiesburg's second woman lawyer, Tommie Leverett Hayes, was born in Webster County on September 21, 1883. Her mother was Roxana Curtis Leverett, and her father was James M. Leverett, a private in the Civil War, 17th MS Infantry.

Tommie married Charles M. Hays in 1899 when she was 16 years old. They had one child during their marriage. Her husband died in 1936.

In 1931, Tommie was a member of the Hattiesburg and Forrest County Bar Associations. She practiced law in Hattiesburg for a number of years. She then moved to the U. S. District Attorney's office in Jackson for 15 years. Ill health forced her retirement at age 69, and she returned to Hattiesburg.

Tommie was a member of Main Street Church in Hattiesburg. She died on May 14, 1960, and is buried in Roseland Park Cemetery in Hattiesburg.

Mrs. Hays, Attorney, Dies At Hub City

HATTIESBURG — Services were held Sunday at Quigley Funeral Home chapel for Mrs. Charles M. Hays, retired attorney, who died early Saturday at Methodist Hospital.

Mrs. Hays was Hattiesburg's second woman lawyer. After practicing here for a number of years, she was in the U. S. District Attorney's office in Jackson for 15 years. Ill health forced her retirement more than six years ago and she returned to Hattiesburg at that time.

She leaves a daughter, Mrs. Rube C. Small of San Angelo, Texas, and a sister, Mrs. James Hays of Hattiesburg.

Mississippi Law Journal

JOURNAL of the MISSISSIPPI STATE BAR

VOL. IX   OCTOBER, 1936   No. 1

MEMBERS OF THE LAW JOURNAL BOARD

BAR COMMITTEE:
HON. D. C. BRAMLETTE, CHAIRMAN
  WOODVILLE
HON. T. C. KIMBROUGH
  UNIVERSITY
HON. HUGH CLAYTON
  NEW ALBANY

EDITORIAL BOARD:
R. GORDON GRANTHAM
  EDITOR

FACULTY ADVISERS:
DR. W. S. MALONE
DR. JOHN W. WADE

CHARLES R. JACQUIN

CONTENTS

Lyda Gordon Shivers ❖ 1930

Growing up in Poplarville as the only daughter of Jack Cocke Shivers and Clyde Miller Shivers, Lyda Gordon Shivers would hardly have imagined her future as a lawyer and a highly recognized North Carolina educator.

She was born on October 11, 1907. Her father was an attorney in Poplarville and was very much involved with local politics, serving in the Mississippi House of Representatives from 1908-1912, as county prosecuting attorney

National Council on Family Relations and various other professional, social, service and civic organizations. She had numerous professional publications including "Twentieth Century South-wide Civic and Lay Organizations for Human Welfare."

She was a frequent speaker on sociological issues and was a consultant with North Carolina's Headstart program. She was awarded a traveling fellowship by the Amer-

(Left): Lyda Gordon Shivers from the 1929 and 1930 Ole Miss yearbook. (Right) Dr. Lyda Gordon Shivers, circa 1965, a professor in the sociology department at the University of North Carolina Chapel Hill.

and as Circuit Court Judge. Lyda received her B.A. and LL.B. Degree with distinction from the University of Mississippi Law School in 1930. She was the first female on the Editorial Staff of the *Mississippi Law Journal*. She was secretary of her senior law class. The bar admitted her to practice in 1930, and she became a member of The Mississippi Bar, as well as the American and Southern Sociological Societies and the National Council on Family Relations. By 1933, she was teaching in the Sociology Department of the University of North Carolina Chapel Hill. She received her Ph.D. from that institution in 1935.

One of her strongest interests was criminology and delinquency. While at the University of Mississippi, she wrote her thesis on "The History of the Mississippi Penitentiary."

During her career, she also taught at the University of Mississippi, Mills College in Oakland, California, and Texas State College for Women. Her tenure from 1954-1968 as Chair of the Sociology Department at the University of North Carolina set a record.

Lyda served as president of the North Carolina Sociological Association and the North Carolina Conference for Social Service. She kept her membership in The Mississippi Bar throughout her life and also belonged to the

ican Council on Education under the auspices of the Commission on Teacher Education to make a study of guidance and personnel in American colleges and universities. Lyda also served as chairman of the Guilford County Board of Public Welfare and as president of the Greensboro Chapter of the American Field Service.

In 1970, she was elected governor at the South Atlantic Region of the Sorgionist Federation of America, an international organization of business and professional women. Dr. Lyda Gordon Shivers died on November 17, 1972, and is buried in the Poplarville, Mississippi City Cemetery.

Dr. Lyda Shivers' Body Brought Home For Burial

A native Mississippian who became a leading educator in North Carolina, Dr. Lyda Gordon Shivers, died last week and her body was brought to Poplarville for burial.

Dr. Shivers, a native of Poplarville, ha dretired as professor of criminology at the Univesity of North Carolina at Greensboro and was making her home there at the time of her death. She had been head of the department of sociology and anthropology from 1954 to 1968.

ation of America, an international organization of business and professional women

Before her work at UNC-G, Dr. Shivers taught for various periods at the University of Mississippi, Texas State College for Women and Mills College in Oakland, California.

She received the A. B. and LL. B. degrees from the University of Mississippi, a doctorate from the University of North Carolina at Chapel Hill. She was a member of the Mississippi Bar, the American and South-

Lucille Brown ❖ 1931

"26 Lawyers Pass Bar Exams Here" was the headline for the *Clarion-Ledger* newspaper on February 26, 1931. "Whether eight Mississippi lawyers are disbarred from practice in the state or not, Mississippi will not suffer for lack of attorneys. A new crop of barristers have just been licensed to practice by the state board of law examiners, according to an announcement of Stewart C. Broome, president of the board."

She was born in 1902 to George Lee Brown and Clyde Steele Brown of Jackson. Lucille had worked as a stenographer prior to passing the bar exam. Lucille Brown passed the bar exam in 1931, along with three other women, Winnie Greer of Jackson, Pearl McClellan of Greenwood and Clara Melton of Jackson.

In 1932 she served as Noble Grand of Rebekah Lodge of Mississippi and as president of the Women's Auxiliary to the United Spanish War Veterans Camp in Mississippi. In the 1950s, she was a member of the Credit Women's Club and the Business and Professional Women's Club. In 1976 she served as president of the Alta Raymond Club.

She passed away in July 1985. Having lived her entire life in Jackson, she is buried in Cedar Lawn Cemetery.

Miss Brown To Assembly In Gulfport

Miss Lucile Brown, as Noble Grand of Rebekah Lodge of Mississippi, will leave Monday for Gulfport to attend the encampment of the Auxiliary of the United Spanish War Veterans as vice-president of the Auxiliary.

Pearl Marie McLellan ❖ 1931

Leflore County's first female lawyer was Pearl Marie McLellan. She was born on May 15, 1890, in Holmes County to Martin Emmanuel and Virginia McLellan. She attended Mississippi College for Women to obtain her higher education. In 1923, Judge S. F. Davis, the presiding judge of the district, appointed Pearl to be the official court reporter for the Fourth Circuit Court District of Mississippi. Pearl was the first woman in Mississippi to be appointed official reporter for the circuit court, and she served for 35 years.

In the February 25, 1931 *Greenwood Commonwealth* newspaper, the headline stated, "Miss Pearl McLellan Passes Bar

Exam." The article continued, "Miss Pearl McLellan, court stenographer, received word this afternoon that she was successful in the bar examination held at Jackson recently and passed with flying colors. Miss McLellan's friends are congratulating her upon becoming a full-fledged lawyer."

She was admitted to the bar in 1931.

In 1938, she was in the *Bench and Bar* listing and was a member of the Leflore County Bar Association. The National Association of Women Lawyers elected her to serve as vice president from Mississippi in 1940. In 1944, she was re-elected president of the Mississippi Court Reporters Association.

At a 1947 Business & Professional

Women's Club meeting, she presented a program on "Legislation — Our Tool." In her talk she stated that "it is our duty to elect statesmen, not politicians at this time, to pass constructive legislation. We must do our best as women to exercise our power to vote, as the ballot is one's greatest tool."

Retirement came in 1959 from her work as both an attorney and a court stenographer. On March 11, 1965, the *Greenwood Commonwealth* reported, "Miss Pearl was a charter member of the Business & Professional Women's Club, but before the club's organization she was already an established business leader. For a number of years, she was Circuit Court reporter for the 4th District. During her membership in Business & Professional Women's Club, Miss McLellan was interested in legislation and provided keen wisdom in this area which helped the club to form an effective constitution and to take an active voice in the local and state legislative responsibilities that were open to women's approval."

Pearl was a member of First Baptist Church in Greenwood and was a resident of Greenwood for 70 years. Pearl died on February 6, 1984, at the age of 93.

Legend of Stronghold, Greenwood's Oldest Home

The year is 1923. I was looking around for a house that I could buy on HOPE and FAITH — I had nothing else. I had a home all of my life and I needed a home for my invalid mother. I wanted one. So one sunny bright day in January 1923, the late Mr. Garrard Barrett, who was looking after the Greenwood property of Mr. D. E. Nichols, a former Greenwood citizen, who had moved to Rhode Island, took me down to look at what turned out to be my "Stronghold."

I fell in love with the old house on first sight. It enchanted, fascinated and intrigued me. I liked its dignity even in its state of despair. You know of course houses have personality. I liked the way the sunlight came streaming in through the west window of what is now my living room. Here was this little old orphaned house, its past greatness and grandeur gone, sad and lonely, unloved and unwanted. Evil days had truly fallen upon it, yet here it sat with dignity still, though embarrassed and humiliated by its environment, as if it hoped to be rescued finally.

The house was located on the north side of String Avenue facing the south with wide open fields, on a dirt street, ruts made by trucks and cars right up to the front steps, cotton stalks then came shoulder high to a big man on the west side right up to the house. There were no flowers. Three scrawny mulberry trees were on the street in front, a big thorn tree in the west front yard, a big cedar tree and a chinaberry tree in the back yard, a coal house and a storage house of sorts. The house was a dingy white clapboard — of pure heart cypress. I later learned — it was Greek Revival architecture but I didn't know it then — there was a long porch down the east side and a wide porch on the front, with ten square columns. The house consisted of three large rooms in a row, doors opening between. The rooms were 16 x 16 feet with 12 foot ceilings; adjoining the back bedroom on the east side was a bath room and a small room back of that; adjoining the middle room was a kitchen with two large pantries and on the north side of the kitchen was a wide back porch. The floors were single, made of wide boards, the doors were Christ doors, sometimes called "witches" doors, with crosses said to keep the witches out. There were three chimneys. We burned wood and coal in those days. There was no gas. The fences around this old house had fallen down and there was an air of general dilapidation and decay all about the place. Painting and repairs were needed badly.

The house was occupied by two families. One used the kitchen and front rooms and one used the back rooms and the bath room, using the lavatory for a kitchen sink. A kitchen stove was set up on the hearth in the back bedroom with the longest stove pipe I ever saw. It extended from the kitchen stove on the hearth across the room, through the window pane of a window on the west side, clear across the wide back porch to the outdoors. The storage closet in the back bedroom had been used for a smokehouse and I thought I would never get rid of the smell of meat there.

My friends all said I was a fool to think of buying this old house. But, remember I told you I had to have a home for my mother and besides that, I was in love with the old home. The price was $2,800 with $500 payable in cash and the balance spread out over several years. I couldn't even afford to pay that price. I had only $100 and HOPE and FAITH. I put the $100 up in escrow and signed a contract to purchase the old house in July 1923 when I became official reporter for the Circuit Court of the Fourth Judicial District of Mississippi and would have a steady income. I had already been appointed to that position. Where to get $400 balance on the down payment and $500 to repair and paint the house and make it fit to live in was more than I knew. But, good lawyers are wise people and they can do a lot of seemingly impossible things. I had a good one on my side. I shall always be grateful to the late Mr. Samuel L. Gwin, who showed me how to finance the purchase of my "Stronghold." Even so, I think I established some sort of record in high financing for I borrowed enough money on a second mortgage to make the $500 down payment and $500 to paint and repair the house and I executed notes for the balance due on the two mortgages. Incidentally, it took me twenty-six years to pay for this old house. It is mine now.

In this lot 100 x 150 is the east wing of the original "Stronghold" plantation residence, which is now located on Strong Avenue facing the south. It was moved across the court yard of the original site and placed in this new location.

In July 1923 my mother and I moved into my "Stronghold" which I believe, since it is part of the original "Stronghold," I have a right to call it "Stronghold."

From time to time I have done such repairs on the house as I could, painted it and planted shrubs and flowers and trees. I cut down the thorn tree, the mulberry trees curled up and died, and I mended the fences and the old place has been a source of much joy to me over the years, and I have always been happy there.

I have made few changes in the original house as it was when I bought it. I covered up the old wide boards in two rooms and wish now I hadn't. I cut a door from the back bedroom to the back porch in place of the window through which the stove pipe extended. I prop my windows up with sticks. The windows are getting a bit feeble now and sometime will have to be replaced but builders who examine the old house say it is still sound, which is a mighty good record, considering how old it is.

Would you like to re-assemble the original "Stronghold?" Then go first to Mrs. Sandifer's residence on River Road. Get there the heavy timbers put into the house from the original old house, go to 1303 on the south side of Leflore Avenue facing north and get a part of the old residence, then to 1309 Leflore Avenue south side facing north and get another part of the old residence, and come over and get my residence which is the east wing of the old residence, put them all together and we will have the original "Stronghold."

I have tried only to have a homey atmosphere at my "Stronghold." I want it to speak a welcome to everyone who comes in its doors. I have not restored its past greatness but I have, at least given it LOVE and a feeling of being wanted. It is a happy house now and I am happy with "Stronghold" as my home.

Presented by Pearl McLellan to the Leflore County Historical Society on April 10, 1956

Anna Clara Melton Sims ❖ 1931

The *Associated Press* reported on September 22, 1931, "Three women are latest additions to membership in the state Bar Association with the right to practice before the state Supreme Court. Expressing the hope that they would become active practitioners before the high court, Chief Justice Sydney Smith formally received the newest members, Missrs Louise and Clara Melton and Allee Dunn, all of Jackson." Martha Louise Melton and Clara Melton were sisters.

Clara was born on June 15, 1885, in Meridian to Jerome Norris Melton and Victoria Barber Melton.

On March 15, 1931, the *Clarion Ledger* published an article stating, "Miss Melton is Now Full-Fledge Member of Firm. Miss Clara Melton, who just passed her bar examination and has had her name put on the letterhead of Green, Green, and Jackson, is the descendent of an illustrious line. With her ancestry including a famous judge and a revered missionary, Miss Melton adopted the profession of one, and the name of the other. Her great-grandfather, Judge J. P. Crisman of Beauregard and Brookhaven, was a signer of the Constitution of 1890. Her full name is of royalty length, Anna Clara Crisman Melton, she being one of twenty-one namesakes of the missionary whose portrait hangs in the Galloway Memorial Church in memory of her services in Brazil and her death in the Jonestown Flood. A life devoted to social engagements was abruptly changed when Miss Melton, a graduate of high school, decided to become a stenographer. A public

stenographer for years, she found her preference growing for handling legal documents. During the world war, she was reporter in federal, circuit, and chancery courts. For a time, she was a secretary in the law offices of J. Edward Mayes and J. Robert Mayes and for the past five years has been with Green and Green, recently made Green, Green and Jackson."

In 1931, she was on the following committees of the Business and Professional Women's Club in Jackson: Employment Committee, Endowment Committee, Chair of the Finance Committee, and Public Relations Committee.

Clara married Walter Scott Sims on August 27, 1936, in Dallas, Texas. The September 9, 1936, *Clarion Ledger* reported, "The couple were married in the Roosevelt Suite of the Adolphus hotel. Mrs. Sims wore a beige sports costume with brown accessories and a corsage of gardenias. After their marriage, Mr. and Mrs. Sims motored to Fort Worth, Houston, and New Orleans, and are at home now in Jackson."

Clara's husband died in January 1955 at the age of 65 after being critically burned at their home on N. State Street in Jackson. He had been a deputy circuit clerk for Hinds County.

Clara was a member of the Ralph Humphreys Chapter of the Daughters of the American Revolution, the Jane Addams Guild and the Mississippi Bridge Association.

In 1968, Clara retired as court reporter. "Glowing tributes were given to Clara Melton Sims and she is most deserving of them," stated the July 7, 1968, *Clarion Ledger*.

Clara Melton Sims died in December 1975 at the age of 90. She is buried with her parents and her sisters Martha Louise Melton and Julia Melton Taylor in Greenwood Cemetery in Jackson.

Woman Lawyer

Miss Clara Melton, Jackson woman, who recently successfully passed the state bar examination, joins ranks of Mississippi's women barristers.

Miss Melton Is Now Full-Fledge Member of Firm

Miss Clara Melton, who has just passed her bar examinations and has had her name put on the letterhead of Green, Green and Jackson, is the descendent of an illustrious line.

With her ancestry including a famous judge and a revered missionary, Miss Melton adopted the profession of one, and the name of the other. Her great-grandfather, Judge J. P. Chrisman of Beauregard and Brookhaven, was a signer of the Constitution of 1890. Her full name is of royalty length, Anna Clara Chrisman Melton, she being one of twenty-one namesakes of the missionary whose portrait hangs in the Galloway Memorial church in memory of her services in Brazil and her death in the Jonestown flood.

A life devoted to social engagements was abruptly changed when Miss Melton, a graduate of high school, decided to become a stenographer. A public stenographer for years, she found her preference growing for handling legal documents.

During the world war, she was reporter in federal, circuit and chancery courts. For a time, she was a secretary in the law offices of J. Edwards Mayes and J. Robert Mayes and for the past five years has been with Green and Green, recently made Green, Green and Jackson.

Marriage Of Miss Melton, Mr. Sims Told To Society

Miss Clara Chrisman Melton and Mr. Walter Scott Sims announce their marriage in Dallas, Texas, on Thursday, August 27.

Mr. Paul Melton, assistant manager of the Adolphus hotel, and Miss Mai Wilkinson of Jackson, were the only attendants.

The couple were married in the Roosevelt suite of the Adolphus Hotel. The ceremony was performed by Reverend Albert Ott, radio minister selected by the combined churches of Dallas.

Mrs. Sims wore a beige sports costume with brown accessories and a corsage of gardenias. Mr. and

(Far Left) 1931 *Clarion Ledger* article about Miss Clara Melton passing the bar and joining the Jackson firm of Green, Green, and Jackson. (Left): Her wedding announcement.

Martha Louise Melton ❖ 1931

Two Meridian sisters became bar members the same year. Martha Louise Melton was born to Jerome Norris Melton and Victoria Barber Melton on July 14, 1882, in Meridian. Her younger sister, Anna Clara Melton Sims, also became a lawyer.

Louise graduated from Mississippi State College for Women, now MUW, in 1902. She worked in Jackson. She then volunteered and served 11 months oversees in Paris for the American Red Cross in World War I.

She taught herself shorthand and with the assistance of her sister, Clara, operated a public stenographer's office in Jackson, by the name "L. and C. Melton."

She attended a law course at night school in Jackson to study for the bar exam. Louise took the bar exam with three other women, Allee Dunn of Jackson, Lena Zama, and Ida Lou Lewis of Hazelhurst. Louise was admitted to the bar in the fall of 1931. She was admitted to the Mississippi Supreme Court along with her sister, Clara Melton, and Allee Dunn.

In 1932, she represented Jackson Business and Professional Women's Clubs in Paris, France. She stayed afterwards in Europe to visit Germany, Poland, Russia, Finland, Sweden, and Norway. She spoke French and German fluently. The following year she was the guest speaker at the Business and Professional Women's Club, in Jackson, telling the audience of her trip through Europe. In 1934 she became the chairman of the "Lawyer Prohibition" Committee of the Business and Professional Women's Club in Jackson. The *Clarion Ledger* reported on January 17, 1934, "Miss Louise Melton is one of the brilliant attorneys of the club."

In 1939, she was an associate with Jaap & Higgins. In the Jackson city directory in 1941, she was an associate with Heidelberg Gordon & Lane in the Lampton building.

She was a member of the Order of the Eastern Star, The Mississippi Bar and the Hinds County Bar Association. In 1954, she became an inactive member of The Mississippi Bar. Louise Melton died at the age of 85 in September 1967 and was remembered in the Bar's Memorial Service in the fall of 1968. She is buried in Jackson.

Miss Louise Melton Is Representing Jackson Business and Professional Women

National Federation Tour of Foreign Lands To Be Enjoyed By Women of Many Countries

Miss Louise Melton, esteemed member of the business and Professional Women's Club of Jackson, will be Mississippi's representative for 1932 on the 5th Good Will Tour to the National Federation of Business and Professional Women's Clubs.

Miss Melton has gone in advance of the party, but will join them in Paris, where they will be from July 13 to 17th—and will attend the meeting of the International Federation of Business and Professional Women's Clubs, headed by an American business woman, Miss Lena Madesin Phillips, an attorney of New York. An international banquet will be held, and member federations from 14 countries will attend.

From Paris, Miss Melton, will continue with the Russian-Scandinavia section of the tour headed by Mrs. Geline McDonald Bowman, president of the National Federation of Business and Professional Women's Clubs, and will visit Germany, Poland, Russia, Finland, Sweden, and Norway.

Louise Melton, who is so fortunate as to enjoy this wonderful trip is truly a self-made woman, having by her own efforts developed an efficiency rarely seen, and still feels she has much to learn and continues to study, and to avail herself of every opportunity to gain more knowledge. She speaks French and German fluently. She taught herself shorthand and with the assistance of her sister, Clara, operates a public stenographer's office in Jackson, where the firm name of "L. and C. Melton" is wide and favorably known. Miss Melton is a native of Meridian, a graduate of Mississippi State College for Women, she has made her home in Jackson for the past twenty years. Louise completed a law course at night school, and passed State Bar examination in 1931.

In 1917 she volunteered for service overseas with the American Red Cross, and was assigned to the secretarial department in Paris and was stationed there eleven months.

It is understood that Miss Melton may not return with the party of American Business women, but may stay awhile to pursue a special course of study, but whatever she may decide to do, Mississippi is proud to have her as their representative at the International Federation meeting where in the words of Josephine Schain, chairman of the International Relations Committee it is "Through the Good Will Tours the Federation offers an unusual opportunity to meet and know the point of view of other countries. Understanding between the different peoples of the world in necessary if we are going to find the pathway to peace."

MISS LOUISE MELTON

(Above) Louise Melton represented Mississippi in 1932 when she traveled to Paris to begin a European tour as part of the National Federation of Business and Professional Women's Clubs.

Alice Lee "Allee" Dunn ❖ 1931

"Few Women Choose Law as Profession in State" was the headline in the July 12, 1931, *Clarion Ledger* newspaper. "Four women took the examination for admission to the bar, the largest number to appear before the board since women were granted suffrage in 1919. The four feminine members of the group of 49 to take the examinations showed on the average the same familiarity with legal procedure as the men, according to Oscar Gober, chairman of the board."

THREE WOMEN ARE LATEST ADDITIONS TO MISSISSIPPI BAR

Miss Allee Dunn, Formerly of Greenville, is Among Those Received as Newest Member – Two Other Ladies Are Included

(by The Associated Press)

Jackson, Miss. Sept. 22, 1931 – Three women are latest additions to membership in the state Bar Association with the right to practice before the state supreme court.

Expressing the hope that they would become active practitioners before the high court, Chief Justice Sydney Smith formally received the newest members, Missrs Louise and Clara Melton and Allee Dunn, all of Jackson.

Alice Lee "Allee" Dunn was born in Greenville on August 1, 1877, the eldest daughter to John Nelson Dunn and Mary Greer Pickett Dunn. Her grandfather was Colonel Ed Burke Pickett of the Confederate Army. In 1895, she taught at the Green School in Indianola.

In 1911, Allee Dunn helped to form the Belvidere Chapter of the Daughters of the American Revolution in Greenville. In 1928, she was a stenographer to Mississippi Supreme Court Judges who helped her study for the bar exam. Allee became a member of the bar in 1931.

In 1934 she was the Chairman of the Resolutions Committee of the Business & Professional Women's Club in Jackson. She was also an active member of the Colonial Dames.

She gave up her law practice due to failing health and returned to Greenville. Alice Lee Dunn died at age 70 on April 23, 1947, and was buried in Greenville Cemetery.

MISS ALLEE DUNN BRILLIANT MEMBER

MISS ALLEE DUNN

Miss Allee Dunn is one of the most brilliant and accomplished members in our club, a fluent linguist and possessed of talents of the highest order.

She is an attorney at law, and we are immensely proud of her.

Studying law at the same time that she filled the responsible position as stenographer in the offices of the supreme judges of the state, Miss Dunn was a few years ago admitted to the bar. She still occupies her position with the supreme court judges, and is one of half dozen or more lawyers in our organization.

Lena Carolina Zama ❖ 1931

Times were hard in Italy in the late 18th century, and many men left to seek their fortunes in foreign countries. Antonia Zama, born in Faenza, Italy in 1857, was one of those who sailed to Argentina to earn his fortune as a gaucho for six years. He returned to Italy to marry Luigia Neri on November 26, 1891. She also was a native of Faenza, having been born there in 1865. They later sailed from La Havre and landed at Ellis Island on December 27, 1892. After a brief stay in New York, the Zamas traveled to Crystal Springs in Copiah County where Antonio took a job in the Piazza tannery there. About two years later, they moved to Hazelhurst where Antonio operated a restaurant and later a dry goods store for the remainder of his life. Antonio and Luigia had three boys and a girl, Lena Carolina. She was baptized on August 30, 1896, at St. Francis of Assisi Catholic Church in Brookhaven.

She excelled as a student in Hazelhurst public schools and attended Soule Business College in New Orleans after graduation.

Carolina returned from New Orleans to take a secretarial job with Myron S. McNeil, and another local attorney in Hazelhurst. Mr. McNeil found her quite capable and undertook to teach her law, and to prepare her for the bar examination. After "reading law" and passing a "rigid bar examination," she was licensed to practice law on September 22, 1931, in Chancellor V. J. Strickler's court. Mrs. Ida Lou Lewis of Hazelhurst was also licensed by the same court decree. They became the first women lawyers to practice in Copiah County. Miss Lena, as she was called at that time, assumed the professional name Lena C. Zama for her entire legal career.

She married Tito Rossi on January 17, 1937 in New Orleans. They were divorced in 1940.

Lena was a partner in the firm of McNeil and Zama until Roy J. Goss came to Hazelhurst from Columbia. She continued as a partner in the firm of McNeil, Goss, and Zama until McNeil's death. Goss and Zama continued the practice a short while until Goss returned to Columbia to practice. She practiced alone thereafter, moving from the McNeil building to her own building in 1949.

Lena's practice was varied like practices for so many lawyers in county seats. She represented individuals as well as companies like Southern Pacific Railroad out of New Orleans and carried a rail pass for business trips there. Her home always had boxes of tomatoes, sweet potatoes, peanuts and other produce from farmer clients. Lena could be seen every day running or walking very fast around town, not having owned a car in her lifetime.

The first woman lawyer to serve as a Bar Commissioner representing the 14th District Court was Lena C. Zama of Hazelhurst. She began her term in 1952.

Lena's contributions were recognized at least three times by her coworkers and friends in Copiah County. She was elected president of the County Bar Association in her late 70s. The Women's Auxiliary during World War I also received her assistance, and she became one of their

members. She also received the first Managers Sweetheart Award in 1978 at the Hazelhurst Chamber of Commerce Ladies Night Banquet. On November 3, 1980, it was declared Lena Zama Day in Hazelhurst at the County Bar

(Opposite page, bottom left) Lena C. "Miss Lena" Zama as a young woman. (Above): Accepting a 50-year service award on November 3, 1980.

Association meeting. This was to celebrate her 50 years as a practicing attorney. Lena is also celebrated posthumously by a Lena Zama section at the Hazelhurst library.

She maintained an active practice at the time she became ill and entered the hospital. Lena C. Zama died on February 1, 1983. She was a member of St. Martin's Catholic Church in Hazelhurst.

Written by Lena C. Zama's nephew Walter Allan Zama, Texas businessman.

Lena Zama To Head Copiah County Bar

HAZELHURST — At its annual meeting, the Copiah County Bar Association elected Miss Lena Zama as president for 1972. Miss Zama has served as secretary a number of years.

31

Ida Lou Simmons Lewis ❖ 1931

Ida Lou Simmons Lewis was born on September 13, 1905, in Hazlehurst to William and Elvia Simmons.

She was admitted to practice in 1931, the same day as Lena Zama. She married Everette M. Lewis, also a Mississippi State Bar member.

An article in the April 28, 1935, *Clarion Ledger* stated, "Lieut. Governor Dennis Murphree at a meeting of his supporters held here at the courthouse organized the 'Copiah County Murphree for Governor's Club' and outlined his platform for the race in this year's election. Mrs. Ida Lou Lewis, a prominent attorney of the county, was appointed county chairman."

In 1935, Ida Lou and her husband established the *Copiah County News* newspaper. In 1963, a merger of the *Copiah County News* and the *Hazelhurst Courier* resulted in a name change to the current *Copiah County Courier*.

Ida Lou was an active member in the Copiah County Bar Association. She was a member of the Hazelhurst Garden Club, the University of Southern Mississippi Alumni Association and the First Baptist Church of Hazelhurst.

Ida Lou passed away on September 28, 1976, at the age of 71. She is buried in Hazlehurst Cemetery.

MURPHREE FORMS CLUB IN COPIAH

HAZLEHURST, April 27—Lieut. Governor Dennis Murphree at a meeting of his supporters held here recently at the courthouse, organized the "Copiah County Murphree for Governor Club" and outlined his platform for the race in this year's election.

Mrs. Ida Lou Lewis, a prominent attorney of the county, was appointed county chairman, precinct leaders under Mrs. Lewis to be appointed later.

32

Winifred (Winnie) Davis Greer ❖ 1931

The Unfair Gods, Winifred Greer's first novel published in 1955, was inspired by visits to her parents' old home in the beautiful countryside, which she describes so well in her book. A novel about the Civil War, she used its events and background as a foil for an absorbing domestic drama. Winnie always enjoyed writing but considered it a hobby along with travel and growing camellias.

Winifred Davis Greer, the daughter of James F. Greer and Vashti Reeves Greer, was born in Brookhaven on October 9, 1893. She received her early education in Brookhaven. She had two brothers and five sisters. She took a business course at Whitworth College and later moved to Jackson. She became secretary to the Attorney General of the State of Mississippi, a position she held until 1929. She attended the Jackson School of Law and became a member of the Mississippi State Bar in 1931. The *Clarion Ledger* reported on December 19, 1931, "The slowly increasing ranks of women barristers were increased yesterday when Judge V. J. Stricker admitted Miss Winnie Greer of Jackson to practice in the local courts." After Winnie Greer was admitted to practice law on June 25, 1931, she worked with the Senior Counsel for Unemployment Compensation Division. That same year she was listed in the *Bench and Bar of Mississippi*.

Winnie held positions in the Legal Department of the Mississippi Employment Security Commission from 1938-1958. She then became Assistant General Counsel of the Commission.

Winnie died on September 24, 1984, in Jackson at the age of 90 and is buried in Lakewood Memorial Park in Jackson.

(Opposite) Winnie Greer was well-known for her novel, *The Unfair Gods*. However, she spent a number of years as Assistant General Counsel of the Mississippi Employment Security Commission.

Winifred Greer Of Jackson Writes Novel Of Interest To Mississippians

THE UNFAIR GODS, by Winifred Greer (Pageant Press, 343 pages, $4.50)

By DR. LOUIS DOLLARHIDE
Professor of English
Mississippi College

Winifred Greer, a Jackson resident, has written a Southern novel which Mississippians will want to investigate for themselves. In a season dominated by novels set in the Southern scene, **THE UNFAIR GODS** can hardly fail to be noticed.

The scene of **THE UNFAIR GODS** is Stuart Hall in the languid plantation era of anti-bellum Mississippi. Against this background of work and play on a great plantation, Harriet, for four years wife of handsome, dashing J e f f Stuart, turns slowly from a beautiful, independent - minded woman to a self-pitying, embittered martyr.

Jeff's easy-going, daring nature leads him into one act of indescretion with a French girl, Cecile Jaubert, for which his wife insists that he pay for the rest of his life. Although she says that she forgives him and even takes his French daughter to rear, she stubbornly refuses to forget. To escape her constant blame, the repentant Jeff volunteers for service in the Mexican War. On his return, Harriet welcomes him with open arms.

The French daughter, however, constantly reminds her of Jeff's unfaithfulness, and soon their relationship degenerates into a succession of quarrels. Jeff welcomes the War Between the States as another opportunity for escape; and when word finally drifts back to them that he has died at Shiloh, Harriet is left grief-stricken and empty.

At this point in the story, another thread emerges as the important narration — the love of Mar-

MISS WINIFRED GREER, author of "The Unfair Gods," is a native of Brookhaven. She is a member of the Mississippi State Bar and legal secretary in the legal division of the Mississippi Employment Security Commission. (Daily News Staff photo by Frank Hains)

garet, the French daughter, for Harriett's n e p h e w, Franklin. Against the desires of his parents, after post-war conditions have reduced their pride, the two a r e married. And where the fathers had planted, the young men now turn to the rich forest lands. The close of the book contains a surprise which should not be disclosed.

Drawn on limited canvas, **THE UNFAIR GODS** is a family annal which traces the fortunes of one group of people through a b o u t twenty years of Mississippi history. The characters, particularly those of Jeff, Harriet, and Margaret, is swiftly paced and compelling.

Like many first novels, the story has some obvious flaws or omissions. The story sometimes lags. Occasionally characters come out of focus, and their talk tends to be stilted or over-formal, or even, perhaps, anachronistically modern. But most of the flaws are those which a good editor should have caught and had corrected before the book saw print.

As a story stressing the corrosive effect of bitterness and hatred on human relations in an age appealing to most readers, **T H E UNFAIR GODS** should be of interest to a great many Mississippians.

Mississippi Scribblers - - -

Few Mysteries Included In Mississippi Writings

By TILLMAN L. MARTIN [Governor of Puerto Rico, has writ-

Ruth Leola Chrismond Franck ❖ 1932

The only woman to be granted a law license in 1932 was Ruth L. Franck. The headline for the *Clarion Ledger* on March 16, 1932, read, "Five Jacksonians Pass in Bar Exam – Only Woman to be Granted License is Mrs. Ruth Franck of Jackson."

She was born on November 3, 1903, in Choctaw County. Her parents were William Riley Chrismond and Willie Florence Stephenson Chrismond. After high school, she began a private study of law.

The *Choctaw Plaindealer* newspaper in Ackerman on March 11, 1932, stated, "Former Ackerman Lady Passes Law Examination – Mrs. Ruth Franck, now of Jackson, who was formerly Miss Ruth Chrismond of Ackerman, took the law examination held in Jackson in February. We know that Mrs. Franck's friends in Ackerman and Choctaw County will be delighted to know that she was successful and passed this

examination. Mrs. Franck is now admitted to the bar and is licensed to practice law in the State of Mississippi. She studied law in a law office in Jackson for about two years, and will practice law in that city."

She was admitted to the bar in 1932 and specialized in legal research and briefing. She was an associate with F. L. Peyton in the 1940s. She was also a member of the Hinds County Bar. In 1938, she was listed in the *Bench and Bar* book.

Ruth was a member of the Retired Federal Employees Association and was a past secretary of the Business

FORMER ACKERMAN LADY PASSES LAW EXAMINATION

Mrs. Ruth Franck, now of Jackson, who was formerly Miss Ruth Chrismond of Ackerman, took the law examination held in Jackson in February. We know that Mrs. Franck's friends in Ackerman and Choctaw county will be delighted to know that she was successful and passed this examination. Mrs. Franck is now admitted to the bar and is licensed to practice law in the State of Mississippi. She studied law in a law office at Jackson for about two years, and will practice law in that city.

FIVE JACKSONIANS PASS IN BAR EXAM

Only Woman To Be Granted License is Mrs. Ruth Franck, of Jackson

Five Jacksonians are now eligible to practice law in the courts of Mississippi, as the result of passing the February state bar examination given 37 applicants, 25 of whom were granted licenses, according to announcement made by the state board of law examiners today.

To one of the younger members of the house of representatives, James L. Whitten, Tallahatchie county, goes the honor of making the highest average in the examination. The only woman to be granted a license was Mrs. Ruth Franck, of Jackson. The other four from this city are

and Professional Women's Association.

She married Clarence Otto Franck, Sr. and had two sons and one daughter. Ruth Franck died June 28, 1981.

RUTH FRANCK

(Opposite) Clippings and photos of Ruth Leola Chrismond Franck from 1932, the year she passed the bar exam. (Left and Right): Photo and biographical sketch from the *Women Lawyers Digest*.

FRANCK, Ruth (Mrs. C. O. Franck, Sr.), Secretary, Federal Works Agency, Bureau of Community Facilities, 414½ W. Capitol St., Jackson, Mississippi; res. 803 Eastview St., Jackson; b. Ackerman, Choctaw County, Miss., Nov. 3, 1904; dau. Senator and Mrs. W. R. Chrismond (Dec'd.). Ch. C. O. Franck, Jr., age 23; Margaret Franck, age 21; William (Billy) Franck, age 18. Adm. Feb., 1932, Mississippi. Mem. Miss. State Bar; Hinds County Jr. Bar Assn.; Navy Mothers Club (Adjutant). Edn. Ackerman High School, Ackerman, Miss.; Draughon's Business College, Jackson, Miss.; six years' private study of law in law offices, Jackson, Miss. Asso. with J. Ed Franklin, Atty., doing title and abstract work, legal research and briefing, 1933-37; asso. with F. Lewis Peyton, Atty., same type of work, 1937-40.

Elizabeth Gwin Kirschten ❖ 1933

The headlines stated, "Elizabeth Gwin Passes Bar Exams" on March 27, 1933, in the *Greenwood Commonwealth*. "Miss Elizabeth Gwin, daughter of Capt. and Mrs. S. L. Gwin of Greenwood, was among the ten successful applicants for admission to The Mississippi Bar, according to an announcement from Harold Cox, secretary of the State Board of Bar Examiners received today. Miss Gwin was the only girl to be admitted by the examiners."

Elizabeth Gwin was born to Captain Samuel L. Gwin and Sallie Gwin of Greenwood in May, 1906. She graduated from Greenwood High School and later attended National Cathedral School in Washington, D. C. She passed the bar exam and was admitted to The Mississippi Bar in March 1933. She soon left to find employment in Chicago, Illinois, where she worked at the Century of Progress Exposition. She married Paul Raymond Kirschten on December 26, 1934, and moved to Evanston, Illinois, after the wedding. She had four children. In 1956, her husband died at the age of 51 and she moved back home to Greenwood, Mississippi.

In 1965, Elizabeth helped to create Pillow Academy, a private school in Greenwood, and served as secretary and on the Board of Directors. Bill Davis, another founding member of Pillow Academy, described Elizabeth as "one of the smartest women" he has ever met. In addition, she was a member of the Daughters of the American Revolution, United Daughters of the Confederacy and Taxpayers for Good Government.

She quilted for over 50 years. Elizabeth stated that quilting was just a hobby, and she used most of the quilts she made for her home.

On December 7, 1994, Elizabeth Gwin Kirschten passed away at the age of 88. She is buried in Greenwood.

Elizabeth Gwin Passes Bar Exams

Miss Eliabeth Gwin, daughter of Capt. and Mrs. S. L. Gwin of Greenwood, was among the ten successful applicants for admission to the Mississippi bar, according to an announcement from Harold Cox, secretary of the State Board of Bar Examiners received today.

Miss Gwin was the only girl to be admitted by the examiners.

W. Y. Humphreys, Jr., son of the late Will Humphreys, of Greenville, was also among the successful applicants.

Others passing the examinations were: R. B. Ricketts, Jr., H. C. Hall and Charles Gordon,

35 Helen Patricia Maltby Lumpkin ❖ 1934

The 9th University of Mississippi Law School female graduate, Helen Patricia Maltby was born in October 1892. In 1925, she was appointed deputy Supreme Court clerk. The *Clarion Ledger* reported, "Miss Maltby is highly desirable for the position, her experience qualifying her for the duties." She graduated from the University of Mississippi Law School in June 1934 with an excellent record. After graduating and being admitted to the bar in 1934, Helen Maltby served as the University of Mississippi Law Librarian and secretary to the Dean of the Law School, Judge T. C. Kimbrough. Her salary was $850 per year. In 1937-1938, Helen was law librarian and instructor, teaching the first year students in Legal Bibliography Lab.

After she married Professor Ben Gray Lumpkin, she moved to work at the University of North Carolina as the Assistant Law Librarian. She was a committee worker for the American Association of Law Libraries, serving in 1936 as a member of the Committee on New Members and in 1937 as a member of the Sub-committee on Law School Library Statistics.

Her husband was called to service in WWII. From 1944-46, Ben wrote technical manuals for the U. S. Quartermaster Generals office at Camp Lee, Virginia. In 1946, he went to the University of Colorado to teach English and folksongs until his retirement in 1969.

In 1947, Helen became law librarian at the University of Colorado. Helen died in 1969.

(Right): Helen Patricia Maltby was appointed deputy Supreme Court clerk in 1925. (Above): She entered law school in the 1930s and graduated in 1934. She served as law librarian and instructor at Ole Miss from 1937-38. She married Ole Miss law professor Ben Lumpkin. In 1947, she was appointed law librarian at the University of Colorado.

Miss Helen Maltby, daughter o Mr. and Mrs. A. Maltby of Nort Jefferson street, has been appoint ed deputy supreme court clerk, i was announced Tuesday morning b Clerk W. J. Buck. Miss Maltby i highly desirable for the position her experience qualifying her fo the duties. She will begin work about November 1, it is declared.

36 Elizabeth Watkins Hulen Grayson ❖ 1934

The first Mississippi female lawyer to argue a case before the United States Supreme Court was Elizabeth Watkins Hulen Grayson. She was born on March 25, 1899, to William and Margaret Elizabeth Watkins. Elizabeth attended Jackson public schools and Millsaps College for one year. She finished her college degree at Agnes Scott College in Decatur, Georgia, in 1919. She married Col. Harry Hulen in 1920 and lived on the Otterburn Planta-

tion in the Mississippi Delta. She often read law in her father's office and decided to pursue her juris doctorate from Jackson School of Law. She was admitted to practice in 1934.

In 1959, she married Thomas J. Grayson, who was state adjutant

MEMBER PIONEER IN REAL ESTATE

One of our club's outstanding members is Mrs. Elizabeth Watkins Hulen, who has recently entered the legal profession. She was brief clerk in the office of Watkins and Eager for five years and was admitted to the Mississippi State Bar in 1934.

general from 1932 to 1936 and from 1940 to 1942. Thomas passed away in 1962.

Elizabeth was president of the Fifth District of the Mississippi Federated Women's Clubs and the Jackson Little Theater from 1938-1940. She was a member of the Mississippi Bridge Association and El Vierners Luncheon Club.

Her father William Hamilton Watkins formed the Jackson law firm of Watkins & Eager in 1916. For almost forty years she was a partner at Watkins & Eager, where she was an expert in appellate advocacy and argued many cases before the United States Supreme Court. A Westlaw search shows 98 Mississippi appellate cases between the years 1943-1976 in which Elizabeth Hulen Grayson was attorney of record.

She was a member of the Hinds County, Mississippi Bar, and the National Women's Lawyers Associations. Elizabeth Watkins Hulen Grayson died on November 4, 1977. She was one of 36 deceased attorneys who were memorialized on September 18, 1979, at the Bar's Memorial Service before the Mississippi Supreme Court.

Elizabeth Watkins Hulen Grayson argued a case before the United States Supreme Court in 1943. She was a well-respected attorney specializing in appellate advocacy. (Top Right): A portrait of Elizabeth Watkins Hulen Grayson that hangs in the law offices of Watkins & Eager.

Local Woman Argues Before High Court

Mrs. Hulen Declares Law Does Not Apply

Washington, Dec. 17 — (AP) — A woman argued today before the Supreme Court that the Federal Wage-Hour Act does not apply to a night watchman who was employed by the Southern Package Corporation of Port Gibson, Miss.

The woman was Mrs. Elizabeth Watkins Hulen of Jackson, Miss., who was admitted yesterday to practice before the Tribunal. She represented the corporation.

Mrs. Hulen said the Wage-Hour Act would apply to a watchman who contributed substantially to the movement of goods in interstate commerce but that there was no proof that the watchman in the case —the late Fred Allen — had made such a contribution. He was employed, she said, only in order to obtain a reduction in fire insurance premiums.

Robert L. Stern, special assistant to the United States attorney general, argued that the watchman was "engaged in maintaining a building so that production could be carried on."

He urged the Tribunal to reverse a decision of the Mississippi Supreme Court which denied the watchman overtime compensation.

Elizabeth Hulen Will Address Law Students

UNIVERSITY — Elizabeth Watkins Hulen, prominent Jackson attorney, will address the School of Law student body at the University of Mississippi on Monday, Feb. 8 at 2 p.m.

Mrs. Hulen, an associate of Watkins and Eager Attorneys and Counsellors at Law in Jackson, will speak in the Moot Court Room in Lamar Hall. Her topic will be "Brief Writing and Appeals."

Her visit to the University is sponsored by the Visiting Lecturer Series, a program begun this year to bring to the campus outstanding members of the legal profession.

Over half of the practice of law which Mrs. Hulen began in 1934 has been concerned with appellate cases in the Supreme Court of Mississippi, the Federal Court of Appeals of the Fifth Circuit, and the United States Supreme Court.

Mrs. Hulen is the daughter of the late William H. Watkins, an honor graduate of the Ole Miss School of Law in 1895 and a distinguished member of the Mississippi Bar for over 60 years. She was educated in the Jackson public schools, attended Millsaps College, and was graduated from Agnes Scott College in Atlanta in 1919. She read law under her father from 1930 to 1934, entered Jackson School of Law, and has been active in law practice since 1934.

Mrs. Hulen is a member of the Hinds County, Mississippi and American Bar Associations, the National Women Lawyers Association, and listed in Who's Who in American Women. She is a former president of the Jackson Little Theater and a former president of the Fifth District of the Mississippi Federated Women's Clubs.

37

Louise Mayo ❖ 1935

*L*ittle is known of Louise Mayo of Jackson. She was admitted to the practice of law in June of 1935. The Mississippi State Bar was not able to locate her after 1935.

Mary Sue Brannon ❖ 1935

Montgomery County's first female attorney, Mary Sue Brannon was born July 2, 1915, in Kilmichael, Mississippi. Her parents were Homa Holland Brannon and Otis E. Brannon. Her father was former Chancery Clerk of Montgomery County. In September of 1935, Mary Sue was admitted to practice law after her graduation from the University of Mississippi Law School. She was the 10th female graduate of the University of Mississippi Law School. The *Winona Times* stated, "Miss Brannon was the only girl graduate of the University of Mississippi Law School this summer. She received her diploma after establishing a remarkable scholastic record. She presented her credentials to Judge Norfleet R. Sledge this morning, who administered the oath of Attorney and Counselor. He then congratulated her and wished her success."

In 1935, she began practicing law in Winona. Defendant Wilson Pullen was the first person in Montgomery County defended by a woman attorney. Wilson Pullen was the confessed slayer of Dave McLelland. Wilson had insufficient funds to employ counsel. According to custom, the names of all attorneys practicing before the Montgomery County courts at that time were placed in a hat and a name was drawn out to defend the man. That name was Miss Mary Sue Brannon. She had just recently passed the state examination and had been admitted to the bar. Her first duty before the Montgomery County jury would be to defend a man for murder. It was a tough assignment for a young woman, but she handled the case remarkably well and was complimented very highly by the Judge of the court. She received $50 in payment for this case from the county funds.

Mary then went to Washington, D. C. where she held a position in the Department of Justice until 1937. In 1936 through 1948, she worked with the United States Justice Department. In both 1944 and 1953 she worked with the United States Government.

She opened an office in Aberdeen, Mississippi as government attorney to investigate war risk cases set for hearing in federal courts. The *Clarion Ledger* reported on February 19, 1938, "Winona Girl Now Federal Lawyer in Upstate Area – Miss Mary Sue Brannon is to have offices in Aberdeen as an attorney to investigate war risk insurance cases that come up for hearing at the federal courts at Clarksdale, Oxford, and Aberdeen. For eighteen months, Miss Brannon has been in Washington, D. C., as an attorney for the war risk division for the Department of Justice. After graduating from Winona High School, Miss Brannon finished a five-year course in four scholastic years and two summer semesters."

She became inactive on the bar rolls in 1966. Mary Sue Brannon died at the age of 59 in 1973 and is buried in Oakwood Cemetery in Winona.

Mary Sue Brannon's first case after being admitted to the bar was a murder defense in a jury trial in Winona. She would later practice law in Washington D.C. and later in Aberdeen, Mississippi.

WILSON PULLEN TO BE DEFENDED BY MARY SUE BRANNON

Young Lady Lawyer Draws Murder Case as First After Graduation

Miss Mary Sue Brannon, charming daughter of Chancery Clerk and Mrs. Otis E. Brannon, drew a tough one for her first case in court when she was selected to defend Wilson Pullen, confessed slayer of Dave McClelland.

After a true bill was brought against him Pullen stated that he did not have sufficient funds to employ counsel. According to custom, Judge Allen placed the names of all the lawyers practic-

Matelyn Floyd Hines ❖ 1936

"Eleven New Attorneys Admitted to the Bar by State Examiners" stated the headline in the May 6, 1936, *Clarion Ledger* newspaper. "The list of successful applicants was announced yesterday by W. Harold Cox of Jackson, secretary of the board. S. E. Travis of Hattiesburg is the chairman of the board and Sam H. Long of Tupelo is the other member. The list of the applicants, who were admitted to practice, included one woman, Miss Matelyn Floyd."

Matelyn Floyd Hines was born in Meridian on Christmas Eve of 1913. Her parents were Earle Norris Floyd and Matelyn Fowlkes Floyd. To follow her desire for higher education, she went first to Newcomb and then to the University of Mississippi. She was formally presented to society in 1934 at the Debutante Ball. The December 13, 1934, *Clarion Ledger* stated, "Mr. and Mrs. Earl Norris Floyd will entertain a debutante ball at the University Club in honor of their beautiful daughter,

Miss Matelyn Floyd, a graduate of the University of Mississippi and one of the most popular members of the younger society set."

She later studied at the Jackson School of Law and was admitted to practice February of 1936.

Matelyn married Lee Douglas Hines in 1937. The *Clarion Ledger* stated on April 26, 1937, "Miss Matelyn Floyd to be Wed to Mr. Hines this Evening in Ceremony Important to Society. A highlight of the season both in beauty and importance to society in Mississippi and surrounding states will be the wedding of Miss Matelyn Floyd of this city and Lee Douglas Hines of Chicago. The Reverend Walter B. Capers, rector of Saint Andrew's Episcopal Church, will perform the service in the home of the bride's parents. After the ceremony, which will be performed in the presence of limited number of relatives and friends, the bridal couple and their wedding party will be entertained at a formal reception to which many of the elite of the city have been invited."

Miss Matelyn Floyd

Matelyn was a member of Chi Omega sorority, the Junior League and a communicant of St. Andrew's Cathedral. She was president of the Jackson Debutante Club.

She went on inactive status with the bar in 1969. She died on March 1, 1975, after a brief illness at age 61 and is buried in Lakewood Memorial Park.

Miss Matelyn Floyd To Be Wed To Mr. Hines This Evening In Ceremony Important To Society

Beautiful Rites To Take Place at 7:30 O'clock In Earle Floyd Home—Miss Mamie Rush Floyd, Weston Segura Will Be Only Attendants

A highlight of the season both in beauty and importance to society in Mississippi and surrounding states will be the wedding tonight of Miss Matelyn Floyd of this city and Lee Douglas Hine of Chicago. The Reverend Walter B. Capers, D. D., rector of Saint Andrew's Episcopal church, will perform the service in the home of the bride's parents, Mr. and Mrs. Earle Norris Floyd, 921 Bellevue place. The groom's mother, Mrs. William Middleton of Okmulgee, Oklahoma, will be one of the interesting out-of-town guests at the wedding.

Maid of honor and the bride's only attendant will be her popular sister, Miss Mamie Rush Floyd of Jackson. Weston Segura, also of this city, will serve Mr. Hines as best man. Mr. Floyd will give his daughter in marriage.

The nuptial music promises to be particularly beautiful. Mrs. G. Garland Lyell will be soloist, accompanied at the piano by Miss Maud Chisholm. Armand Coullet

This Week With The Seniors

THURSDAY

Thursday, one—Mrs. Leon Hendrick, 1424 Pinehurst, at luncheon for Miss Mary Carraway.

Thursday, four-thirty—Mrs Elmore Stickney, 733 North Jefferson, at seated tea for Miss Patricia O'Brien.

Thursday, ten until two—Jim Livesay and Raymond Martin at dance at Armory.

Edna Loeb Friedman Fischer ❖ 1936

Edna Loeb was born December 16, 1913, in Columbus to Joseph Albert Loeb and Edna Belle Washer. She was a very good student and progressed very quickly through school, completing high school at 16. She entered Mississippi State College for Women, now MUW, that fall and completed her studies there in three years. When she entered Duke University Law School at age 20, she was only one of a few women to do so. She graduated magna cum laude and was admitted to practice law in Mississippi on September 21, 1936. With a great deal of confidence, she arrived in Washington, D. C. where she found she could not obtain a job where she could use her legal knowledge and skills. In defeat and desperation, she took a job at the Library of Congress.

Edna was strikingly beautiful, and she soon had many suitors. She traveled and enjoyed her life as a single woman until captured by Joe Friedman, an attorney with the Department of Justice. They married and had three children. Edna and Joe moved to Somerset, Maryland. Joe was struck down with an aneurysm and died in 1951. Edna was able to find a legal job through a friend who needed help with a book about broadcasting law so that she could support her young family. In 1953, she was invited to a dinner party by Elaine and Eli Nobleman where she met Ben Fischer and his wife, Hana, who was then dying of cancer. Hana died shortly thereafter and Ben called Edna to let her know

that, though he was moving back to Pittsburgh with his two children, he would be in Washington frequently on business and intended to call her. They married in Pittsburgh in July 1954, surrounded by their five children whom they later cross adopted.

For several years, Edna did not work. She learned how to play golf, played cards with women she met at the country club in Pittsburgh and participated in theater productions. When the two older children went to college, Ben and Edna moved from their very large four story home to a modern house. The house required very little in the way of management, and Edna took a part time job in the firm of family friends. The job eventually became full time, and she threw herself into her family law cases with passion. She also developed an informal network of women lawyers in Pittsburgh who provided support for one another. She took on the issue of gender discrimination in credit, membership in their country club and elsewhere.

Then she became ill with a rare form of pleural cancer. She entered hospice on July 12, 1979, and died a few hours later.

She will be remembered as a brilliant lawyer with uncommon vitality and strong opinions. Her southern upbringing and accent did not always mesh well with her life in Pittsburgh and her New York-raised, labor union-involved husband, but she left a definite impression behind when she left far too early.

Edna L. Fischer

Edna L. Fischer, a lawyer with the Pittsburgh firm of Baskin & Sears, died Thursday at the Forbes Hospice of East Liberty.

Mrs. Fischer, 65, of 154 N. Bellefield Ave., Oakland, was active in developing the halfway house program of the National Council of Jewish Women and was a member of the National Women's Political Caucus. She was also active in the local Histadrut, and recorded books for the blind.

Surviving are her husband, Ben; two sons, Fred of McLean, Va., and Mark of Pietown, N.M.; three daughters, Susan

Marguerite Ardella Williams ❖ 1936

The 11th female to graduate from the University of Mississippi Law School was Marguerite A. Williams, also known as Peggy. She was a native of Picayune. She received her undergraduate degree from Mississippi Women's College. After she graduated from law school, she was admitted in September 1936. She became the first female lawyer in Picayune. She worked a few months with an older established lawyer. She then established an of-

fice of her own. Peggy decided not to continue in law practice and dropped her active status.

She was a retired school teacher and a member of the Picayune First Baptist Church. She died at the age of 82 on November 5, 1986, in Pineland, Texas. Peggy is buried in Poplarville Cemetery.

Marguerite Ardella Williams was Picayune's first female lawyer, but she ultimately returned to teaching.

Josephine Louise Hood ❖ 1936

Madison County's first female lawyer was Josephine Louise Hood. She was born on January 25, 1912, to parents Mr. and Mrs. Oscar Gross of Canton.

Josephine was admitted to the bar on September 24, 1936. She was active in the newly formed Junior Bar of the Mississippi State Bar, and in 1940 she was on the Bar's Public Relations Committee and the Legislative Drafting Committee. During her career as a lawyer, she was selected Business Woman of the Year in October 14, 1971.

In the January 26, 1984, *Clarion Ledger* newspaper, she was known as "Canton's Longtime Lady Lawyer."

The Jackson Daily News featured Josephine Hood on January 26, 1984. "After 48 years as a practicing attorney, Miss Hood has become something of an institution. Her office is tucked away on the town square and could easily be used as the set for a

(Above): The Madison County Courthouse. Josephine Louise Hood was Madison County's first woman lawyer.

movie about small-town lawyers. Only a simple shingle bearing her name marks the door that faces the Madison County Courthouse. A steep, narrow flight of 24 well-worn wooden steps leads to her office. Inside her office are tables heavily laden with law books, legal papers, and letters. 'I've been up here every day of my life since I've been practicing law. I guess it's been a law office for 100 years, that's how old this building is,' said Miss Hood. She couldn't afford to go to law school after she graduated from Canton High School in 1932, so she apprenticed or read law under the tutelage of a local attorney until they both felt confident she could ably represent her craft. It had been her dream to become an attorney, even as a child."

Miss Josephine Hood died in May 1987. Services were held at the Sacred Heart Catholic Church in Canton.

Zelda Siegel Labovitz ❖ 1937

Sunflower County's first female attorney, Zelda Siegel Labovitz was born on February 10, 1917, in Greenwood. Her parents were Samuel Siegel and Sadie Curland.

Zelda graduated from Sunflower Junior College. To pursue her dream of becoming an attorney, she attended the University of Mississippi Law School and was the youngest woman to graduate from the law school at that time. The *Clarion Ledger* newspaper on April 28, 1937, re-

> The little town of Sunflower soon will have the distinction of having the youngest girl law graduate in the state. She is Miss Zelda Siegel, who will graduate from the law department of the University in June. Chancellor Jackson has removed her minority disability, for she is only nineteen.

ported, "Ole Miss Girl, Minor, Granted Permission to Practice Law. Disability to practice law in the state of Mississippi because of minority was removed from Zelda Siegel, Sunflower, 19 year-old senior law student at the University of Mississippi, by Chancellor R. E. Jackson, Cleveland, according to Dean T. C. Kimbrough of the law school today. Miss Siegel will be the youngest law student ever to graduate from Ole Miss. It is the first time the minority exemption has been a necessity here." She was secretary of her Senior Law Class. Once she was admitted to practice law in May of 1937, she moved to Indianola and established her practice.

Zelda married Samuel Labovitz in 1940, who was a Lt. Col. in the US Air Force. In 1942, a significant change happened to the Junior Bar. For the first time, a woman, Zelda Siegal Labovitz of Sunflower, had been elected to serve on the Junior Bar's Executive Committee.

In 1938, she was listed in *Bench and Bar*. Zelda was a member of both the Sunflower County and the Mississippi State Bar Associations. In 1993, Zelda received an award from the Sunflower County Bar Association for her service as president of the organization for three years. She served as president from 1990-1993.

Zelda Siegel Labovitz died on January 5, 2005, and is buried in the Ahavath Rayim Congregation Cemetery in Greenwood. The saying "Many women do noble things, but you surpass them all" is inscribed on her tombstone.

(Above): Zelda Siegel Labovitz started practicing law in Sunflower County when she was 19 years old.

OLE MISS GIRL, MINOR, GRANTED PERMISSION TO PRACTICE LAW

UNIVERSITY, April 27— Disability to practice law in the state of Mississippi because of minority was removed from Zelda Siegel, Sunflower, 19-year-old senior law student at the University of Mississippi, by Chancellor R. E. Jackson, Cleveland, according to Dean T. C. Kimbrought of the law school today.

Miss Siegel will be the youngest law student ever to graduate from Ole Miss. It is the first time the minority exemption has been a necessity here.

Graduation from the University law school permits a person to practice law in the state without taking the state bar examination.

Miss Siegel will be formally admitted to the bar, with other graduates, by Chancellor L. A. Smith, Holly Springs, of the local chancery district, or by

Award for three years of service

ATTORNEY Zelda Labovitz of Sunflower (center) was given an award Monday by the Sunflower County Bar Association for her service as president of the organization for the past three years. Mrs. Labovitz served as president of the organization from July, 1990, to July, 1993. Pictured are (from l.) Chancery Clerk Jack Harper, Circuit Court Judge Howard Q. Davis, Mrs. Labovitz, Supervisor/Attorney Carver Randle and Attorney Johnny McWilliams.

Rhoda Catherine Bass ❖ 1937

"Smartest Girl Lawyer" read the headlines when Rhoda Catherine Bass graduated from law school.

Rhoda Catherine Bass was born on October 7, 1905, in Hazelhurst. Her parents were James Morgan Bass and Nancy Ann Robertson Bass. She graduated from Monmouth College, Illinois. While she was a student at the University of Mississippi Law School, she served as secretary to Judge Kimbrough and also served one year as Law Librarian. She graduated from the University of Mississippi Law School in 1937. On August 19, 1937, the *Greenwood Commonwealth* newspaper reported, "Judge T. C. Kimbrough, dean of the Ole Miss law school, announced today the graduates of the summer session. In point of outstanding work, Catherine Bass, one of the two women to complete the law course during the past year was especially cited. Miss Bass was awarded the only diploma with distinction out of the 47 graduates of the whole year. Previous of this recognition she was selected by the faculty to receive the Phi Delta Phi award given each year to the outstanding law student. Friday the graduates will be admitted to The Mississippi Bar by Chancellor L. A. Smith of Holly Springs."

Catherine was a law faculty member. In 1938, she taught "Legal Bibliography Lab" to first year students and "Damages" to second and third year students.

She joined the firm Brady, Brady, Phillips, and Bass in Brookhaven until she began her own firm in Hazlehurst. In 1940, she became a member of Commissioner of Admissions to the Bar. *The Daily Mississippian* paid tribute to her work in an article in 1940, and she was featured in her Ole Miss yearbook. She was legal adviser for the State Welfare Department in Jackson.

Catherine was also executive secretary of the Children's Code Commission in the Children's Division of the Mississippi Department of Public Welfare. Evelyn Gandy succeeded Catherine Bass in this position.

She was a former president of the Ole Miss Law School Alumni. During the 1948 legislative session, Catherine was active in seeking passage of statutes dealing with children.

Catherine died at the age of 42 on April 22, 1948, while attending the National Conference of Social Work in Atlantic City, New Jersey. The YWCA Board memorialized Catherine Bass with a resolution adopted at a meeting of the board of the Mississippi District, Young Women's Christian Association. "Whereas, God in His infinite wisdom saw fit on April 22, 1948, to terminate the earthly labors of Catherine Bass, and whereas, the Citizens of Mississippi, and especially the children, have lost a public servant whose devotion to their interests was matched only by the brilliance with which she served them, and whereas the members of the State Legislature who are keenly concerned with humane and forward-looking legislation in the field of child welfare will sorely miss her because she possessed an unusual degree of technical knowledge, a warm personal interest and familiarity with legislative procedures, and whereas the Mississippi District Y. W. C. A. is infinitely richer because of her many years of service as a Board member, as Personal Friend, and as a Legal Counselor, now therefore, be it resolved, by the Board of Directors of the Mississippi District Y.W.C.A. that in the passing of Catherine Bass the Mississippi District Y.W.C.A. has sustained a heavy loss and wishes now to record its sorrow."

Smartest Girl Lawyer

RHODA CATHERINE BASS AND DEAN KIMBROUGH

Rhoda Catherine Bass of Hazlehurst, Miss., is shown receiving congratulations from Dean T. C. Kimbrough of the Mississippi University Law School for winning top honors in a class of 47 which included a State Senator and a U. S. Court Clerk. "Smartest lawyer in the bunch," said the Dean as he handed her the diploma.

YWCA Board Memorializes Catherine Bass

The following resolutions of sympathy and respect over the recent death of Miss Catherine Bass were adopted in a recent meeting of the board of the Mississippi district, Young Women's Christian association:

"Whereas, God in His infinite wisdom, saw fit on April 22, 1948 to terminate the earthly labors of Catherine Bass, and

"Whereas, the Citizens of Mississippi, and especially the children, have lost a public servant whose devotion to their interests was matched only by the brilliance with which she served them, And

"Whereas, the members of the State Legislature who are keenly concerned with humane and forward-looking legislation in the field of child welfare will sorely miss her because she possess

Betty Bartee Tucker ❖ 1938

The first female lawyer to attain judgeship in Hinds County was Betty Bartee Tucker.

She was born on February 10, 1900, in Louisville, Kentucky, to Chesley Thomas Bartee and Laurs Evelyn Compton Bartee. She graduated from Jackson High School in 1916. Her ties to the high school remained, and she later became president of the Alumni Association in 1925. She attended Mississippi State College for Women, now MUW. During the depression, Betty was involved with the Works Progress Administration before she went to law school. The Jackson School of Law accepted her into their program and she graduated in 1938. After she was admitted to the bar in 1938, her outstanding career began as she worked for the firm Pyles and Tucker. She then was appointed to the Chancery Bench, making her the second woman chancellor in the state and the first in Hinds County. She served as a judge from 1973-1979. Apart from her achievement in her profession, she also worked for the advancement of women and won the Susan B. Anthony Award for her voice and leadership for the equality for women in the workplace.

She is quoted after receiving the Susan Anthony Award at the Mississippi Women's Day symposium in Jackson: "For anyone to be elected, the right time and the right situation have to combine. That's not always true for women running. Women can't afford to pass the buck and make the same mistakes as a man. Women in politics have to be like Harry Truman – the buck stops here."

"There's opportunity in every area, the girl just has to take advantage of it."

"Society conditions a girl to look forward to marriage and to live happily ever after. If a girl has a mind above average, she is looked at suspiciously and called a bookworm. Fortunately this is changing and women are being encouraged more to academic achievement."

She married Joseph Wofford Tucker, Jr.

The Mississippi Federation of Business, the Conference of Local Bar Associations and the Professional Women's Club asked her to be their president, all of which she accepted. She was named "Woman of the Year" by the Riverside Business and Professional Women's Club. Betty was also a past president of the MUW Alumni Association and served on its board of directors from 1925-1927. In 1957, she was elected president of Soroptimists Interna-

(Above): Betty Bartee Tucker served as president of the Alumni Associations of both Jackson High School and Mississippi State College for Women (now MUW). (Left and Opposite Page): Better Tucker served as a Chancery Court Judge in Hinds County from 1973-1979.

Help Elect
Judge Betty B. Tucker
Chancery Judge,
Hinds County,
Fifth District, Place 1
Experience, Knowledge & Understanding

HELP ELECT A WORKING CHANCELLOR

★ In over 25 years of practicing law, Judge Betty B. Tucker has missed only one day of work.

★ Since her appointment as Chancellor, Judge Tucker has not missed a single day from her duties.

★ In 1974 alone, Judge Tucker has handled over 37% of all cases filed in Hinds County Chancery Court. This means that she has handled more cases than any Chancellor in the State of Mississippi.

Ask your lawyer, he will tell you Judge Betty B. Tucker works. You need her as Chancellor. 3

tional of Jackson. She was a member of the Hinds County Bar Association.

Betty led the 25-year fight for women's jury duty and was central to the discussion surrounding the Equal Rights Amendment. In 1974, she was named State Woman of Achievement. Betty also wrote and produced a play which helped reorganize and save The Jackson Little Theater from closing. She attended St. Andrew Episcopal Cathedral. Betty Bartee Tucker died on April 3, 1994, at the age of 94.

SUSAN ANTHONY AWARD TO BETTY TUCKER

Women's Day Recalls Suffrage Anniversary

By NANCY STEVENS
Daily News Staff Writer

Mississippi women had their day Saturday.

More than 300 Mississippi women, in Jackson Saturday for the first Mississippi Women's Day symposium, came together with a common goal in mind—equal rights for women, and now—and left with the same thing in mind.

"What do women want anyway?"—the all-day symposium's theme—was considered as speakers in various fields led discussion sessions and participants planned "strategy" for passage of the Equal Rights Amendment by the Mississippi Legislature.

Women's Day, commemorating the 53rd anniversary of the passage of the women's suffrage amendment, though a "first" for Mississippi, has been an annual event in other states in recent years—and Mississippi women plan the same.

Miss Betty Tucker, longtime Jackson attorney who for 25 years led the fight for women's jury duty, was selected to receive the first Susan B. Anthony Award for her contributions to women's rights during past years.

Pledging to continue her fight for equality under the law for women, Miss Tucker in accepting the award, said, "I cannot understand why our legislature hesitates a minute to ratify the ERA," adding that Mississippi women now have more rights than women in other states.

CONTINUING FIGHT

She was appointed a Hinds County chancery judge in June.

The award is in honor of the pioneer women's rights activist in the 19th century, whose fight for women's rights grew out of her earlier crusade against slavery.

Women of varied interests and fields, and a sprinkling of interested men, heard and participated in discussion of the Equal Rights Amendment, women and politics, psychology and religion, sex stereotyping and the history of the women's movement.

An afternoon workshop focused on the matter they consider of pressing importance—the ERA.

Education of legislators and their constituents, the women decided, is the first overriding issue in achieving support for the amendment, which has been ratified by 30 states and requires 38 for passage.

Detailed plans of organization for pro-ERA work by numerous women's groups during the upcoming legislative session were discussed, with an "intensified crusade" to begin soon.

TRY AGAIN

Leading a session on the ERA, Miss Euple Dozier, Fulton attorney said, "Perhaps we didn't holler loud enough to be heard last year. We're just interested in full rights under the law for all."

Arguments used by ERA opponents during the last session are the same arguments used throughout history when women tried to achieve certain rights, she said.

Dr. Thomasina Blissard, Jackson psychiatrist said "a male-centered orientation" in culture and environment, not physical traits, and treatment of women traits, and treatment of women as "second rate men" has hampered, and hampers, women's development as full human beings.

An "awareness" is coming to women that they have been "notoriously neglected," she said. "I just wonder why it's taken so long for women to voice their dissent."

Some 51.5 per cent of Mississippians are women, she

See WOMEN, Page 16A

FIRST ANTHONY AWARD — Miss Betty Tucker, Jackson attorney for 38 years, was named recipient of the First Susan B. Anthony Award at Saturday's Mississippi Women's Day symposium in Jackson. Selected from women nominated for their contributions to women's rights, Miss Tucker led the 25-year fight for women's jury duty and serves as a Hinds County Chancery Judge. Dr. Beth Hoskins of Jackson, sculptor of the award honoring the pioneer women's rights activist, presented the award.—Photo by Jimmy Lay.

(Above): Tucker receives the Susan B. Anthony Award. (Left): Being sworn in as Chancery Judge. (Below): More accolades and headlines. (Opposite): A letter of support she received after one of her first appearances.

Mrs. Betty Tucker Named President Of BPW Club

At the business meeting of the Jackson Business and Professional Women's club held Monday night at the YWCA, following members were chosen as officers of the club for the new year beginning in June, 1946: Mrs. Betty Tucker, president; Miss Mabel Bridges, first vice-president and membership chairman; Mrs. Bertha Yarborough, second vice-president and program chairman; Mrs. Halla May Pattison, third vice-president and news service chairman; Miss Susie Selzer, recording secretary; Miss Kathleen Thornton, corresponding secretary; Miss Minnie Powell, treasurer.

Club members who will represent the Jackson club as delegates at the Mississippi Federation of Business and Professional Women's club convention to be held in Jackson May 17-19, by right of their office are: Mrs. Kate Lamkin, president, Jackson club; Mrs. Betty Tucker, chairman, steering committee; Mrs. N. F. Cotter, chairman, public affairs; Miss Ferris Cotter, editor, Mississippi Business Women.

Delegates elected by the club at the Monday meeting were: Miss Flo Lehman, Miss Mable Bridges, Mrs. Addie McBryde, Mrs. Halla May Pattison, Miss Susie Selzer, Miss Minnie Powell, Mrs. Ruby Rogers, Mrs. Velma Rogers, Miss Kathleen Thornton, Miss May

Mrs. Betty Tucker Elected President of Soroptimists

Mrs. Betty Tucker was elected president of Soroptimist International of Jackson at the club's monthly luncheon meeting, held in the Jackson Room of the Robert E. Lee hotel. She succeeds Mrs. Daphyne Pridgen, under whose leadership this new Jackson service club is filling a real need in the community. Chartered in November, 1955, much groundwork has been laid in living up to Soroptimist ideals and goals of service. Today there are more than 30,000 professional and executive business women in Soroptimist Clubs in over 25 countries of the world.

Other officers elected include Miss Louise Williams, vice-president; Mrs. V. Ray Wadlington, secretary, and Mrs. Mat Lavail, treasurer.

Progress was reported on the club's project for the children at University Hospital. A much needed record player was selected as the Soroptimists gift to the children's ward at Easter.

Members attending this luncheon meeting included Mrs. Daphne Pridgen, president; Mrs. Betty Tucker, Miss Katie Smith, Mrs. Mat Lavail, Miss Minnie Powell, Mrs. Dollie Strahan, Miss Loryce Wharton, Mrs. Ruth King, and Miss Louise William

Miss Koops Engaged to Lt. Budner

Lt. Col. and Mrs. Fred W. Koops Jr., of Fort Hood, Tex., and former residents of Jackson, have announced the engagement of their daughter, Shirley Louise, to Alfred Martin Budner, son of the late Mr. and Mrs. Martin Budner of Chicago, Ill.

Miss Koops attended Mississippi Southern college where she was a member of Chi Omega sorority. She is a graduate of Baylor University and she is presently

WILLIAM A. BACON
POST OFFICE BOX 15
JACKSON, MISSISSIPPI
39205

June 28, 1973

Dear Betty -

After appearing in your court the other day I told Dink how pretty and distinguished you looked in your judicial robe.

The only trouble with your appointment is that I understand it is not permanent. You would grace the office.

I send you my congratulations and best wishes.

Sincerely yours,

Billy

Lulie Reynolds Eddins Walker ❖ 1938

(Above): Lulie Eddins was not only one of the youngest members of her law school class, she was also one of the top graduates. She obtained a decree freeing her of her minority in order to practice law.

"Meridian Girl is Youngest Lawyer — Miss Lulie Eddins Can Hang Out Her Shingle at Age of 20," stated the *Clarion Ledger* on May 31, 1938. "Miss Lulie Eddins, 20, who became the youngest lawyer in Mississippi when she was admitted to the bar, previously appeared before Chancellor A. B. Amis, Sr. in Meridian to obtain a decree freeing her from disabilities of minority. She is a cousin of Misses Margaret and Annelle Hodges of Meridian."

She was the daughter of Commander Henry Eddins and Natalie Eddins and was born on March 23, 1918, in New Hampshire.

Lulie was a resident of Bay Springs. She attended All Saints College in Vicksburg and the University of Mississippi Law School. She ranked high in her class of 24 students. She also won honors in beauty contests at All Saints and the University of Misissippi.

Lulie was employed as the secretary to the dean of the University of Mississippi Law School and was admitted to the bar in 1938. She was a member of Daughters of the American Revolution and was a Girl Scout leader.

She married George Wilbur Meek in 1940. They lived in Washington, D.C. in the early 1940s, but were divorced in 1943. Lulie then married Mark Anthony Walker, a Tennessee Judge, in Biloxi in 1948. The wedding was followed by a reception at the Longfellow House in Pascagoula. They had three children together and moved to Covington, Tennessee, after their marriage.

Lulie Reynolds Eddins Walker died on October 10, 1984, at the age of 66 and is buried in Covington, Tennessee.

MERIDIAN GIRL IS YOUNGEST LAWYER

Miss Lulie Eddins Can Hang Out Her Shingle At Age Of 20

Mary Caruthers Gholson Berger ❖ 1939

The second female on the Editorial Staff of the *Mississippi Law Journal* and the 15th female student to graduate from the University of Mississippi Law School was Mary Caruthers Gholson.

Born on January 27, 1917, in Holly Springs, Mary Caruthers Gholson Berger was one of two children of Norman Glasgow Gholson and Eliza McNeel Penick Gholson.

She attended the University of Mississippi Law School with Catherine Bass, Zelda Seigel Labovitz, Viola Lee James Hilbert and Lulie Reynolds Eddins Walker. Also attending was her brother Daniel P. Gholson. She was admitted along with her brother to The Mississippi Bar in June 1939. She was also admitted to the Tennessee Bar in October 1947. Mary was married to Fred Berger.

Rieves and Smith hired Mary in 1948 as their legal secretary, and after working with them for two years she was employed as a policy writer by Mid-South Title Company in Memphis. Following her move to Memphis, she then left for Lexington, Virginia, to work as a note teller for Rockbridge National Bank. Once in Virginia, she expanded her work and took on the job of caseworker and child welfare worker. She moved to Washington D.C. and worked in the Examining Attorney Copyright Office.

An attorney in the Office of the Solicitor, United States Department of Labor, Mary was active in the National Women's Party before 1960. She provided data and arguments for the NWP to submit to Congress to aid in securing passage of the sex discrimination amendment of Title VII of the Civil Rights Bill of 1964. She attended the organizing conference of NOW in October 1966, and worked as a volunteer attorney on nearly all of the early Title VII test cases in the U. S. appellate courts. Because of her government position, she worked on these cases without signing her name. Mary was a founder and member of the board of directors of Human Rights for Women, established in 1968. She left NOW in 1968. She is the author of "Equal Pay, Equal Employment Opportunity and Equal Enforcement of the Law for Women," published in the *Valparaiso University Law Review* (1970), as well as numerous papers on sex discrimination in employment and Women's Constitutional Rights for the National Women's Party and NOW.

Mary Caruthers Gholson Berger died on June 1, 1984, at the age of 67 and is buried in Holly Springs, Mississippi.

EQUAL PAY, EQUAL EMPLOYMENT OPPORTUNITY AND EQUAL ENFORCEMENT OF THE LAW FOR WOMEN

CARUTHERS GHOLSON BERGER*

INTRODUCTION

The right to work, I had assumed was the most precious liberty that man possesses. Man has indeed as much right to work as he has to live, to be free, to own property. It does many men little good to stay alive and free and propertied, if they cannot work. To work means to eat. It also means to live.[1]

It is hoped that Justice Douglas, the author of the above quote, used the word "man" generically to include all human beings. In a democratic, capitalistic system there is no more important right than the right of an individual, whether man or woman, to work for a livelihood.[2] Women as well as men should have equal opportunities "to work," "to eat" and "to live." But this is not the case. Women are discriminated against in employment by state governments whose legislatures have passed laws barring them from certain employment. They are also discriminated against by private employers, labor unions and employment agencies in hiring, job placement and promotional opportunities. They

(Above): Mary Caruthers Gholson during her years at Ole Miss. She was the second female on the *Mississippi Law Journal* editorial staff. (Left): A 1970 article by Caruthers Gholson Berger published in the *Valparaiso University Law Review*. Berger was not only active in the National Women's Party, she attended the organizational conference for the National Organization of Women (NOW).

THE LATE 1930S

The late 1930s saw a boon in women enrolling at The University of Mississippi Law School. From 1936-1939, six women graduated from the law school and joined The Mississippi Bar — Marguerite Ardella Williams, Catherine Bass, Zelda Seigel (Labovitz), Viola Lee James (Hilbert), Lulie Reynolds Eddins (Walker), and Mary Caruthers Gholson (Berger). They worked together in notable undergraduate leadership positions while at Ole Miss, including officers and cabinet members of the YWCA, president and officers of Pan Hellenic Council, and founding members of the Tassel Senior Honorary for Women. Most importantly, they were among the first women who could call fellow female law students "friends and colleagues" when they entered law school.

MARY
CARUTHERS
GHOLSON

CATHERINE
BASS

VIOLA LEE
JAMES

GHOLSON

JAMES

LULIE
REYNOLDS
EDDINS

ZELDA
SEIGEL

Viola James Hilbert ❖ 1939

*V*iola "Vi" Lee James was born on August 17, 1915, in Manila, Philippine Islands. Her father, Fred James, was the grandson of an early settler in Logan, Ohio. Her mother, Floy Garner James was a pioneer in education in the Philippine Islands, as well as the Mississippi Coast. Both parents instilled in Vi the inherent value of education, a sense of adventure, and a belief in the inherent value of every individual, regardless of race, religion, or nationality.

Breaking Gender Boundaries

Fred and Floy preached to Vi that nothing was out of her reach — and they supported her in roles that were atypical of women in the 1920s and 1930s.

The May 28, 1932 edition of the *Daily Herald* carried a story about the Gulfport High School class of 1932:

"Viola Lee James, daughter of Mr. and Mrs. Fred James, received the highest honors which may come to a senior at the school both academically and in athletics. Among her honors were: vice-president of senior class; valedictorian; Newcomb scholarship; D.A.R. medal in American History; American Legion Auxiliary award for highest average in English for four years; Eta Sigma Phi Latin medal for highest average in Latin for four years; National Honor Society; editor of *Tiger's Claw* and *Quill and Scroll*; Girl Reserve ring; state, regional, and Big Eight tennis singles champion; best record for girls baseball and basketball throws in Big Eight; winner of Big Eight debate; winner of regional championship tennis for girls; letters in basketball, track, tennis, and debate; captain of girls basketball team."

(Above) Viola James, far left, with her father, Fred James, and brother and Sister, Garner James and Elizabeth James, circa 1917, Philippine Islands; Fred James served as Manila City Commissioner for 15 years; Floy started a school for Amerian children whose parents were stationed in Manila.

Early Adulthood
Marked by Adventure

Vi entered adulthood with a gusto for life. She enrolled in Brookhaven's Whitworth Junior College in 1932 and graduated in 1934 as valedictorian.

The following year, Vi enrolled at Ole Miss where she received her B.A. and

(Above) Garner James and Viola James in 1936. Viola was a student at Ole Miss. Garner was a speechwriter for Mississippi Gov. Hugh White.

LL.B. degrees. While at Ole Miss she was president of Chi Omega sorority, Pan Hellenic, and the Ole Miss YWCA. She was also a founder of the Tassel Women's Honorary Society.

Vi's law school years were interrupted due to financial hardship. She accepted a one-year position at Copiah-Lincoln Junior College where she coached the girls basketball team and led them to a state championship.

Vi returned to the Ole Miss law school in 1938 and served on the law journal staff (the third woman to do so, see photo next page). She graduated with distincton (the sixteenth female to graduate) and accepted a position with the Brookhaven firm of Brady, Brady, and Phillips.

The Brady (pronounced *Braddy*) firm was dominated by men who were staunch segregationist, but were progressive in hiring women. Prior to Vi's tenure, the firm had hired Catherine Bass (see profile page 57).

Mr. Thomas Brady, Jr., the patriarch of the firm, told Vi he wanted her to experi-

Viola Lee James (Third from Right) surrounded by the other members of the *Mississippi Law Journal*. James was the third woman to serve on the law journal.

(Above) Viola James, age 24, started her legal career with the firm of Brady, Brady, and Tullius in 1939. (Right) In 1945, Vi joined the American Red Cross.

ence the law "from the bottom up." Vi documented her time at the Brady firm (1939-1941) through a series of letters she wrote to her mother and father. The letters describe in great detail what law practice was like for a woman in the 1930s (see excerpts facing page).

Vi spent two years with the Brady firm until the outbreak of World War II.

Vi moved to Washington D.C. where she served as an associate attorney for the National Labor Relations Board. Then, Vi transferred to Atlanta to work for the War Food Administration.

In 1945, she joined the American Red Cross in China-Berma-India Theater. While there she served as a hospital counselor in and around Calcutta, India, in the last years of the Bangal famine.

In 1946, Viola returned to the United States.

Young, Single Attorney

Vi returned to the U.S. with the financial resources to

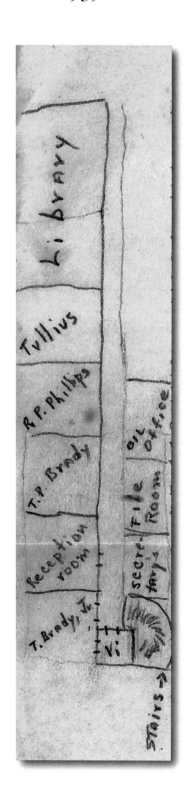

Brady, Brady, Phillips & Bass

ATTORNEYS AT LAW

Brookhaven, Miss.

T. BRADY, JR.
THOMAS P. BRADY
TULLIUS BRADY
R. PEARCE PHILLIPS
R. CATHERINE BASS

Oct. 12, 1939

Excerpts from a letter from Viola James, October 12, 1939

Both of the sons in the firm and Mr. Phillips are rather young, and all three are unusually attractive. The oldest Mr. Brady received his training at Ole Miss, Tom at Yale, Tullius at Wisconsin, and Mr. Phillips at Ole Miss. They have deep, resonant voices, and when a discussion is going on and they start knocking heads, I wouldn't miss it for the world. There is still another son, whom I haven't met. He is primarily a journalist at heart, but runs a Pontiac agency on the side.

Yesterday I spent one of the most enjoyable days of my life. I went with Tom over to New Hebron where he was to try a J.P. case. It was set for 10 O'clock. At about 10:30 we strolled in a little grocery store and on out through the back. A few minutes later the jedge came in. He is 79 yrs. old, and can't write as well as the worst WPA client I had. He got his docket and the code off a sack of sugar and we gathered in the courtroom which was in back of the store under a couple of trees. He and I had the only chairs. The docket and code were put on an empty fruit crate, and the lawyers and witnesses sat on stumps. Ïhexxxxxlxexxx Mr. Brady had told me to go with Tom to start from the bottom up. He especially wanted me to examine the docket book. When I did, the last case recorded before ours was in 1938, tho there have been numerous cases since then no doubt.

The case itself was one in which the plaintiff, a shrewd old fellow did his own arguing, and he was suing to recover for the value of a cow he alleged had been killed by a G. & S. I. train. My side was trying to show that the cow died rather gracefully in a corn field trying to "find a calf", the expression used. Though the whole affair may sound rather inelegant, I was spellbound through it all, especially with the way in which Mr. Brady handled himself. He is a brilliant lawyer.

He and I ate lunch at a typical old hotel in the big dining room with anybody who wanted to come and sit down with us. It was a good country meal, and everyone was as friendly to me as they could be. The old judge was there, and I had nice chat with him, as well as the plaintiff, who was friendly enough while the trial was not in progress.

On the way to New Hebron, Tom (Mr. Brady to me) showed me a letter he had received in the morning mail from Paul Johnson, asking him to be a colonel on his staff. I don't know whether he will accept or not.

(Above) Fred Hilbert and Viola James happy on their wedding day in Gulfport, Mississippi.

travel to visit friends she had made while in D.C. and Atlanta.

In the Summer 1946, she accepted an invitation to visit with friends in New England's White Mountains. While vacationing there, she met Fred Hilbert. Fred was a perfumer — a nose — for the Fritzsche Brothers Chemical company of New York, a manufacturer of essential oils and perfumes.

Fred courted Vi and the two married on October 19, 1946, in a ceremony in Gulfport. They moved together to Patterson, New Jersey to start a life together.

A Difficult Marriage

Vi's hopes for an adventuresome partner in life were dashed in short order. Fred, it turned out, would not "allow" Vi to work outside the home. He threw tantrums over the slightest missteps; he imposed his sense of scarcity on their household; he slowly chipped away at her self-esteem.

Vi, who had always been joyful and light, found herself trapped. Vi was also devoutly religious and did not believe in divorce.

Vi was separated from the family

and the career she loved. She forfeited nine years of her legal career.

In 1953, ostensibly to care for her aging parents, Vi moved back to Gulfport. The couple never divorced and Vi chose to retain her married name. Fred Hilbert died six years later on November 26, 1959. Vi was not mentioned in his obituary.

A New Start

When Vi returned to Gulfport, she started practicing law again. In 1956, she argued a case in the Fifth Circuit Court of Appeals. She would argue two more in the next three years, as well as two before the Mississippi Supreme Court.

Vi had a thrving legal practice and in 1959 she was named one of the "Outstanding Women in America" (a class that also included Eudora Welty).

An Old Family Friend

Dan Russell had a long history with the James family. In 1932, when Russell enrolled at Ole Miss, his roommate was Garner James, Viola James' older brother.

Garner was, in fact, somewhat of a prodigy. He entered Ole Miss at the age of 15. In addition to being an honors student, Garner was president of the Ole Miss Intercollegiate Debate Team, vice president of the Hermaean Literary Society, and an officer in just about every other academic honors fraternity on campus.

(Above) Mr. Hilbert refused to "allow" his wife to work outside the home. Vi did not practice law for nine yeas. Vi left the marriage in 1956, but never filed for divorced. The year she returned to Gulfport, she opened a law practice.

Dan Russell and Viola James were classmates and he understood her skill sets. In 1965, after being appointed U.S. District Court Judge Russell joked with James, "If you don't join me as a clerk, I will turn down the appointment."

At Ole Miss Viola James was President of the YWCA, Pan Hellenic, and Chi Omega, as well as a founding member of the Tassel Honorary. She was also a member of the law journal staff.

Russell helped Garner adjust socially. Garner helped Russell academically. On more than one occasion, Russell said, "Garner James got me through my freshman year at Ole Miss."

Two years later, Viola James enrolled at Ole Miss and Dan Russell was witness to her academic and leadership qualities.

Cajoling

Dan Russell was charming and charismatic. He flew to Ole Miss football games with Dizzy Dean. He was known to carry a pistol when meeting with clients involved in circumspect businesses, and he was friends with the powerful Senator James Eastland (Dan Russell's father taught Eastland at the Ole Miss law school). In 1965, after the retirement of U.S. District Court Judge Sidney Carr Mize Senator Eastland pushed for the appointment of Dan Russell.

On September 24, 1965, Russell was nominated to the bench by President Lyndon B. Johnson.

When Russell received news of his nomination one of his first calls was to Viola James Hilbert. Russell wanted Vi on his team. He asked her to serve as his law clerk. Initially, she was reluctant; she enjoyed her private practice. But Russell continued to press. He explained that she would have a marvelous federal retirement and that together they could make a difference. And finally, in a last-ditch effort, he joked, "Vi, if you don't join me, I'll turn down the nomination."

Dan Russell received his commission on October 2, 1965. Vi stood by his side, just as she would for the next 11 years.

They tackled more civil rights cases (48) than any other U.S. District Court Judge. Judge Russell, his family, and his staff received death threats. They often traveled with armed U.S. Marshals. Vi felt the weight of the courts decisions and dedicated her waking hours to working with Russell to craft the meticulous legal arguments to support the court's decisions. The job, particularly the civil rights cases, took a toll.

Vi retired in 1976. She never remarried; she had no children. She spent the remainder of her days golfing, gardening, teaching Sunday school, talking to her best friend and fellow attorney Tommy Thompson, and doting on her dogs, nieces, and nephews.

Viola Lee James Hilbert died on February 28, 1988.

Written by Neil White, III, Viola James Hilbert's great-nephew

U.S. District Court Judge Dan Russell with Viola James Hilbert at her retirement party in 1976, forty-one years after they were classmates at Ole Miss.

69

49 Doris Chastine Hartford ❖ 1939

Doris Chastine

*L*iving to be 101 years old, Doris Chastine Hartford was the last female attorney admitted to The Mississippi Bar in the 1930s.

She was born on December 22, 1910, in Mendenhall to parents Bessie Tolles Chastine and Marcus Morgan Chastine.

Doris lived most of her life in Jackson. She attended Mississippi State College for Women. She graduated from the Jackson School of Law and was admitted in 1939 by Judge V. J. Stricker in Hinds County. While attending law school, she met her husband Lt. Robert W. Hartford, an attorney and CPA.

Doris was an adjudicator for the Veterans Administration for many years.

She was a member of St. Luke Methodist Church. Doris Chastine Hartford died on August 28, 2012, and is buried in Cedarlawn Cemetery in Jackson.

1928-1929 Scholarship

Success of the scholarship girls and the joy of service being experienced by members of the Jackson Business and Professional Women's Club grew, so the that in the fall of 1928-1929 three scholarships were awarded. One going to Doris Chastine, helped with make it possible for her to spend office her freshman year at M.S.C.W., Columbus, Mississippi. Doris became interested and wanted to return for her second year, and by self-help, a student loan and assistance from home, Doris completed requirements for a degree in 1932. During the summer Doris did excellent work in the Playgrounds in Jackson, saved her earnings, and thus paid her way through her senior year in college.

Following her graduation Doris taught several years. Salaries were small and paid irregularly. Doris decided to take a business course after which she secured employment with the Treasury Department of the PWA.

Miss Chastine Becomes Bride Of Lt. Hartford

Mrs. Marcus Chastine of Jackson is today announcing the marriage of her daughter, Doris, to Lt. Robert Walton Hartford of Greenwood and Jackson, son of Mrs. Ora Walton Hartford of Lewisburg, Ky. The wedding was quietly solemnized on July 6th at the parsonage of Capitol Street Methodist church, with Dr. Roy H. Kleiser officiating.

The bride was lovely in a poudre blue chiffon dress made on princess lines. She wore a small off-the-face hat with a shoulder-length veil, and her corsage was of gardenias.

Miss Olive Chastine, the bride's sister, was her only attendant. Ralph Boughman served as best man. Miss Chastine wore a summer model of navy blue chiffon with white accessories.

Mrs. Hartford graduated from Mississippi State College for Women at Columbus where she was prominent in student and social activities. She received her law degree from the Jackson School of Law and is a member of the

1940s

Duquote during the 1940s, the number of women practicing law in the United States increased 50%. Female enrollment in law schools, during the same period, nearly doubled. The Japanese attack on Pearl Harbor in 1941 left a huge void in American law schools. Biloxi native Clare Sekul's law school class at the University of Mississippi went from 28 to 2. The war also created new opportunities for women lawyers in the workplace. With most young American men scattered around the Pacific and Europe, women lawyers made inroads into law firms, small practices, and government positions. In Mississippi, Evelyn Gandy served as the first female editor of the *Mississippi Law Journal*. A few years after graduation, she was elected to the state legislature. Zelma Wells Price joined her mother, Zelma Price, in her Greenville practice, making the first mother-daughter legal team in the state. But the triumph of women lawyers was short-lived. Attorneys returning from the war were, for the most part, given their jobs back after 1945. By 1947, law schools were churning out male attorneys again, most of whom had taken advantage of the GI Bill. Women lawyers were often demoted or relieved of their newfound duties. It would be decades before women lawyers represented a respectable percentage of practicing attorneys in Mississippi. Case in point: between 1950-1964, the University of Mississippi law school would award degrees to only eleven women, and during eight of those years, no woman graduated from the law school.

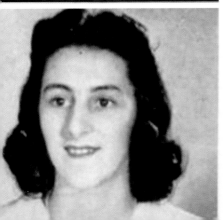

All-Around Marshal

MISS HELEN BLOEDORN is an all-around marshal.

During the day she marshals arguments for the anti-trust division of the Justice Department in Washington. By night she is marshal at Rosecroft Raceway, Maryland's newest harness track.

If a trotter or pacer breaks away at the Oxon Hill oval it is up to this young lady, who is a graduate at law from National University, to retrieve the ill-behaved horse.

A bad actor among the harness racers is rather rare, however, consequently Miss Bloedorn, who is billed as marshal on the Rosecroft programs, has little chance to exhibit her finesse in catching a runaway.

A New Job For Her

Her chief duty is to appear pretty, but capable, in leading the colorful post parades of horses and sulkies and accompanying the victor to the winner's circle after each race. This she effects exceedingly well.

Attired in riding breeches, traditional fox-hunting pink coat, with her blond hair tucked under a black cap, few spectators in the nightly crowds at Rosecroft would suspect that leading trotters and pacers was not Miss Bloedorn's life-long occupation.

Actually it is quite new to her. She had never seen a trotter or pacer race on a regular track before she started working at Rosecroft on May 26. When she accepted the position as marshal she thought it was an honorary one and did not expect to be paid.

William E. Miller, sometime dealer in Wash-

50   Sarah Adeline Chalk Tipping ❖ 1940

Lincoln County's first female lawyer and the 17th female to graduate from the University of Mississippi Law School, Sarah A. Chalk was from Brookhaven. Sarah was admitted to practice law on February 1, 1940. She was the only female attorney admitted to The Mississippi Bar in 1940.

Sarah was born on June 24, 1908. She married Frank Merton Tipping. Sarah died at the age of 61 on January 17, 1970, and is buried in Rose Hill Cemetery in Brookhaven.

51   Zulah Mayo Purvis ❖ 1941

Rankin County's second female lawyer was Zulah M. Purvis of Puckett. She was born in 1898, and graduated from high school in Mendenhall. She attended National University, which is now George Washington University, where she earned her juris doctorate. Through a June 22, 1941, Legal Notice in the *Clarion-Ledger*, Earle Wingo, secretary of the state board of bar admissions, announced that she was eligible to take the state bar examinations to be offered July 7-9, and she was admitted to practice in 1941.

She practiced law in Washington, D.C. as a Civil Service employee, and was licensed to practice before the U. S. Supreme Court.

She was appointed honorary assistant attorney general of the state of Mississippi by Governor Coleman and was active in civic affairs. Zulah was a Worthy Grand Matron of Order of the Eastern Star, a Masonic body open to both men and women; and she was a past chair of the Board of Trustees Auxiliary of Rankin General Hospital.

The *Clarion-Ledger* ran an

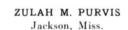
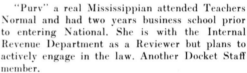

ZULAH M. PURVIS
Jackson, Miss.

"Purv" a real Mississippian attended Teachers Normal and had two years business school prior to entering National. She is with the Internal Revenue Department as a Reviewer but plans to actively engage in the law. Another Docket Staff member.

article on July 30, 1961, stating, "Sixty prominent women from Mississippi have been included for the first time in 'Who's Who of American Women' according to the editors of the newly-published second edition." Zulah M. Purvis was included in those listed from Jackson area.

In 1961, she retired from the practice of law and moved back to Puckett to reside.

Zulah died in July, 1975. Her burial service was at Puckett Baptist Church and she is buried in Rock Bluff Cemetery.

(Above): From the *Docket*, National University's yearbook. Zulah was features editor for the yearbook, as well as a member of the Cy Pres Club, a women's legal sorority. (Left): Zulah Purvis as a first-year law student at National University.

Genevieve Yonkers Schaffer ❖ 1941

Genevieve Yonkers took The Mississippi Bar exam in July 1941. She was one of two women lawyers admitted to the Mississippi Bar in 1941. She attended the National University Law School where she served as class historian. She was born in Mount Savage, Maryland, on September 10, 1911, to Harry and Grace Yonkers. Genevieve married Robert Weber Schaffer and had one son. She lived in Monticello, Mississippi in 1941.

She served in the U.S. Army Marines during WWII and did not have to pay Mississippi Bar dues during that time.

Genevieve retired from the Department of the Interior as an attorney. She died at the age of 87 on May 10, 1999, in Flintstone, Maryland, and was buried in Lockbourne, Ohio.

(Above): Genevieve Yonkers from the 1941 Docket, National University's yearbook. (Right): The Senior Class History of National University Law School, as published in the *Docket*, written by Genevieve who served as class historian.

SENIOR CLASS HISTORY

This, the history of the class of 1941, must be brief because the life of the class is short. But it does have a history and each of its members has one, interesting, if we could but tell it. They have come from all parts of the country; north, south, east and west. They have come from all walks of life. They are of many races, of many religions, and of various political philosophies. With similar desires, hopes and ambitions their life history lines converged steadily upon one focal point—the entry into the class of 1941.

Perhaps this class is no different from other graduating classes of the Law School of National University although we, ourselves, believe it is the best. It has the distinction of being the largest. It had an enrollment of 538 students in 1938 and the graduating class numbers approximately 314. It has the honor of being the first class to graduate since the school has been professionally approved by the American Bar Association as a Grade A law school. It is proud that it is solvent. During its first years lasting friendships were cemented. The second year has been one of understanding, cooperation and loyalty. Only graduation remains before the class members will again spread into all parts of the country. It is safe to predict its members will take their place in the arena of public affairs and bring credit to our beloved Alma Mater.

During the life of the class the school has taken many strides forward. The Midnight Oil school paper was organized. Apex Honor Society was formulated. The Debating Club was revived. A Flying Club was founded. The Coronation Ball became an added attraction to the Docket activities. The Commencement Ball became an annual feature of the graduating festivities. Many of the foregoing were the result of active participation and promotion by the Class of 1941 and its members.

It is regrettable that the active life of the class must close. But we should console ourselves with the thought that during its life we have made enduring friendships and have found inspiration and guidance from professors and fellow classmates. We are comforted that we can, and should, in after years meet frequently to review and to relive the happy and fruitful days of the Class of 1941.

GENEVIEVE A. YONKERS, *Historian.*

[87]

Mary Elizabeth West ❖ 1942

Mary Elizabeth West of Jackson was admitted to the bar on February 5, 1942. She practiced for two years until she retired in 1944, when she requested an inactive status from the bar. Her last known address was Lake Village, Arkansas.

Wells, Robert, Jackson
West, Mary Elizabeth, Jackson

Little is known about Mary Elizabeth West. She was listed as a member in the 1942 edition of the Mississippi Law Journal. She retired two years later and requested inactive status.

THE EARLY 1940S

Five of Mississippi's first one hundred women lawyers graduated from National University Law School in Washington D.C. between the years 1940-1942. The graduates were Zulah Mayo Purvis, Genevieve Yonkers (Schaffer), Helen May Bloedorn, Ivy Lee Buchanan, and Sarah A. Charles. National University Law School (which later merged with George Washington Law School) welcomed female and non-traditional law students. Upon graduation, Purvis was 43 years old; Yonkers was 30; Bloedorn was 24; Buchanan was 40; and Charles was in her late 30s. All five women were members of the National University Cy Pres Club, a woman's legal sorority organized in 1920 to promote women in the profession.

SARAH CHARLES

ZULAH PURVIS

HELEN MAY BLOEDORN

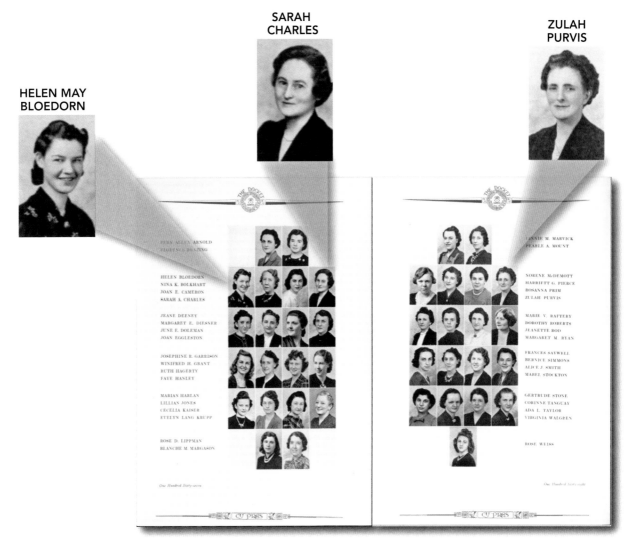

Cy Pres Club

THE CY PRES CLUB is the oldest woman's organization in National University, having been organized October 2, 1920, by Miss Jane Elizabeth Newton of North Carolina. On May 5, 1932, the Club was duly incorporated and a charter granted in the City of Washington, District of Columbia.

The purpose of the Club is to help its members advance in the study of the law, to promote closer friendships, and to stimulate the members to a keener interest and deeper understanding of the legal profession.

IVY LEE
BUCHANAN

SARAH
CHARLES

GENEVIEVE
YONKERS

The Cy Pres Club attained legal age this year, as it was 21 years ago that the club was organized by a small band of National University women students to promote closer friendship, good fellowship and educational advancement of its members.

The Freshman Tea, the Fall Luncheon, the George Washington Birthday Banquet and the Spring Breakfast are the Cy Pres' outstanding annual social events.

An inspiring address by Mrs. Franklin D. Roosevelt made this year's George Washington Birthday Banquet an unforgetable occasion—and to our Gracious First Lady, Cy Pres extends its deepest gratitude.

In 1941, at the Cy Pres Club's annual George Washington Birthday Banquet, Eleanor Roosevelt spoke to the fifty women members. Helen May Bloedorn, Sarah Charles, Ivy Lee Buchanan, and Genevieve Yonkers were all in attendance at that banquet.

75

Helen May Bloedorn ❖ 1942

Helen May Bloedorn was admitted to practice in Mississippi in February of 1942, and worked in both Cleveland, Mississippi and Washington D.C. She was born on July 8, 1918, in Washington, D. C. to parents Lieutenant Commander Walter Andrew Bloedorn and May Howard Bloedorn. Helen grew up in Washington D. C., attending Central High School in Washington.

HELEN MAY BLOEDORN

BLOEDORN, Helen May, Attorney, Criminal Division of Department of Justice, Washington, D. C. (trial and appellate work), Dept. of Justice, Washington, D. C.; res. 835 Richmond Ave., Silver Spring, Md.; b. Washington, D. C., July 8, 1918. Adm. 1942, Virginia; 1943, Maryland. Mem. Md. State Bar; Va. State Bar; Federal Bar Assn. (Chairman, Chapter Liason Committee, 1946; Chairman, Membership Committee, 1947; Editor, Federal Bar News, 1944-45; Asso. Editor, Federal Bar Journal, 1945-48); Women's Bar Assn. of Baltimore City (Vice-President, 1947-48); American Bar Assn. (Committee of Criminal Law Section on Cooperation with the Editors of the American Bar Assn. Journal, 1947, and Committee of the International and Comparative Law Section on Comparative Penal Law and Procedure, 1944); Inter-American Assn. (Penal Law Committee, 1946 and 1947). Edn. George Washington Univ., pre-legal; National Univ., LL.B., 1940 and LL.M., 1941. Former Claims Adjuster, Capital Transit Co., Washington, D. C.; former

She moved to Maryland in 1943 and became a member of the Maryland Bar. She worked for both the antitrust division and the criminal division of the Justice Department.

From 1944-45, Helen served as editor of the Federal Bar News and from 1945-48 she served as associate editor of the Federal Bar Journal.

(Left): Helen May Bloedorn as a law student at National University. (Top): Photo and profile from the 1949 edition of the *Digest of Women Lawyers and Judges*.

(Right): A June 19, 1949, feature story from the *Baltimore Sun* about Helen's role as Marshal of the Rosecraft trotting track.

May Spencer Ringold ❖ 1942

Living to be 100 years old, May Spencer was born on May 1, 1914, in Winona. Her parents were Thomas Harrison Spencer and Mary Beard Spencer. She received her B. A. degree from Mississippi State College for Women. She received her Masters from the University of Mississippi and her Ph.D. from Emory University. May graduated from the Jackson School of Law and was admitted to practice in February 1942. In 1939, she was married to Rupert Marion Ringold, who was also a Mississippi Bar attorney. They had three children during their marriage. As well as practicing law, May also joined the faculty of Clemson University in South Carolina as an historian in the Department of Social Science and assisted in establishing their college library. She also held a teaching fel-

lowship at the University of Mississippi. Beginning the fall of 1967, she joined the staff at MSCW as a history professor.

In 1966, Dr. Ringold's book she authored, entitled, *The Role of State Legislatures in the Confederacy*, deals with the practical rather than the theoretical aspects of state rights in action. It concentrates on the programs by which Confederate governors and general assemblies sought to relieve domestic crises, trying to protect and maintain as nearly as possible normal economic, social, and political institutions. Secession conventions were a part of the investigation insofar as their ordinances initiated or supplemented policies of the legislatures. The research for her work obligated her to travel all over the South studying legislative records.

Besides being a professor and researcher, she was in real estate since 1942. She worked in Winona in real estate sales and became a broker in 1971, forming her own business. Winona attorney, Donald W. Bond, stated "May was a very remarkable woman and was way ahead of her time as far as women in business and taking their place in what was a man's world in those years. She was very feminine and gracious."

She sold her real estate business in 1984 and moved to Greenwood in 1984.

She became Greenwood's Cottonlandia Museum public relations officer. She achieved some important accomplishments as an historian. She spoke fondly of research she did transcribing old letters of the Gourdin family, cotton factors and export-import brokers. From Charleston, South Carolina the research took her to the English cities of London and Liverpool, and she wrote several scholarly articles concerning the Gourdin letters.

She acknowledged that working at the museum and learning about Indian cultures of the Mississippi Delta was fascinating.

In the early 2000s, she was listed as Active Exempt living in Memphis, Tennessee. She was a member of Moore Memorial United Methodist Church in Winona. May Ringold died on March 22, 2015, with all three of her children passing away before she died. May is buried in Oakwood Cemetery in Winona.

Cottonlandia Communique

May S. Ringold brings view of historian to museum job

By STEVE RUSSELL
Staff Writer

MAY SPENCER RINGOLD, Cottonlandia Museum's public relations officer, is one of the people you are likely to meet if you take a tour of the museum's many exhibits.

She hails from Winona and attended school there before attending Mississippi State College for Women (now Mississippi University for Women) from which she was graduated in 1936 with a bachelor's degree in English. She went on to receive a master's and a doctorate

cruel treatment administered to Indians by whites had been upsetting for her.

But she acknowledged that working at the museum and learning more about Indian cultures of the Mississippi Delta have been fascinating. Conducting tours of the museum seems to be an activity that Mrs. Ringold enjoys greatly.

MRS. RINGOLD has lived in Greenwood since June and should feel very much at home; she has a sister, Mrs. H.T. Odom, and a brother, M.B. Spencer, who both

R. Whittington, and a grandson, Joshua Spencer Glazer, reside in Schlater.

I have visited Cottonlandia Museum several times and have usually met interesting people who work there. This visit was no exception. Mrs. Ringold is the kind of person who can talk knowledgeably on many different subjects to almost any person. You are in for a treat if you get a chance to meet May Ringold at Cottonlandia Museum.

Upcoming events: the Cottonlandia Foundation will hold its annual meeting 2 p.m. Sunday, Jan.

Alice Porter Nevels ❖ 1942

"Mrs. Alice Nevels is not only the Secretary-Treasurer of the Mississippi State Bar, she is . . . Secretary of the Board of Bar Admissions, Secretary of the Junior Bar Section. . . mother confessor of the individual lawyers of the State of Mississippi, the head of her family, a devoted mother, and a doting and admirable grandmother, and she is a delightful and lovable person, and as far as I am concerned, she is Mrs. State Bar." stated Bar President C. Sidney Carlton in 1963.

Alice P. Nevels was born September 30, 1900, in Lexington, and received her B.A. from Millsaps College. From 1932 to 1942, she worked as the secretary-treasurer of the Mississippi State Bar. She was the first non-lawyer to hold the position. Her interest lay in law, so she attended the Jackson School of Law and graduated in 1942. She was admitted to the Bar on March 23, 1942.

Alice Nevels was re-elected as secretary of the Mississippi State Bar. The June 25, 1942 *Clarion-Ledger* stated, "Re-election of Mrs. Alice Nevels as secretary of the Mississippi State Bar, announced by Charles F. Engle of Natchez, president, was hailed with approval by lawyers throughout the state. Mrs. Nevels' re-election was done unanimously at a meeting of the commissioners and officers of the Bar in Jackson."

Alice then resigned from working at the Bar to take a commission in the W.A.A.C.

During World War II, Alice enlisted in the Women Army Corps in 1942 becoming a First Lieutenant. She wore silver bars of a second officer in the Women's Army Auxiliary Corps. She was stationed at Camp Ruston, Louisiana as an intelligence officer and inspector general, and she was notified of her promotion from third to second officer by a telephone message from the

Jackson Mother And Son In The WAAC And The Air Corps To Beat The Axis

MOTHER AND SON TEAM — Lieut. Alice Porter Nevels, and her son, Lieut. R. E. Nevels, are both doing their part in this war. Lieut. Nevels is stationed at Camp Ruston, La., as intelligence officer. Her son has been on duty in the South Pacific for the past year.

W.A.A.C. headquarters in Washington, D.C. Her new rank was the same as that of her son, First Lieutenant Robert Ernest Nevels of the Army Air Corps, who served in the New Guinea sector. She became Captain of the W.A.A.C.

At the Mississippi State Bar, five other women served as secretary-treasurer and then in 1951 Alice was asked by the Commissioners to take the job again. She was paid $2,400 per year. Her title was changed in the by-laws in 1963 to executive director and secretary-treasurer, a position she held until 1966.

She was a member of the Hinds County Bar, the American Bar Association, and the American Judicature Society. She served as a member of the Council of Delegates of the National Association of Women Lawyers.

She was a widow to Joseph Galloway Nevels. Alice Porter Nevels died on August 1, 1969, at the age of 68. She was a member of St. Luke's Methodist Church. A special resolution was presented at the Bar's Fall Memorial Service in 1969 for the late Alice P. Nevels being the former executive director of the Mississippi State Bar.

MRS. ALICE NEVELS
Secretary-Treasurer Mississippi State Bar

The Mississippi State Bar owes much of its progress and efficiency to the efforts of its capable and charming Secretary, Mrs. Alice Nevels. Known to most of the lawyers throughout the state as "Miss Alice", she is called upon to perform many and varied duties, and her unfailing good humor and friendliness have endeared her to all.

Mrs. Nevels served as Secretary of the Mississippi State Bar from 1932 to 1942, when she enlisted in the Women's Army Corp. (WAC). She was separated from the army with the rank of Captain. In 1951 she was again appointed to her present position, and as the State Bar has grown both in membership and in service to the lawyers and the community she has continued to carry a heavier load and to make her own fine contribution toward such advancement.

Mrs. Nevels is a graduate of the Jackson School of Law and a member of the Bar of Mississippi. She holds a B.A. degree from Millsaps College in Jackson. She is a Methodist, and a member of the Hinds County Bar as well as the American Bar Association and the American Judicature Society.

She is a past secretary and past president of the Pilot Club of Jackson, and has

(Above): A photograph of the 1963-1964 Mississippi Bar officers and commissioners. Alice Porter Nevels, fourth from left, is surrounded by men. (Below): Alice Porter Nevels at the 1962 Mississippi Bar Convention held in Biloxi, Mississippi

At the annual Friday night banquet of the State Bar Convention is pictured Sherwood W. Wise, outgoing president of the State Bar; Senator E. K. Collins, Laurel, receiving recognition from the Bar in the field of legislation; Mrs. Alice Nevels, Secretary of Bar, who received special recognition for outstanding service to the Bar; Banquet Speaker Rear Admiral W. C. Mott from Washington, D.C., C. Sidney Carlton, incoming president from Sumner and Charles M. Hills, who was presented a plaque for journalistic excellence. (Award winners not pictured are Webb Overstreet (Jackson) and Rep. Thompson McClellan (West Point), both receiving awards in the field of legislation.

57
Margaret Norman Yarborough McLean ❖ 1942

Jackson attorney Margaret Yarborough McLean was born on November 1, 1915. She was a native of Bentonville, Arkansas. Her parents were J. S. Norman and Mollie F. Norman. Margaret was known by "Sally." She was a graduate of Draughton Business School. She attended the Jackson School of Law. In March of 1942, she was admitted to practice. She formerly served as secretary-treasurer of the Mississippi State Bar from 1946-1947 after secretary-treasurer Alice Nevels left to be in the W.A.A.C. during the war. She was a communicant of St. James Episcopal Church, where she was previously the Wedding Coordi-

nator. Former President Richard Nixon appointed her to the executive position of the National Small Business Administration. Margaret was a lobbyist for the Equal Rights Amendment.

Margaret married Lewis Everett Yarborough in 1932. They were divorced in the 1930s. Her second husband was Sam H. McLean.

Margaret Yarborough McLean died on May 19, 2000. She was listed in the Bar's Memorial Service in Fall 2000 with Chief Justice Lenore Prather presiding over the program and Bar President Dick Bennett presenting the Eulogy.

MISSISSIPPI STATE BAR
1946-1947

OFFICERS

R. C. STOVALL OF COLUMBUS	PRESIDENT
TOXEY HALL OF COLUMBIA	FIRST VICE-PRESIDENT
CHAS. S. TINDALL, JR. OF GREENVILLE	SECOND VICE-PRESIDENT
MRS. MARGARET MCLEAN OF JACKSON	SECRETARY-TREASURER

58
Ivy Lee Buchanan ❖ 1942

Warren County's first female lawyer was Ivy Lee Buchanan. She was born on December 13, 1902. After graduating from National University, Ivy was admitted to practice law in Mississippi on April 6, 1942, and she worked both in Vicksburg, Mississippi and also in Washington D.C. Ivy died at the age of 54 on December 7, 1957. She is buried in Louin Cemetery in Jasper County.

IVY LEE BUCHANAN
Dallas, Texas

A Texan in every sense of the word, that's Ivy Lee. After attending State College for Women and Southern Methodist in Texas she settled down at National. Horseback riding is her hobby and Dr. Cassidy her favorite professor despite his remarks about her miscellaneous hats. She experienced a great moment when she passed the Mississippi bar. Good luck, Buckey—for your private practice either in Washington or Texas.

Cy Pres Club

Sarah A. Charles ❖ 1942

Lowndes County's first female attorney was Sarah A. Charles. She was married to Gorman A. Charles. Sarah received her juris doctorate from the National University in Washington D.C., and was admitted to practice in Mississippi on April 6, 1942.

She worked in various aspects of legal work in Washington in the Business Veterans Administration and then in Columbus, Mississippi.

SARAH AGNES CHARLES
San Francisco, California

Mississippi State College For Women in Columbus, Mississippi not only gave "Charley" a B.S. degree, but also a lovely, gracious manner. She has resided in many parts of the country, but claims Sunny California as her legal residence; however, the Bar Examiners of Mississippi were so impressed with her legal knowledge, that they admitted her to practice law there. She has many outside activities, which accounts for her hobby of "touring", but for the "duration" this will be her sacrifice in the interests of victory.

Cy Pres Club
Kappa Beta Pi

(Left): The 1942 Docket yearbook profile of Sarah Agnes Charles from National University. (Right): The photo of Sarah from the New York Lit Club section of the Docket.

Martha Virginia Clarke Bunting ❖ 1942

Born on April 24, 1911, in Brookhaven was Martha Virginia Clarke. Her father was Carus V. Clarke and her mother was Mattie Goza Clarke. She graduated from Brookhaven High School in 1928. She attended Belhaven College to obtain her bachelor's degree and from there attended Jackson School of Law.

Upon her admittance to the bar, she opened a law practice in Jackson and stayed in Jackson until 1943. She moved to Seattle in 1943 to get married to Douglas Bunting, Jr., sergeant U.S. Army, stationed at the time in Seattle.

She then moved to Birmingham, Alabama, and worked for the Social Security Administration for the next forty years. Her daughter-in-law remarked: "She set a great example for the women who worked under her and let them know that they can do it, too." Virginia was a member of the Home Garden Club and the Cauldron Literary Club.

She was a member of Independent Presbyterian Church. Martha Virginia Clarke Bunting died April 22, 1994, at the age of 82.

Edythe Evelyn Gandy ❖ 1943

In 1920, the 19th Amendment to the United States Constitution gave women the right to vote. That same year, Edythe Evelyn Gandy, who would be called "The 'Lady' Who Hit Mississippi's Glass Ceiling" and "A Giant in Mississippi Politics" was born in Hattiesburg, Mississippi. The date was September 4, 1920. She would become the most successful woman in the history of Mississippi politics and would open doors for women in politics on all levels of state government. She would be the first woman elected to the state legislature from Forrest County, the first woman to serve as an Assistant Attorney General, the first woman elected to a statewide constitutional office, the first woman to serve as State Treasurer, the first woman to serve as Commissioner of Public Welfare, the first woman to serve as chair of a major policy making state board, the first woman to serve as Commissioner of Insurance, and the first woman to serve as Lieutenant Governor. "There can be no discussion of 'firsts' in Mississippi without a long list of Ms. Gandy's accomplishments being included. Evelyn Gandy paved the way for so many of us, while serving as a role model for all of us," stated Joy Lambert Phillips, the Mississippi Bar's first female President.

(Above): Evelyn Gandy's yearbook photo from her senior year at the University of Southern Mississippi. (Right): Evelyn lived and thrived in a man's world, long before most women were afforded that opportunity.

Evelyn Gandy and her sister Frances were raised in the Glendale Community by their parents Kearney C. and Abbie Whigham Gandy. Evelyn developed an interest in politics at an early age. As a student at Hattiesburg High School, she excelled in debate and oratory. While a teenager, she began making political speeches for friends of her father. In the Hattiesburg High School annual of 1938, her class prophecy predicted that Gandy would be the first woman elected Governor of Mississippi.

After graduating high school with high honors, she enrolled at the University of Southern Mississippi. She continued to be an active debater and a participant in many programs. She was voted "Most Intellectual Girl" of her class.

She graduated from the University of Southern Mississippi with a desire to become a lawyer. Few women had attended the University of Mississippi Law School, and many people said that she would never be admitted. Her father responded by saying, "When they see her record, she'll get in," – and she did. She

EVELYN GANDY
DICK STRATTON
ERICH MERRILL
MARTHA GERALD

The Journal of the Mississippi State Bar
Association issued by the School of Law.
Co-edited each year, the publication is an
outstanding campus publication, and its
editorship is one of the most coveted of
publication heads.

MISSISSIPPI LAW JOURNAL

STAFF

EDYTHE EVELYN GANDY . . . . *Editor*

RICHARD E. STRATTON, III . . . . *Editor*

WILLIAM H. WARD . . . . *Business Manager*

ERICH W. MERRILL . . . . *Ass't Business Manager*

MARTHA W. GERALD . . . . *Assistant Editor*

PROFESSOR JOHN WADE . . . . *Faculty Advisor*

PROFESSOR WILLIAM ETHRIDGE . . . . *Faculty Advisor*

won the state oratorical contest. She was also the first woman editor of the *Mississippi Law Journal* and the first woman to be elected president of the Law School Student Body.

Upon graduating in 1943, Evelyn was admitted to The Mississippi Bar on January 30, 1943. She began her law career as a Legislative Assistant in the United States Senate in Washington, D.C. After three years, she returned to Hattiesburg to open her own law office.

In January 1947, Evelyn ran for the Mississippi House of Representatives and won. Her first time to hold public office also made her the first woman representative of Forrest County in the state legislature. Her work for education and human services in this term set the theme for the programs that she would support during her career. Gandy was connected to bills supporting community colleges and institutions of higher learning. She was listed as co-author of both the statute that established the University of Mississippi Medical Center, Mississippi's only four-year medical school, and the first law that provided financial assistance to the disabled.

In 1959, Evelyn was appointed Assistant Attorney General of Mississippi, again becoming the first woman to hold this position. Later that year, she announced her candidacy for the office of State Treasurer. Her victory made her the first woman to be elected to a state-wide constitutional office in Mississippi. As State Treasurer, she implemented a program that ensured the fair and equitable distribution of state funds to all Mississippi banks.

Evelyn was appointed Commissioner of Public Welfare in 1964, in the midst of civil rights reform. She brought the Public Welfare agency into complete compliance with all new civil rights requirements. She was also responsible for the successful expansion of the state's food stamp program into all 82 counties.

Evelyn put her name on the ballot again in 1967 for a second term as State Treasurer. This time, she was elected without opposition. She convinced the legislature to enact the practice of placing all state funds in interest-bearing accounts. Millions of dollars in interest was earned for Mississippians in the decades that followed.

In 1971, Gandy was elected Commissioner of Insur-

(Opposite): Evelyn was the first female editor of the *Mississippi Law Journal* — and Martha Gerald wasn't far behind her.
(Below): Again, surrounded by men

THE ESSENTIALS OF GOOD CITIZENSHIP

"Governments must depend on men rather than men upon governments," William Penn once declared.

Truer words than Penn's were never spoken, and it is because of the truth of the statement that good citizenship is so important to the government of to-day. However, before a citizen can fully understand how governments depend on men through citizenship, he must have some conception of this relationship of government and citizenship.

There are two principles underlying civil society--the principles of obedience and independence. The former in excess leads to despotism while the latter in excess means anarchy. It is a reasonable medium between the two principles that establishes a free and popular form of government.

The spirit of independence is very important--men must govern independently or they must be governed by others. Our government is a republic--one in which the people govern. If it is to remain a government "of, by, and for the people" each citizen must know and practice the essentials of good citizenship.

Good citizenship cannot be learned; it must be lived. However, it is possible to recall a few of the characteristics of a good citizen.

The good citizen must be intelligent. He must be able to understand the interests of his community. To fully understand the needs of his government, the citizen must know the history of his country. He must be familiar with the governmental structure and with his duty as connected with it. His intelligence must give him an appreciation of what his country has done for him. If the citizen has a real appreciation of the rights and privileges which his ancestors fought for, he will realize the importance of his duties and discharge them faithfully.

Excerpts from an award-winning 1938 essay — "The Essentials of Good Citizenship" — written by Evelyn Gandy when she was a student at Hattiesburg High School. Although the standard at the time, the use of the male pronoun is ironic considering the barriers she broke through during her legal and political career.

Third, service to the government is necessary. The good citizen must be willing to serve as a juror; therefore, he must face this responsibility without shirking. Some citizens must go further and serve their community in public office. In this respect, however, the motto should be, "Not for one's self but for others."

Law is the free will of the people; therefore, in the United States law means liberty. The citizen must possess self-control in order to submit his will to the higher authority--the authority of law. Thus, self-control lies at the base of all popular government and without it successful government is impossible.

The citizen, who possesses the ideal community spirit, receives more enjoyment from seeing his fellow citizens healthy, peaceful, and happy than from his own personal interests. The citizen can realize this desire by working individually and by working in and cooperating with civic organizations.

says the words but feels them. As he feels these words, he realizes that he does not depend on his government but his government depends on him; and, being fully conscious of this fact, he strives to be a good citizen and to possess all the essentials of good citizenship.

ance, making her the first woman in the United States to be elected State Insurance Commissioner. During this term, she strengthened the regulation of insurance companies and agents and initiated a program of field representatives throughout the state to assist policy holders with insurance-related information and to assist policy holders with small claims against insurance companies.

In 1975, Evelyn became the first woman to be elected Lieutenant Governor of Mississippi. Her term was marked by successful legislation in improving education, economic development, and health care. Under her direction, some state agencies were reorganized, and the Ethics Commission was created.

Evelyn ran for Governor in both 1979 and 1983 but lost to William Winter and Bill Allain, respectively. Despite her loss, Governor William Winter held Gandy in high regard and called her "one of Mississippi's most conscientious and able public leaders."

From 1980-1981, she was the Deputy Director of the State Department of Mental Health.

In 1994, she stated in a speech to the Mississippi Women's Political Network, "This democracy will never be what it was destined to be – our civilization will never be truly refined – until men and women work together in every phase of our society, including government at every level, in full equality, equal partnership and mutual respect."

Evelyn did not run for public office again. She continued to serve on multiple local and national policy making boards and commissions. The Mississippi Supreme Court appointed her Honorary Chair of the Gender Fairness Task Force, where she served until 2003. And, she continued her service to Mississippians in the private practice of law as a member of the Hattiesburg law firm Ingram & Associates. Carroll H. Ingram, founding member of the firm, says of Evelyn: "She was a person who served the State without regard for her own financial or political gain and always did what she thought was in the best interest of the people – all of the people, not just some of the people. She truly was a public servant, not only in her service through public office, but also in her private practice of law. The people of the State truly loved and cherished her. She made a real difference for the long term. She always did her duty, always did what was right, and always followed the law. This is why she continues to be held in such high esteem."

Evelyn Gandy's life in public service was recognized by many awards and honors, both locally and nationally. She received the Service of Humanity Award from Mississippi College, 1976; an Honorary Degree of Doctor of Law from Blue Mountain College, 1977; the Humanitarian Award from the National Mental Health Association, 1979; the Mississippi Woman of the Year Award from Mississippi State University, 1980; the Mississippian of the Year in Government Award from the State of Mississippi, 1981; the Award for Excellence in Law from Mississippi College School of Law, 1984; Susan B. Anthony Award for Outstanding Service to the State of Mississippi from the Mississippi Women's Political Caucus, 1984; a Medal of Excellence from Mississippi University for Women, 1991; Lifetime Achievement Award from The Mississippi Bar, 1994; the First Annual Award for Distinguished Service from the Women's Political Network, 1994; the James O. Eastland Award from the Mississippi Democratic Party, 1995; the Margaret Brent Women Lawyers of Achievement Award from the American Bar Association, 1997;

the Lifetime Achievement Award from the Mississippi Association of Women Lawyers, 1998; the Leadership Award from the Hattiesburg Women's Forum, 1998; the Chief Justice Award from The Mississippi Bar, 1998; and the Susie Blue Buchanan Award from The Mississippi Bar Women in the Profession Committee, 2003. Evelyn was inducted into the University of Southern Mississippi Alumni Hall of Fame and the Mississippi Hall of Fame. The Mississippi Bar named its annual women lawyers conference the "Evelyn Gandy Lecture Series" in her honor.

(Opposite): Evelyn Gandy portrait. (Above): Lieutenant Governor Evelyn Gandy, center, with City of Jackson Mayor Dale Danks, second from left, and Governor Cliff Finch, far right.

Evelyn Gandy died on December 23, 2007. Forest attorney Constance Slaughter-Harvey stated, "Governor Gandy, shaped by her deeds and actions, made state government responsive and held it accountable, through shared wisdom-making, as it served all of its citizens. This state is better because of the commitment of this trailblazer to all of us, and her integrity in providing services is a great testament to her legacy."

Evelyn Gandy's memorial statue, commissioned by the Women in the Profession Committee of The Mississippi Bar, is located in the Old Supreme Court Chamber of the Mississippi State Capitol.

Evelyn Gandy First Woman To Hold Post

Evelyn Gandy, 70, says she hopes that Mississippi women will make the same strides in politics on a statewide level as women in other states have. Gandy, who now practices law in Hattiesburg, also hopes that people will remember her for being a political pioneer and not just for her two unsuccessful gubernatorial races.

(Above): Evelyn Gandy at the end of her career. (Below): She was known for often quoting a poem that she read in a magazine as a child. Evelyn stated it expressed her philosophy:

Dear Lord, In the battle that goes on in life,
I ask but a field that is fair.

A chance that is equal with all in the strife,
The courage to strive and to dare.

And if I should win, let it be by the Code,
With my faith and my honor held high.

And if I should lose, let me stand by the road,
And cheer as the winners go by.

Hilda Howell ❖ 1943

Lawrence County's first female lawyer was Hilda Howell from Wanilla. She was admitted to practice law on February 2, 1943.

Lottie M. Steele ❖ 1943

Lottie M. Steele was born June 20, 1912. She was a native of Silver Creek and was reared in Rockport. After completion of Clarksdale High School, Lottie attended Millsaps College and the University of Mississippi for her undergraduate degree. In pursuit of her interest in law, she attended the Jackson School of Law and was admitted to practice on May 29, 1943. The VA employed her beginning in 1944.

She was married to Horace Steele. In 1946, she did not practice law but continued to pay Bar dues. While not practicing law in the 1950s, she became an artist. The Art Department of Protective Paint Company presented the works of Lottie Steele. She studied art and painted a collection of children's portraits in watercolor. She remained on inactive status, not practicing law. She was a resident of Jackson for more than 50 years and attended the Unity Church. Lottie died in February, 1988.

Statham, Bill Dan, Magnolia
Steele, Mrs. Lottie M., Jackson
Steene, R. E. Picayune

Ruth Rose Miller Deterly ❖ 1943

"Twelve Applicants Admitted to Bar" read the headline on April 16, 1943, in the *Greenwood Commonwealth*. Two of the twelve applicants were husband and wife, H. G. Deterly and Ruth Deterly.

Ruth was born on May 4, 1906, in Beaver Dam, Wisconsin. She was a graduate of the Wisconsin State Normal School and the Jackson School of Law. She was a member of the Hinds County Bar Association. She was a member of Calvary Baptist Church.

Early on Sunday morning, July 7, 1957, Ruth shot herself to death in her home. She had been very despondent because of illness. She was found by her husband. Ruth had left two notes, one to the finder of her body and the other addressed to her husband.

Ruth is buried in Cedarlawn Cemetery in Jackson.

Unfortunately, Ruth's suicide was not the last in our profession. Subsequent research has shown that lawyers suffer from substance abuse and depression at a rate higher than the general population and may be at a greater risk for suicide. As such, the Women in the Profession Committee strongly encourages the use of The Mississippi Bar's confidential Lawyers and Judges Assistance Program (LJAP).

Local Woman Kills Self In Her Home

A Jackson woman attorney shot herself to death in her home early Sunday morning, despondent because of illness, according to relatives.

The body of Mrs. Ruth Miller Deterly, 51, was found lying across a bed of her home at 236 Mt. Ver-

Adeline N. Morris ❖ 1943

*A*deline N. Morris was one of nine persons passing the Bar exam in July, 1943. The *Hattiesburg American*, on July 29, 1943, reported, "Nine applicants are reported today to have passed bar examinations conducted by the state board of bar admission on July 5, 6, and 7. Earl Wingo, secretary of the board, stated that twelve students of law stood for the recent examination." Another female, Zelma Wells Price of Greenville, also passed the examination.

Adeline was admitted to practice in July of 1943, after which she then moved and practiced in Washington D.C.

Zelma Wells Price Schuetta ❖ 1943

*T*he first "mother and daughter" law partnership in this state was Zelma Wells Price Schuetta and her mother Zelma Price, a prominent woman member of the bar from Greenville. She was born on February 7, 1922, in Greenville. Her parents were Robert Price and Zelma Wells Price. She was a graduate of Greenville High School. Zelma graduated with a law degree from the University of Southern California.

After being accepted to practice law on August 14, 1943, she began practicing with her mother, Mrs. Zelma W. Price, in the Weinberg Building in Greenville. She was Washington County's fourth female attorney.

On January 1, 1945, Zelma married Captain Lawrence

Victor Schuetta from Franksville, Wisconsin. They were married in Greenville. He served in WWII, the Korean War and the Vietnam War.

In 1946, she practiced law in Starkville. Her husband was attending Mississippi State University, completing his training in Aeronautical Engineering. In 1947, Zelma and her husband moved to Madison, Wisconsin. In October, 1954, Zelma and her 10 month old son, Kenneth R. Schuetta, left from New York City bound for Southampton, England.

She died on February 26, 1980, in Pinellas, Florida.

(Left): Zelma Price Wells (center) with her two daughters, both of whom became members of The Mississippi Bar. (Above): Zelma's wedding announcement to Captain Lawrence V. Schuetta of the U.S. Army. (Below) Zelma's biography from *Women's Lawyers Digest*.

SCHUETTA, Zelma P. (Mrs. Lawrence V. Schuetta), Attorney, Price & McIlwain, Attys., Greenville, Mississippi; b. Corinth, Miss., Feb. 7, 1922; dau. Mrs. Zelma W. Price. Adm. Aug., 1943, Mississippi. Mem. Miss State Bar Assn.; Washington County Bar Assn.; National Assn. of Women Lawyers; American Bar Assn.; Business & Professional Women's Club of Greenville, Miss.; American Assn. of Univ. Women, Greenville. Edn. grad. Univ. of Southern Calif., Los Angeles, B.A. in Speech, June, 1941. Formerly af. with L. W. Brown, Atty., Starkville, Miss.; now af. with mother, Mrs. Zelma W. Price, Atty., Greenville, Miss. Academic Latin and French. Little theatre work; sports.

Dessie E. McManus ❖ 1943

Gulfport's third female lawyer was Dessie E. McManus. She was born on July 10, 1892. Her parents were Hugh and Mary McManus. Her father was a sheriff. She was admitted to The Mississippi Bar in 1943. Dessie served as the Deputy Clerk at the Harrison County Courthouse. She was a member of the Gulfport Business and Professional Women's Club. Dessie McManus died on January 31, 1966, at the age of 73.

Martha Wilson Gerald ❖ 1944

The first female President of the Hinds County Bar Association was Martha Gerald.

The first President of Mississippi Women Lawyers Association was Martha Gerald.

Born on October 4, 1919, in the small Mississippi Delta hamlet of Leland to a lawyer/farmer father and a mother who taught second graders in a little red schoolhouse, Martha experienced the Mississippi River Flood of 1927, the Great Depression, and the effects of World War II on their close-knit community.

She graduated *cum laude* from Millsaps College in 1941. Martha was one of three women students to enter the University of Mississippi Law School in the fall of 1941, just months before the United States entered World War II. She received her law degree from the University of Mississippi in 1944, where she served as the Editor-in-Chief of the *Mississippi Law Journal*.

Once she was admitted to practice on January 28, 1944, she worked for the firm Wells, Gerald, Brand, Watters & Cox, becoming senior partner of Gerald & Brand. One of her former partners, Joe Jack Hurst, once wrote, "She is one of the state's outstanding women lawyers, and without peer among oil and gas lawyers in Mississippi."

Martha served as president of many professional organizations. In 1974 to 1975, she was the first female President of the Hinds County Bar. She was President of the Mississippi Oil and Gas Association in 1966 and was President and co-founder of the Mississippi Association of Women Lawyers in 1976. She also served on the district Board of Directors for the National Association of Women's Lawyers. She was chairwoman of the Board of Directors of the YWCA of Jackson and served on the Board of Directors of Central Mississippi Legal Services. In 1980, she was awarded the Millsaps Alumnus of the Year.

One of her good friends, United Methodist Bishop Clay Lee, who knew Martha long before she became the first chairwoman of the governing body of Jackson's Galloway Methodist Church, and who nominated her for service on

(continued next page)

(Left): Martha from the 1943 Ole Miss yearbook.
(Below): A photo from the 1975 *Mississippi Lawyer*

Hinds County Bar Ass'n officers. Seated, Martha Gerald, outgoing President. Standing, from left, Pat H. Scanlon, President; Ross R. Barnett, Jr., Vice-President and President Elect; and Alex Alston, Secretary-Treasurer.

the General Council on Finance and Administration for the United Methodist Church, stated she was, "an authentic human being who understood and accepted her vulnerability, and offered it in the best spirit possible, by not taking herself too seriously and by not seeing others as objects to be manipulated and exploited."

Upon my graduation from law school, I asked her opinion as to the most important quality, apart from competence, that a lawyer should possess. "Integrity" she replied, without hesitation.

The Mississippi Women Lawyers Association formed the Martha Wilson Gerald Scholarship for students at the University of Mississippi Law School.

Martha Gerald died on January 6, 1997, at the age of 77. She is buried in Leland-Stoneville Cemetery in Leland.

Written by her nephew, Mississippi attorney Jim Fraiser

Millsaps Alumnus of the Year recalls her days as a student

By JANA BRUCE STEVENS
FOCUS Writer

When Martha Wilson Gerald, a Northeast Jackson lawyer, was a student at Millsaps College, one of the college's most popular activities was to meet at the drug store across the street and play the nickelodeon.

This year's winner of the Alumnus of the Year Award at Millsaps, the 1941 graduate recently recalled her days as a student there at a time when World War II was just beginning.

"People were just coming out of the Depression then, not many students had a car on campus," the Leland native said. She said she knew of only one girl among the about 600 students who had a car on campus. "There was no problem then," she said.

Miss Gerald began her college career in 1937 at Belhaven College, which was then a girls' school. "I went to Belhaven mainly because other girls from Leland were going. After a year I wanted to change. Belhaven was a strict girls' school," she said.

"I thought Millsaps was a very modern school even at that time. I lived in a dorm which had its own dining room. The next year they put in a cafeteria, which was quite an improvement of the food," she said.

Free time could be spent at 28-cent movies — "one of the few reasons you'd go downtown," she said. Afterward "You'd go to Primos for a Coke and fudge square if you could afford it." Transportation around town could be had for a nickel on the city bus.

Although dancing and drinking were forbidden on campus, Miss Gerald, president of Kappa Delta sorority, said the fraternities and sororities would hold their dances off campus.

Martha Wilson Gerald

in January, she said her graduation class consisted of herself and another woman.

"The war was hard on all the schools," she said, adding that at Ole Miss, three former student body presidents were killed in succession.

"They had an Army ROTC unit at Ole Miss. At that time a boy could go three years and then get his commission as a second lieutenant his fourth year," she said. "Many of these young men, like student body presidents, were called out to serve on the front lines."

Her first job after graduation was with the Jackson

Listing of top lawyers in U.S. includes 1 woman from state

By Mac Gordon
Clarion-Ledger Business Writer

Martha Gerald's colleagues in the Jackson legal community aren't surprised she's on the latest listing of *The Best Lawyers in America*.

But Gerald sounds surprised that she is the only female attorney in Mississippi included on the biennial survey of the nation's top lawyers.

"It's a profession that I think is peculiarly suited to the talents of women. They don't mind working and so much of the practice of law is what you do before you get to the courtroom," said Gerald, senior

Grantham, Grower & Hewes, has often butted heads with Gerald.

"Martha has some very faithful and loyal clients who think an awful lot of her," said Grower. "I'm sure she has earned that faith. She came along when there weren't many lady lawyers — in fact, she was the only one we dealt with for a long period of time."

Larry Houchins, executive director of the Mississippi State Bar, said there are 743 women practicing law in the state, out of 4,800 attorneys.

Gerald's interest in law came nat-

dealings with the oil and gas board, litigation, title work, contracts, environmental work. When you say oil and gas, it covers a multitude of sins."

The oil and gas specialty is among 14 categories of law in which Mississippians are listed in the recently published book.

Grower is one of four from the Brunini, Grantham firm in the oil and gas category. Gerald is among three from her firm.

Overall, the Jackson firm of Butler, Snow, O'Mara, Stevens & Cannada leads the Mississippi list with

Martha Gerald: Law is "peculiarly suited to the talents of women."

Bar.

Alston credits Gerald for helping

69 Allie D. Zeller ❖ 1944

"*F*ive Jacksonians Pass Bar Exams" stated the March 4, 1944, *Clarion-Ledger*. "Three women and a corporal in the U.S. Army were included in a list of 10 Mississippians who passed the recent bar examination, it was learned yesterday from Earl Wingo, secretary of the State Board of Bar Admissions at his office in Hattiesburg." Mrs. Allie D. Zeller of Jackson was accepted to practice law in 1944.

Five Jacksonians Pass Bar Exams
3 Women, One Soldier Included

Three women and a corporal in the U. S. Army were included in a list of 10 Mississippians who passed the recent bar examinations, it was learned yesterday from Earl Wingo, secretary of the State Board of Bar Admissions at his office in Hattiesburg.

Five of the successful candidates gave their address as Jackson and included:

Jos. B. Mackey, 1126 E. Fortification; John G. Tyler, 732 Arlington; Mrs. Allie D. Zeller, Carl E. Sankhauser, and Raymond W. Miller, 721 North State street.

The other five were Miss Bonnie Smith, Collins; John M. Gardner, Gulfport; Wm. R. Cunningham, Booneville; Miss Frances McBride, Meridian, and Cpl. John M. Giansorte, Laurel Base Detachment, Laurel.

Other two members

Bonnie Earline Smith ❖ 1944

Covington County's first female lawyer was Bonnie Earline Smith. She was born on November 10, 1901, in Collins, Mississippi. Her father, Luther Otis Smith, was 21 and her mother, Blanche Edith Mercer Smith, was 19. She is a graduate of Collins High School. Her law education came from working at a law office run by lawyer E. L. Dent for twelve years. After passing the bar exam, she was admitted to practice on March 4, 1944, and sworn in by Chancery Judge Lester Clark.

According to Bonnie's niece, "Bonnie Smith began working for Judge Dent in the last half of the 1920s and gradually took on

Bonnie Earline Smith practiced law for 37 years. She lived to see her 100th birthday.

more and more of the writing of documents and briefs on her own. In the late 1920s, Judge Dent was very busy and away from the office a lot doing the job of Circuit Judge and asked Bonnie to be ready to take the bar exam as he had signed her up to do so. She went to Jackson, took the exam, and passed it on her first try."

She continued to practice at Dent's firm for many years. She retired in 1981.

At the age of 100, on October 4, 2002, Bonnie Earline Smith died in Fort Worth, Texas. She was a member of Collins Presbyterian Church and is buried in Collins City Cemetery.

Marie Luter Upton ❖ 1944

The author of numerous genealogy books which helped hundreds of American families research their Colonial roots and locate lost cemeteries in the backwoods of Mississippi was Marie Luter Upton of Jackson.

She was born on January 11, 1904, to Hosea Davis Luter and Rosa Belle Gin Luter. She followed her passion for the law and graduated from Jackson School of Law. From there she was admitted to practice on July 11, 1944. She was married to Robert Chester Upton.

The patriotic and lineage societies were encouraged by her membership, as well as her work within various groups including: Daughters of the American Revolution, Daughters of American Colonists,

Marie Luter Upton was the author of dozens of genealogical books. She died at the age of 100.

Dames of the Court of Honor, Colonial Dames of America, United Dames of the Confederacy, Scottish Dames, Knights of the Garter, Descendants of Colonial Clergy, and Magna Charta Dames.

She was the founding regent for the Annandale Chapter of DAR. Marie was one of the organizers of the Order of First Families of Mississippi and served as their Registrar General.

Marie Upton died on January 19, 2004, at the age of 100. She is buried in Lakewood Memorial Park.

MARIE LUTER UPTON, a resident of Madison, recently received an award in Natchez, given by the Order of the First Families of Mississippi, for meritorious leadership in history and genealogy. Upton has served the order in an official capacity since 1967. She was organizing regent of the Annandale Chapter of Daughters of the American Revolution in Madison and is still active in that organization.

72 Cecile Cambre Alford ❖ 1944

Born in Jackson on June 24, 1905, was Cecile Cambre. She had five sisters and one brother. She was married to Thomas W. Alford, Jr. on August 15, 1933. He died at the age of 39 in WWII. Cecile graduated from the Jackson School of Law after which she was admitted to practice on August 14, 1944. Cecile's main focus in law was working as an Attorney Legal Rating Specialist for the Veterans Affairs in Jackson.

Cecile Cambre Alford died on December 25, 2000, at the age of 95. She was a member of St. Richard Catholic Church and is buried in Lakewood Memorial Park.

73 Lura Mae Womack ❖ 1944

Lura Mae Womack was born on August 6, 1909, in Lincoln, Mississippi. Her father was William David Womack and her mother was Martha Ann Kyzar Womack.

She was a stenographer for United Gas Pipe Line Company before she took the bar examination. After rigorous study and dedication, she was admitted on September 25, 1944.

Lura worked for the Veterans Administration in Jackson. After many years of service, she retired in 1973, and her status was changed to inactive. She passed away on February 14, 1980, at the age of 70 in Florence. She is buried in Bogue Chitto in Lincoln County.

74 Dolsie Earline Williams Doerr ❖ 1944

The 20th female graduate of the University of Mississippi Law School was Dolsie Williams.

She was born on August 21, 1922, to Mr. and Mrs. B. L. Williams of Raymond. She married Donald D. Doerr in 1946. They had one son and one daughter.

Dolsie attended the University of Mississippi for her B.A. and she graduated from the University of Mississippi Law School in 1944. She was the sixth Editor-in-Chief of the *Mississippi Law Journal*. She was admitted to the bar in 1944. Dolsie was then employed in New Orleans.

She lived in Pennsylvania in the 1980s. She was appointed the position of administrative chair at Butler County Community College in Butler, Pennsylvania. Her responsibilities included scheduling, budgeting, evaluation and adjunct hiring of the physical education, social studies and humanities departments of the college.

Her husband passed away in 1988 and she moved to Gulf Shores, Alabama.

Dolsie Williams Doerr died on May 1, 2014, at the age of 91 and is buried in Lakewood Memorial Park in Jackson.

MISS DOLSIE EARLENE WILLIAMS of New Orleans and Raymond is the bride-elect of Donald D. Doerr of Butler, Pa. Her engagement is made known today by her parents, Mr. and Mrs. B. L. Williams of Raymond.

(Left): Dolsie Earline Williams from the 1943 Ole Miss yearbook.
(Above): Her 1946 wedding announcement in the *Clarion-Ledger*.

Margaret E. Fisher ❖ 1945

argaret E. Fisher was born on October 2, 1901, and after completing high school, she continued her education at George Washington University. She then attended VA State Teachers College. Upon graduation and receiving her acceptance to practice in Mississippi in 1945, she began working in Roanoke, Virginia. She then moved to Perry Point, Maryland, and later in 1952 moved to Gonyon, Virginia. Margaret practiced until 1957 which is when she moved to St. Petersburg, Florida.

Margaret E. Fisher died May 29, 1978. She is buried in Gulfport.

ROANOKE, VA.
Fisher, Mrs. M. E.
c/o Veteran's Adm. Hos.

Virginia C. Searcy ❖ 1945

irginia C. Searcy of Lebanon, Tennessee, was admitted to practice after taking the Mississippi Bar exam in February of 1945 and proceeded to work in Florida. She worked in the statutory revision division of the Florida Attorney General's office. She was a graduate of Cumberland University Law School, which was not on the Florida accredited list. She did hold a license to practice in Mississippi. As she was out of state, she did not have to pay bar dues.

On October 31, 1945, the *Tampa Tribune* in Tampa, Florida reported, "Court Refuses to Relax Bar Exam Rules. A petition by Attorney General Watson for relaxation of a state bar examination rule to give one of his clerks a chance to take the test was denied by the Supreme Court today. The action came after a lengthy hearing which produced a verbal outburst between lawyers rare in the Supreme Court chambers. Watson asked the court to permit the state board of bar examiners to waive the 1941 rule requiring candidates for the examination to be graduates of accredited law schools if it is shown the applicant has training equivalent to the college work. He said he asked for the change after the board had informed him it had no discretion to permit Mrs. Virginia Searcy to take the examination."

COURT REFUSES TO RELAX BAR EXAM RULES

TALLAHASSEE, Oct. 30.—(AP)—A petition by Attorney General Watson for relaxation of a state bar examination rule to give one of his clerks a chance to take the test was denied by the supreme court today.

The action came after a lengthy hearing which produced a verbal outburst between lawyers rare in the supreme court chambers.

Watson asked the court to permit the state board of bar examiners to waive the 1941 rule requiring candidates for the examination to be graduates of accredited law schools if it is shown the applicant has training equivalent to the college work.

He said he asked for the change after the board had informed him it had no discretion to permit Mrs. Virginia Searcy to take the examination.

She is a graduate of Cumberland University Law School, which is not on the Florida accredited list and holds a license to practice in Mississippi. She works in the statutory revision division of the attorney gen-

Clare Sekul Hornsby ❖ 1945

Biloxi attorney Clare Sekul Hornsby was a first generation American from a Yugoslavian family from Dalmatia Brac'. She was born on August 16, 1921. Her father owned and worked on a fishing boat on the Mississippi Gulf Coast. He then began a seafood packing business while her mother ran the family-owned grocery store. A rather large population of Yugoslavians lived in Biloxi and supported the Slavonian Lodge where the Yugoslavian immigrants held meetings, weddings, family suppers and dances. Clare served as queen of the Slavonian Lodge in 1938, beating out her competitors for the crown by collecting the most money.

For two years, Clare attended Perkinston Junior College. She then attended the University of Mississippi and was enrolled in the University of Mississippi Law School when World War II began. The class dropped from 28 students to two. Another student transferred in, so Clare graduated in a class of three in 1945. She was admitted to The Mississippi Bar on May 1, 1945. To Clare and her family, law was the highest and noblest calling next to ministry.

After graduation, Clare returned home and became the second female lawyer to practice on the Mississippi Gulf Coast. In 1946, she met her future husband Warren Hornsby, who was stationed at Pass Christian in the Merchant Marines. In 1947, they were married. Her husband thoroughly supported her career and accompanied Clare to numerous law conventions where he regaled in telling convention-goers that Clare finished third in her law school class.

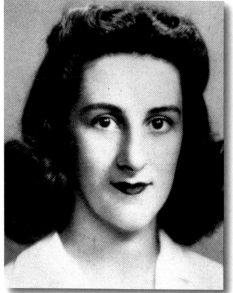

(Above): From the 1943 Ole Miss yearbook
(Below): From the 1965 Mississippi Lawyer

Mr. and Mrs. Dan Monroe Russell, Jr., right above, Bay St. Louis, were honored guests Sunday night of Biloxi Bar Association at a cocktail and buffet party where they are shown with Louis Hengen, president of the association, and Mrs. Clare Sekul Hornsby, secretary and treasurer and hostess for the occasion. (Herald Photo by Campbell)

She was a sole practitioner in Biloxi. Clare then became President of Sekul, Hornsby, and Tisdale law firm. Her brother, John M. Sekul, also became a Mississippi lawyer. In 1958, they were both admitted to the United States Supreme Court, believed to be the first brother/sister team to be so admitted. Although she began her career with a general practice, she later concentrated on family law. Her husband Warren advised her to develop her legendary flare for patterned stockings and a mouse pinned on the back of her left shoulder so that people would remember her.

Clare soon became known as "Queen of the Biloxi Bar." Clare was the president for decades and was famous for inviting Judges from all over the state as its speakers. She also served as the first woman President of the Harrison County Bar Association.

Biloxi lawyer Karen Sawyer, 1998-2001 Mississippi Bar Women in the Profession Committee Chair and 2011 Mississippi Bar Foundation President stated, "Everyone remembers Clare as an unstoppable force in the legal community, in her church and in her family. But she was also a remarkable friend to many women lawyers, including me. She promoted me professionally and nominated me for many leadership roles in the Bar. She entertained me for hours with stories about her very amazing life. There is no doubt that Clare earned the honor of being called a 'legal legend'."

Among other outstanding achievements, she was honored with the Susie Blue Buchanan Award in 1999 from

The Mississippi Bar Women in the Profession Committee. She served as a Master in the Chancery Court of the Second Judicial District of Harrison County, Mississippi Women's Cabinet on Public Affairs, and Harrison County Family Court. Clare was a member of the National Association of Women Lawyers, American Trial Lawyers Association, Mississippi Trial Lawyers Association, American Judicature Society, and International Federation of Women Lawyers. She received the following awards: Biloxi's Outstanding Citizen – 1990; Fellow of the Mississippi Bar Foundation – 1993; Life Patron

Honorable Clare Sekul Hornsby presents gavel from Harrison County Bar Association to Honorable Boyce Holleman, President of Mississippi State Bar.

and Honorary Commander of the 81st Training Wing of the John C. Stennis Chapter of the Air Force Association (first woman to serve as President); Recipient of the "Iron Magnolia" Award sponsored by WLOX television; 2009 Coast Young Professionals "4 Ever Young" Award; and in 2016 was inducted into the University of Mississippi School of Law Hall of Fame.

In 1999, the Senate of the State of Mississippi bestowed Clare Sekul Hornsby as a Woman of '99 "Power of One."

(continued next page)

OFFICERS of the Harrison County Bar, shown after their recent election are from left, Harry Hewes, Gulfport, Second vice-president, Mrs. Clare Sekul Hornsby, Biloxi, President, Sherman Muths, Jr., Gulfport, First vice-president and Virgil G. Gillespie, Gulfport, Secretary. Not pictured is Harry R. Allen, Gulfport, Treasurer.

1999 Senate Resolution 23

WHEREAS, Governor and Mrs. Fordice are hosting the third annual conference to recognize women in the state who are outstanding volunteers in their community, which is entitled Mississippi Woman '99: The "Power of One"; and

WHEREAS, Chare Sekul Hornsby has practiced law in Biloxi since 1945; and

WHEREAS, she learned early that understanding the law gave her the power to help people, which she does with the understanding imparted to her in childhood by her parents that the law is the highest and best calling next to the ministry; and

WHEREAS, she and her brother John had the rare honor of being admitted to practice before the United States Supreme Court; and

WHEREAS, Clare Hornsby has been a pioneer who has experienced many "firsts" in her career, including her election as President of the Harrison County Bar Association in the early 1970s; and

WHEREAS, Mrs. Hornsby is a valued role model in the law profession who mentors, nurtures, and encourages younger lawyers; and

WHEREAS, she is also extensively involved in community service, having been brought up to do for others and treat everyone fairly; and

WHEREAS, past honors include having been named by the Lion's Club as Mother of the Year in 1960; and

WHEREAS, despite her work and community involvement her family has been of utmost importance to her, including her late husband, Warren, and her four children and her grandchildren; and

WHEREAS, it is the policy of this body to recognize the honors and achievements of the citizens of this state;

Now, therefore, BE IT RESOLVED by the Senate of the State of Mississippi, That we do hereby commend Clare Sekul Hornsby for the honor bestowed upon her as a Woman of '99 "Power of One" honoree.

CLARE SEKUL HORNSBY

HORNSBY, Clare Sekul (Mrs. Warren Haywood Hornsby), Attorney, Asso. with brother (John Marshall Sekul), Barq Bldg., No. 217, Biloxi, Mississippi; res. 1046 W. Howard Ave., Biloxi; b. Biloxi, Miss., Aug. 16, 1922; dau. Mr. and Mrs. Steve M. Sekul. Adm. May 28, 1945, Mississippi. Mem. Miss. State Bar; Harrison County Bar Assn.; American Bar Assn.; National Assn. of Women Lawyers; Miss. Jr. Bar Assn.; Business & Professional Women's Club; Girl Scouts (Biloxi Council and Board of Directors); Little Theatre (Secretary); American Red Cross; Gulf Hills Golf Country Club; Perkinston Jr. College Alumni Assn. (President; first woman president since organization in 1929). Edn. Biloxi High School; Perkinston Jr. College, Perkinston, Miss.; Univ. of Miss., Oxford, Miss., LL.B. Jugoslavian, academic Spanish and French. Golf, swimming, collecting old coins, tennis, Little Theatre.

(Opposite): A Senate Resolution to honor Clare; (Left and Above): from the 1949 *Digest of Women Lawyers and Judges*; (Below): A portrait; (Bottom): Clare at the 2015 Mississippi Bar annual meeting surrounded by friends and colleagues.

Clare was a member of the following civic organizations: Biloxi Chamber of Commerce, Biloxi Lions Club (First Female President), Lions International, Altrusa Club, MGCJC Foundation (Past President), American Cancer Society (Past President), March of Dimes, and Biloxi Business and Professional Women's Club.

Former Lieutenant Governor Evelyn Gandy, a friend from law school, said "Clare Hornsby opened many doors for women in general

and certainly for women lawyers." Evelyn called her "one of our state's most distinguished leaders."

Grounded on solid family values, steeped in religion, and endowed with boundless energy, a positive attitude, a genuine love for her fellow man, and a passion for life, Clare Sekul Hornsby attained a loving following of clients and friends. She died on January 24, 2017, at the age of 95.

Walterrene Price Roderick ❖ 1945

The daughter of Mississippi's first female Judge, Zelma Wells Price, was Walterrene Price Roderick. She is also the second daughter of Judge Price to become a Mississippi lawyer, following in the footsteps of her sister Zelma Wells Price Schuetta who had been admitted in Mississippi in 1943. Walterrene was Greenville's fifth female lawyer.

Walterrene Price Roderick was born April 6, 1918, in Greenville, Washington County. She graduated from Mississippi State College for Women in 1937 with a teaching degree. She received a master's degree in French from the University of Southern California in 1939. She taught high school English in Magnolia in 1941 and married Morgan D. Roderick in December 1942.

She received her law degree from George Washington University Law School. She was admitted to The Mississippi Bar on June 14, 1945. Walterrene practiced with her mother, Zelma Price, in the Weinberg Building in Greenville. While her husband was serving overseas during World War II, she worked in the legal department of the office of Price Administration in Seattle, Washington. After the war, she and her husband settled in Arlington, Virginia. She was a charter member of the Gov. Thomas Welles Chapter, Mississippi Society of the National Society Colonial Dames XVII Century.

She died July 17, 2003, in Arlington, Virginia, and is buried there.

> *Mrs. Zelma W. Price*
> *Mrs. Zelma Price Schuetta*
> *Mrs. Walterrene Price Roderick*
>
> *Law Offices*
> *Zelma W. Price*
> *Weinberg Building*
> *Greenville, Mississippi*

(Left): Walterrene from the 1940 *Ole Miss* yearbook. (Above): the letterhead from the law offices of Zelma W. Price that listed three attorneys — Zelma and her two daughters.

Mary Frances Ray Holloway ❖ 1945

Mary Frances Holloway was born March 2, 1916, in Corinth, and received her juris doctorate from Columbus University in Washington D.C. After her exam in July 1945, Mary moved to Takoma Park, Maryland. In 1955, she was working on Capitol Hill. The *Hattiesburg American* newspaper on October 24, 1955, reported, "One Congressional junket is composed of two women staff members of the Senate Appropriation Committee. Mrs. Grace E. Johnson, who has worked on Capitol Hill for more than 15 years is directing the study. Assisting her is Mrs. Mary Frances Holloway, a former government lawyer, who recently joined the staff."

She died on May 22, 2007.

After serving as a government attorney for ten years, Mary Frances Holloway joined a commission to study foreign aid in 18 countries. Her duties included international junkets.

One congressional junket is composed of two women staff members of the Senate Appropriations Committee. Mrs. Grace E. Johnson, who has worked on Capitol Hill for more than 15 years is directing the study. Assisting her is Mrs. Mary Frances Holloway, a former government lawyer, who recently joined the staff.

They are making a staff study of foreign aid operations in 18 countries.

"This is strictly a working junket," Mrs. Johnson told reporters before taking off from the capital. "There'll be no headlines. Our inquiries will be made as quietly as possible. There'll be no newspaper interviews and very little entertain-

Ethel Ramsey Arrington ❖ 1945

*M*arried to Mississippi Supreme Court Justice Richard Olney Arrington, Sr. was Ethel Ramsey Arrington. She was born on March 16, 1905, in Hazlehurst to parents Simeon Ramsey and Lillie Pharebee Ramsey. Following her completion of school, she was accepted to practice in August of 1945. In Hazlehurst, she practiced with Arrington & Arrington and was a member of the Copiah County Bar. Ethel was Hazlehurst's fourth female lawyer.

She was one of the first women trial lawyers. To Ethel, to practice law meant to represent justice and fairness in the community, no matter the clientele.

She practiced law to the day of her final hospitalization. Ethel Arrington died on November 25, 1990, at the age of 85. She is buried in Hazlehurst.

Ten Pass State Bar Exams

Names of ten applicants who passed the bar examinations in Jackson on July 2 and who are qualified to practice law in Mississippi, were announced here today by Earle L. Wingo, secretary and treasurer of the State Board of Bar Admissions.

The ten are:

Captian O. Willard Holloway, and his wife, Mrs. Mary Frances Holloway, 1457 Park Road, N. W., Washington, D. C. (The Holloways are from Crinth, Miss.); Robert L. Purser, 721 North State street, Jackson; William Neely, Jackson; Colte E. Cloninger, 817 N. Jefferson street, Jackson; L. B. Porter, Union; R. Earl Roberson, Pascagoula; Champ Clark Gipson, Lebanon, Tenn.; Ethel R. Arrington, Hazlehurst; and Troy Case, Brookhaven.

Mrs. Arrington is the wife of R. O. Arrington, assistant attorney general of Mississippi.

Seven other applicants failed to qualify.

The next examinations will be held in Jackson on the first Monday in February, 1946, according to Mr. Wingo.

Members of the board are: Leon F. Hendrick, Jackson, chairman; J. E. Caradine, West Point, vice chairman; and Mr. Wingo, Hattiesburg, secretary-treasurer.

Ethel R. Arrington

Services were held on Tuesday at the First Baptist Church in Hazlehurst for Ethel Ramsey Arrington, 85, of Hazlehurst, who died Nov. 25, 1990 at St. Dominics Jackson Memorial Hospital.

Dr. Robert Hanvey officiated. Interment was in the Hazlehurst Cemetery.

Mrs. Arrington practiced law at Arrington and Arrington, Attorneys at Law, until the time of her death. She was a member of the First Baptist Church of Hazlehurst. She was native and lifelong resident of Copiah County. She had practiced law since 1944, and was a member of the Mississippi State Bar. She had operated the Copiah Feed Mill for a number of years. She was preceded in death by her husband, Judge Richard Arrington Sr., who was a Supreme Court judge; one son, Richard Arrington; and one daughter, Nancy Arrington Bryant.

Survivors include one son, Dr. Myron Lamar Arrington of Prentiss; one daughter, Melinda Bryant Arrington of Hazlehurst; one brother, Sim Ramsey of Hazlehurst; six grandchildren; and six great-grandchildren.

Stringer Funeral Home in Hazlehurst was in charge of arrangements.

Maxine Brunn Crain ❖ 1946

*M*eridian's fourth female lawyer was Maxine Brunn Crain. She was born on July 24, 1913, in Wabash, Indiana. Maxine married Harold G. Crain of Omaha, Nebraska, in 1933. She attended Cumberland University School of Law, where she graduated in 1946. Maxine and her husband took the Bar exam at the same time. After being admitted to practice in Mississippi on March 22, 1946, she and her husband practiced law in Meridian.

In 1956, she was elected to serve as a Board of Bar Commissioner for The Mississippi Bar. Maxine was Treasurer for the Meridian Pinnacle Chapter of the American Business Women's Association for 1963-1964. In 1967, she moved back to Wabash, Indiana, and became inactive with The Mississippi Bar.

Maxine died July 18, 1999, and is buried in Florida.

Lauderdale Bar Plans Law Day Program May 1

MERIDIAN — Plans for the 1964 observance of Law Day during the week of May 1 were discussed when the Lauderdale County Bar Association met at Weidmann's Restaurant for its March meeting with President William J. Gunn, Jr., presiding.

Joe Clay Hamilton is chairman of the Law Day committee.

A memorial resolution for Richard G. Lord, Jr., who died two weeks ago, was unanimously adopted after it was read by J. L. Prichard.

Committees named by Gunn for this year are as follows:

Winston Cameron, chairman, Roger Shows, George Ethridge, Lawrence Rabb, Howard Pigford, Hunter Harmon, Gerald Adams, Grievance and Professional Ethics committee.

Dan Self, chairman, Roy Pitts, Jim Singley, Marvin Williams, G. R. Gaillard, C. D. Shields, J. L. Prichard, Professional fees and Economics; Joe Clay Hamilton, chairman, Michael Corrigan, Billy Ray Covington, Tom Bourdeaux, David Wilton, Tom Stennis and Harvey

Odom, Bill Ready, Paul M. Busby, Russell Wright, Constitutional Rights.

Richard Wilbourn, chairman, Henry Woodall, Harold Crain, Mrs. Maxine Crain, Dan Coit, Tom Hendricks, Fledell Chain, Legal Aid; Lyle Corey, chairman, J. A. Covington, T. K. Holyfield, Nate S. Williamson, J. V. Gipson, Knox Huff, Constitution and By-Laws.

Billy Gunn, chairman, Thomas Minniece, A. S. Bozeman, Jr., Dal Crenshaw, Tom Ward, Frank Buchanan, H. C. Watkins, Program; Walter Eppes, chairman, E. L. Snow, Betty Long, R. B. Deen, J. Pat Wiley, Tom Goldman and J. C. Floyd, Library.

Gibson Witherspoon chairman, George Warner, Tom Dunn, Thomas R. Jones, Kenneth Watts, Lee Kirk, Public Relations; Dennis Goldman, chairman, Ed Clayton, Danny Beard, Champ Gipson, Granville Jones, Donovan Ready, Entertainment.

82 Elsie Cambre Parker Purser ❖ 1946

Following her sister, Cecile Cambre Alford, who was admitted in 1944 and featured ten women lawyers before her in this book, Elsie Cambre Parker Purser also attended Jackson School of Law and became a lawyer.

Elsie was born on August 20, 1915, to parents Mr. and Mrs. Frank Octave Cambre. Her first husband was Ben Parker, who passed away in 1941. She married Robert Purser, Jr. of Brookhaven in 1946.

Nineteen of twenty-one candidates passed the bar exam in February, 1946. Upon her admittance to practice law on April 4, 1946, she practiced law in Brookhaven. In 1948, she was included in the *Mississippi Law Journal.* Ten years later she became inactive with The Mississippi Bar.

She was a mother of three children and a communicant of St. Francis of Assisi Catholic Church. Elsie died on November 9, 2005, at the age of 90 and is buried in Lakewood Memorial Park.

83

Iva Lea Stringer Greer ❖ 1946

Born on December 19, 1912, in Crystal Springs, Iva Lea Stringer Greer lived most of her adult life in Jackson. While working as a paralegal at the law firm of John Satterfield, she went to the Jackson School of Law and obtained her law degree.

She was married to James Hebert Greer, Sr. They had two sons.

Iva was admitted to practice on April 27, 1946, after her examination in February. Immediately after her acceptance, she practiced law with Alexander & Alexander.

She was a charter member of St. Mary's Catholic Church. Iva Lea Stringer Greer died on April 25, 2007, and is buried at Lakewood Memorial Park.

(Below): In February of 1946, five women passed the bar exam, representing over 25% of those who passed the test.

19 of 21 Pass State Bar Exams

Nineteen out of twenty-one candidates successfully passed the Mississippi state bar examinations held in February, Earle L. Wingo, secretary of the State Board of Bar admissions, announced today.

The successful candidates are:

Joe B. Coursey, 938 North Main street, Hattiesburg; Mrs. Elsie Parker, H. T. Ashford, jr., Howard Lee Lindsey, Iva Lee Stringer, Josephine M. Jameson, Jay R. Jameson, jr., Irwin W. Coleman, all of Jackson; Wendell R. Lutes, Biloxi; R. E. Townsend, University; Robert M. Rutledge, William K. Dutledge, both of Dicksburg; Vernon D. Rowe, jr., and Johnston Rowe, both of Winona; James M. Fleming, jr., Tupelo; Edward T. Steele, Laurel; W. W. Brand, Houston; Harold G. Crain and Maxine B. Crain, both of Meridian.

Mr. Wingo said that the 19 candidates represent the largest percentage to pass the state bar examination in about ten years. A number of veterans took the examination.

Included in the 19 were two FBI men, two husband-and-wife couples, twins, and a circuit clerk.

Other members of the State Board

Mary Emma Bullock McGee ❖ 1946

Brandon's second female lawyer was Mary Emma Bullock McGee. She was born on April 8, 1922. She was the youngest child and only daughter of Harvey Hasty Bullock and Mary Williams Bullock. Mary Emma graduated from Brandon High School in 1939. She earned a Bachelor of Arts degree in Mathematics from Mary Hardin-Baylor College in 1943. After teaching mathematics for a year, she began her legal studies at Jackson School of Law.

Her father was a prominent lawyer in Brandon. He had previously served as county superintendent of education. In June 1944, he died from a bullet wound to the head.

Mary Emma was admitted to practice law in July of 1946. She held her practice in Brandon.

Two years later, she was wed to Rev. Tildon S. McGee, and moved to live in California. They had three children. Prior to their marriage, he had participated in the Invasion of Normandy, been imprisoned in Germany, and was awarded the Distinguished Service Cross, the second highest medal for gallantry in action awarded by the War department.

She died December 7, 2019, in Los Angeles, California.

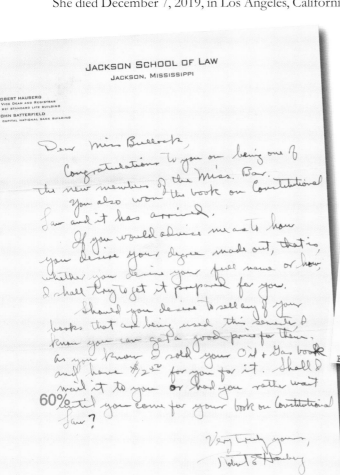

(Top): Mary Emma Bullock McGee circa 1946; (Left): A congratulatory letter from Robert Hauberg, Vice Dean and Registrar at the Jackson School of Law; (Above): Letter notifying she passed the bar and her bar admission certificate.

85 Martha Rose Moffitt Parsons ❖ 1946

"Love, goodness, sweetness in her fair person shines" was written in her 1939 Central High School yearbook. Martha Rose Moffitt was born in Corinth, Mississippi on May 6, 1921. Her parents were Mumford Moffitt and Ida Cole Moffitt. She attended Blue Mountain College. In 1940, she was elected President of her college orchestra. Her husband was Thomas Cade Parsons and they had one daughter.

After being admitted to practice law on August 31, 1946, she worked as a paralegal for the next 27 years in various agencies.

For the last 22 years of her life, she lived in Tracy, California. Martha Rose Parsons died on the last day of the year, December 31, 2005, at age 84. The following year, she was recognized at the 2006 Memorial Service Program for her dedication to the legal profession.

86 Lottie Berniece Russell Pickard ❖ 1946

Lottie Berniece Russell was born on September 12, 1921. She graduated from the University of Tennessee Extension School. Berniece was accepted to Southern Law University and graduated in 1946. She married John R. Pickard. They had four children.

On August 21, 1946, she was accepted into The Mississippi Bar and moved to work in Memphis, Tennessee.

Berniece died on May 5, 2011, at the age of 89. She is buried in Memphis, Tennessee.

20 Candidates Pass State Bar Examination

Twenty of the 29 applicants who took the Mississippi State bar examination in July will be admitted to the practice of law in the state, Earle L. Wingo, secretary-treasurer of the State Board of Bar Admissions, announced today.

Candidates who successfully passed the examination are:

E. T. Wooton, 100 Twenty-fifth ave., Hattiesburg; M. E. Collum, jr., Mrs. Aline J. Collum, Magruder Lee Mansell, C. C. Richmond, Mrs. Claribel Hunt Moncure, Martha Rose Moffitt, Ted Russell, James A. Townes and William T. Neely, all of Jackson;

Joseph W. Lloyd, Greenville; Harry Hooker, Gulfport; Miss Berniece Russell, Memphis; Woodrow C. Jones, Waynesboro; Volney H. Campbell, Brookhaven; Mrs. C. E. Slough, Oxford; S. W. Craft, Sylvarena; David E. O'Donnell, Inverness; Walter S. Gordon, Lebanon, Tenn., and Mary Emma Bullock, Brandon.

The examinations are held twice a year in Jackson.

Other officers of the State Board of Bar Admissions are: Leon F. Hendrick, Jackson, chairman; and J. E. Carradine, West Point, vice-chairman.

Aline Jones Collum ❖ 1946

A native of D'Lo, Aline Jones Collum was born on March 30, 1911. She graduated from Hillman College and also attended Mississippi College and Bowling Green Business University. She was married to Marvin E. Collum, also a graduate of Jackson School of Law, in 1933. They had one son.

To further pursue her interest in law, she attended the Jackson School of Law, and on September 7, 1946, Alina was permitted to practice law. She was hired by Tighe and Tighe in Jackson, then known as Tighe and Ross, and Tighe and Barksdale. In 1958, her law office was on North State Street. She became inactive in 1980.

Aline Jones Collum died on September 5, 1993, at the age of 82. She was a long-time Sunday School teacher at the First Baptist Church.

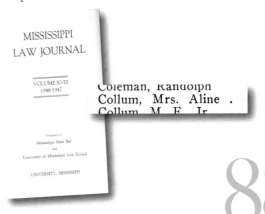

MISSISSIPPI LAW JOURNAL

VOLUME XVIII
1946-1947

Published by
Mississippi State Bar
and
University of Mississippi Law School

UNIVERSITY, MISSISSIPPI

Coleman, Randolph
Collum, Mrs. Aline .
Collum, M. E., Jr.

Josephine Myrick Jameson ❖ 1946

Josephine Myrick Jameson was destined to be a lawyer from birth. She was born on September 29, 1915. Her mother had attended the University of Texas Law School. She graduated from Harlingen High School in 1932, then at Baylor earned two degrees, the second in law. She was admitted to practice law in Texas on September 12, 1938. She continued her education and was the second woman to receive a Master of Arts in Law degree from the University of Texas Law School. She practiced with her father in Harlingen. During WWII, she was a War Department investigator at the New Orleans Port of Embarkation, then from 1943-1946 she worked for Tidewater Associated Oil Company

She had met Jay Reese Jameson, Jr. in Baylor Law School and they married in 1941. They established their home in Houston, Texas. He worked for Woodley Petroleum in Texas and Mississippi. The couple became Mississippi lawyers in 1946. She only practiced law in Mississippi for one year. They then moved to Abilene, Texas where he practiced law and she established a home.

She was the first president of the Junior League of Abilene. Josephine's husband died and she began practicing law in her husband's old law firm, first as an associate and

then as a partner. She was appointed as judge of the Abilene Municipal Court, becoming the first woman judge in her area. Josephine served less than one year, as she died from a brain tumor on September 11, 1969.

Written by Barbara Rollins, a Texas County Court Judge

(Left): Josephine as a student at Baylor; (Below): A 1969 story from the *Abilene Reporter* about Josephine's appointment to a judgeship. The caption reads: "Judge Jo Jameson . . . some show shock."

Her Honor, the Judge

By NANCY JACOBS
Reporter-News Staff Writer

A woman's work is never done, Lawrence Rusden told a graduating class at Cambridge, England, in 1714. In today's world it still holds true -- and doubly so when the woman is a judge

Mrs. Josephine Jameson has been Corporation Court judge for Abilene since Jan. 1. So far, she's experienced "no problems," she said.

"IF PEOPLE expect more leniency from me because I'm a woman, I haven't been aware of it," she said.

Mrs. Jameson is the first woman to serve as judge in any Abilene court. She doesn't feel that being a woman has given her a different outlook or approach to her job.

"I tend to see two sides of any question, but I'm not sure this is a feminine characteristic," she said.

Mrs. Jameson, who holds law degrees from Baylor University and the University of Texas, puts in busy hours at her office. First business of the day is seeking the prisoners from the jail, those who have not posted bond.

"Some of them are pretty shocked when they see me," she said.

She deals with those charged with being drunk in public; simple assault and battery (no lethal weapon involved); aggravated assault; using profane, abusive language; shoplifting, $5 and under; animal violations such as no rabies tags; and traffic

JUDGE JO JAMESON
. . . some show shock

bench, they can't do much else," she joked.

In general, she believes that "people reflect my attitude towards them."

Male judges are also treated courteously, she believes. She explained that she had eighteen Corporation Court several times before taking office in January. "I found that people were respectful to Don Lane (her predecessor, now County Court-at-Law judge) too."

Mrs. Jameson doesn't wear a black robe in the courtroom. "The bench adds to her dignity. The 5'2" judge believes, "I may ask for a robe in the next budget, though," she said.

A FEW MORE women than men take personal offense to a traffic ticket, she's found. And generally the older the person, the more apt he is to be offended.

"Women sometimes treat a violation as a personal matter and my fining as a personal thing. A grandmother charged with running a red light asked me if I thought a grandmother would actually do such a thing."

Older people are less willing to admit their mistakes, she said. She explained that if it's a first ticket the older person doesn't see why he should have to have one now.

"Teens are apt to agree that they did something wrong and "say I'm sorry," she said.

Those upset about a first-time traffic violation have a chance to clear their record one time, providing the violation doesn't fall into certain categories.

For six or seven years, a driver improvement school sponsored by Corporation Court has been taught by Miss Eudora Hawkins and Officer Paul Warren. The class meets for four sessions. If the student makes a specified score on the exam at the end, the fine will be refunded and the ticket dismissed, Judge Jameson said.

THE CLASSES are held almost every two weeks, Judge Jameson said, with the exception of Christmas and summer vacation time. The next class begin tonight at 7:30 and continues Tuesday evening, as well as the following Monday and Tuesday.

Being a lawyer was pretty much a family thing for Mrs. Jameson. Her late husband, Jay,

Wendell Bedichek Said Satisfactory

Wendell Bedichek, executive

Claribel Hunt Moncure ❖ 1946

A native of Utica, Claribel Hunt Moncure was born on May 30, 1908. She graduated from Jackson Central High School and attended Millsaps College for her bachelor degree. Claribel married Edwin Conway Moncure of Terry in 1929. She received her law degree from Case Western University. Afterwards, she was admitted to practice law on December 28, 1946. She was sworn in by Chancellor V. J. Stricker.

She was a member of Jackson Business & Professional Women's Club.

She held several positions with the Veterans Administration, including at the Regional Office in Waco, Texas from 1948-1950; Chief Social Worker at the VA Center in Shreveport, LA, 1950-1952; Chief Social Work Services at the VA Hospital in Syracuse, N.Y.; Chief Social Worker Services at the VA Hospital in Washington, D.C.; Specialist in Program Development and Appraisals in Washington, D.C.; member of the VA Central Office Committee on Aging; and chairman of the Subcommittee on Social Services and Family Relationships and on Community Planning.

She moved back to Jackson and retired as a social worker. Claribel Hunt Moncure died on December 21, 1993, at the age of 85.

Claribel Hunt Moncure (far left) with railroad and steel officials who make donations to the American Red Cross. Claribel was the local Jackson leader of the Red Cross during World War II.

Helen Daniel White ❖ 1947

The *Greenwood Commonwealth* stated, "Names of 35 applicants who passed the February state bar examinations were announced. They are: Fred P. McRae, Robert S. Moore, Christopher C. Isbell, Wayne A. Bigner, James R. Brannon, Mrs. Helen D. White, W. E. Robbins, George B. Grubbs, Miss Frances Porter, J. Hubert Dodd, Harry D. Owen, and Charles D. Kilgore, all of Jackson." Helen Daniel White of Jackson had passed the Bar exam in February, 1947.

Helen's husband's name was Thomas S. White.

35 Applicants Pass Bar Exams

Earl Wingo, Secretary Of Board, Lists Names

Fred P. McRae, Robert S. Moore, Christopher C. Isbell, Wayne A. Bigner, James R. Brannon, Mrs. Helen D. White, W. E. Robbins, George B. Grubbs, Miss Frances Porter, J. Hubert Dodd, Harry D. Owen and Charles D. Kilgore, all of Jackson.

Mildred Wells Norris ❖ 1947

Hattiesburg's first female judge was Mildred Wells Norris.

Mildred Wells was born on August 2, 1913, in the little town of Ovett. When she was an infant, the family moved to Laurel where her father operated a barbershop.

She attended schools in Laurel, and she stated, "As children we were never prodded about our lessons . . . We just took it for granted that we had the greatest honor and privilege in the world, just to attend school." After high school, she studied college for one year, and then returned home because of health reasons. She started working as a secretary in the law office of T. Webber Wilson, a former Congressman, and F. Burkitt Collins.

Mildred married Walter Thomas Norris in 1940.

During WWII, she worked for the United States Department of Agriculture and the War Department. With her experience as a legal secretary, she read the law and passed the bar exam in February, 1947. She was admitted on March 22, 1947.

In 1961, Mildred was appointed judge of the Municipal Court of Hattiesburg. She then returned full time to her law practice.

She worked actively for the advancement of women. She was the first woman to serve on the Forrest County Industrial Development Board and was appointed first chairman of the Mississippi Governor's Commission on Women. Mildred was honored with national office when named first vice-president of the Interstate Association of Commissions on the Status of Women.

Mildred was a longtime member of the Mississippi Federation of Business and Professional Women. She was appointed by Governor Paul B. Johnson, Jr. to serve on the Governor's Commission on the Employment of the Handicapped.

She died on February 8, 1981, at the age of 67 and is buried in Hattiesburg.

Excerpts printed with permission from The University of Southern Mississippi Center for Oral History & Cultural Heritage

Judge Norris--

(Continued from page 1)

Forrest County Industrial Development Board, an appointment she received through her membership in the Hattiesburg Area Chamber of Commerce.

A member of the Church of Christ, Judge Norris served several terms on the YWCA board of directors in addition to being a past president. She was also a member of the Mississippi Women's Cabinet of Public Affairs, the local and state bar associations, the National Assn. of Women Lawyers, the International Platform Committee and the Assn. of Retired Persons.

She was listed in Who's Who in American Women and in Who's Who of Women in the World.

Survivors include her husband, Tommy Norris; a sister, Mrs. Charles

Mildred Norris is B&PW Club Woman of the Year

Judge Mildred Norris was selected as Woman of the Year by a unanimous vote of the Hattiesburg Business and Professional Women Club members at a luncheon meeting Tuesday at the YWCA, Mrs. Lula Grace Sikes, club publicity chairman, announced.

Judge Norris is married to Walter Thomas Norris, who is a colonel on the staff of Gov. Paul B. Johnson. She is president of the Mississippi Federation of Business and Professional Women's Club; is an attorney and judge of the city court; a member of the Forrest County Bar Assn., Mississippi Bar Assn., Mississippi Women's Cabinet, and chairman of the State Traffic Committee.

Judge Norris is author of the novelette, Bees Don't Sting, People Do. She is a member of the Church of Christ where she teaches an adult Bible class.

Mrs. Millie Fowler, president, was in charge of the meeting. Mrs. Letha P. Jones, state corresponding secretary, was named as a candiate for third vice president of the Mississippi Federation of B&PW Clubs. Members of the local club voted to support Mrs. Jones to this office.

Mrs. Fowler announced she had received as a gift from the Corinth B&PW Club to the local club, a copy of the song, A Yellow Rose, which was composed by Mrs. Onie Potts, a member of the Corinth Club. On request, the song was played by a guest, Mrs. T. P. Ramsey, on the piano.

Judge Norris announced that Dr. Frances Whitehead, national recording secretary and international funds chairman, is requesting contributions from all clubs. This fund will be used by the hospital in China, spon-

JUDGE MILDRED NORRIS

Bridge tourney slated here March 13-15

The third annual South Mississippi Sectional duplicate bridge tournament will be held here March 13-15 at the Community Center.

Games begin at 2 p.m., Friday, March 13, and end following the night session on Sunday, March 15.

Several hundred players from sourrounding states are expected to participate in the tournament. All games will be held at the Community Center. The Forrest Hotel is tournament headquarters.

Officers of the Hub Bridge Assn. are Marvin Reuben, president; Bernard Callendar of Columbia, vice-president; and T. H. Livringhouse, secretary-

JUDGE NORRIS

Judge Norris, whose home is presently in Hattiesburg, is a graduate of the high school in Laurel, where she spent her girl-

Amy Burkett ❖ 1947

A native of Natchitoches Parish, Louisiana, Amy Burkett was born on January 2, 1890. She decided to pursue her interest in law by taking the bar exam in July of 1947. Amy was one of three women to pass the bar exam – Miss Helen J. McDade of DeKalb, Mrs. Marguerite L. Williams of Gulfport, and Miss Amy Burkett of Biloxi.

Amy Burkett was sworn into the Bar by Judge Russell of Jackson County. Her practice included representing families on property law matters, as reflected by her three published cases which all involve land title issues. See *Burkett v. People's Bank of Biloxi*, 255 Miss. 291 (Miss. 1955), *DeFraites v. State*, 227 Miss. 496 (Miss. 1956), and *Calloway v. Showers*, 231 So. 2d 797 (Miss. 1970).

From 1953 through 1978, she was the attorney of record for twenty cases before the Supreme Court. She was a resident of Ocean Springs for 30 years. She retired from practice in 1982, two years before her death. Amy Burkett died in July of 1984.

(Above): The Mississippi Supreme Court Building. From 1953-1978, Amy Burkett was the attorney of record for twenty cases before the Mississippi Supreme Court.

Helen Jacobs McDade ❖ 1947

Kemper County's first female lawyer was Helen J. McDade. She was born on May 15, 1918, in Randolph Bib, Alabama to parents George W. McDade and Emma F. Jacobs McDade. They moved to Mississippi in the 1930s.

She was admitted to practice in July of 1947 by Judge Gillis. Once accepted, she practiced at the McDade Law Firm for the following 53 years in DeKalb.

Beginning in 1968, Helen served twelve years in the Mississippi Legislature as a State Representative. Only two women lawmakers were in the Legislature.

She was a member of the American Judicature Legal Society, National Association of Women Lawyers, Daughters of the American Revolution, Charter

VOTE FOR AND ELECT HELEN J. McDADE AS YOUR CHANCERY JUDGE
PLACE 1
6th CHANCERY COURT DISTRICT
JUNE 4, 1974

- Successful, experienced Attorney of proven ability, qualified and competent to serve you constructively as your Chancery Judge, and pledged to a loyal, dedicated, constructive and progressive administration in the best interest of the citizens of Kemper, Neshoba, Winston, Choctaw, Attala and Carroll Counties.
- Actively engaged in the Practice of Law for 27 years, admitted and qualified as Attorney and Counsellor in all State and Federal Courts, including the Supreme Court of the United States of America.
- Attorney for Kemper County Board of Supervisors, Kemper County Board of Education, Town of Scooba, Kemper County Hospital
- Member Mississippi State Bar Association
- Member American Judicature Legal Society
- Member Daughters of American Revolution—Samuel Hammond Chapter Kosciusko, Mississippi
- Served 16 years as Official Chancery Court Reporter of the 6th Chancery Court District comprising Kemper, Neshoba, Winston, Choctaw, Attala and Carroll Counties
- Member International Platform Association
- Member Executive Committee of the East Mississippi Council
- Charter Member Chamber of Commerce of Kemper County, Mississippi
- Dedicated Member De Kalb Baptist Church
- Member Mississippi Farm Bureau
- I am also a member of the Mississippi State Legislature, House of Representatives, representing Kemper and Neshoba Counties from 1968 to 1972, and from 1972 representing Kemper and Lauderdale Counties.
- I shall ever be grateful and appreciative for your vote, support and influence extended in my behalf, ever mindful of the confidence you placed in me, shall ever serve as your Chancery Judge with honor and dignity, and you shall never regret having so honored me.
Gratefully,

Member of the Kemper County Chamber of Commerce, Executive Committee of East Mississippi Council, and member of the Mississippi Farm Bureau.

Helen served for sixteen years as the court reporter for 5th Chancery Court District. She was the Attorney for Kemper County Board of Supervisors, Kemper County Board of Education, Town of Scooba, and Kemper County Hospital.

Helen was a member of the DeKalb Baptist Church. Helen J. McDade died at her home on October 18, 2003, at the age of 85.

(Left): Helen served successfully in the Mississippi Legislature for twelve years, but she did not win her bid for Chancery Judge. (Opposite): A house resolution honoring Helen Jacobs McDade.

Mississippi Legislature
House Resolution 6 (1999)

A Resolution commending Miss Helen J. McDade for her many years of public service to Kemper County, Mississippi.

WHEREAS, Miss Helen J. McDade has been a lifelong resident of Kemper County, Mississippi, where she has worked in the legal field for over fifty years; and

WHEREAS, Miss McDade began her career as a legal secretary and court reporter in Kemper County; and

WHEREAS, in July 1947, Miss McDade was admitted to the practice of law before the courts of the State of Mississippi; and

WHEREAS, representing the citizens of Kemper County, Miss McDade was elected to the Mississippi House of Representatives, where she faithfully served from 1968 to 1980; and

WHEREAS, Miss McDade, County Prosecuting Attorney since September 1992, has won justice for the victims and families of Kemper County by prosecuting and obtaining convictions for numerous criminals; and

WHEREAS, in June 1998, Miss McDade was dutifully recognized by the Mississippi Bar for her outstanding service in the legal profession in the State of Mississippi for over fifty years; and

WHEREAS, the House of Representatives finds it most appropriate to pay special tribute to such an outstanding citizen as Miss Helen J. McDade, who has served the citizens of Kemper County, Mississippi to the best of her ability in carrying out her many duties of public service in the legal profession for over fifty years.

Now, therefore, BE IT RESOLVED by the House of Representatives of the State of Mississippi, that we do hereby commend Miss Helen J. McDade on the many professional accomplishments of her career and extend to her our appreciation for her many years of dedicated service to the citizens of Kemper County and the State of Mississippi."

94   Marguerite L. Williams ❖ 1947

*G*ulfport's fifth female lawyer was Marguerite L. Williams. She was admitted to practice in July of 1947.

Biloxi, Gulfport Residents Pass State Bar Exams

Hattiesburg, Miss., Aug. 13 (*AP*) Names of 41 persons who successfully passed the July Mississippi State Bar examination were announced today by Earle L. Wingo, secretary-treasurer of the state board of bar admissions.

Among them were: Abner E. Hughes, Daniel D. Guice, Stephen L. Guice and Miss Amy Burkett, all of Biloxi.

Mrs. Marguerite L. Williams and Ewart G. Lindsey, Gulfport.

95   Nannie-Mayes Crump ❖ 1947

"*35* applicants Pass Bar Exam" in February 1947 stated the newspapers with one of the applicants being Nannie-Mayes Crump. The other two women passing the bar at the same time were Mrs. Mildred W. Norris and Mrs. Helen D. White.

Nannie-Mayes Crump, daughter of John Thomas Crump and Linda Taylor Crump, was born in Bienville Parish, Louisiana on February 2, 1895. She graduated from Vassar in 1918. She then worked for a year as a superior of art at the schools of Breckenridge, Texas from 1920 – 21. Nannie-Mayes later worked as a reporter for the *Gulfport Daily Herald* and *Bay St. Louis Sea Coast Echo*.

She then received an LL.B from George Washington University Law School in 1944. She was admitted to The Mississippi Bar in 1947.

She had a career in both law and real estate. She lived in Shreveport, Louisiana and Washington, D. C. She died on March 1, 1985, in Caddo, Louisiana and is buried in Evergreen Cemetery in Gulfport.

(Above): Artwork by Nannie-Mayes Crump. (Right): Nannie-Mayes was the featured speaker at the Gulfport Business and Professional Women's Club meeting at the Markham Hotel on December 11, 1946.

Tells of Christmas In Nation's Capital

Miss Nannie-Mayes Crump was the principal speaker at the Christmas banquet of the Gulfport Business and Professional Women's Club Tuesday night in the Gold room of Hotel Markham.

Miss Crump, a graduate of Vassar College, obtained her LLB from George Washington University, is a licensed attorney in the District of Columbia and is preparing for her bar examinations in Mississippi. She is a former resident of Gulfport and was on the social desk of The Daily Herald for several years.

Miss Crump spoke of Christmas in Washington. She spoke informally as a member of a family returned for Christmas. She told of her arrival in Washington, a stranger, and of the welcome extended by people of all races, bringing out the fact that she had been unconscious of any race prejudices. She told of the decorations of the city, some three miles of Santa Claus land with lighted trees every fifty feet, of the President's tree and how she had seen President Roosevelt light it by a switch from his chair, and later, during the war when the tree was lighted for just a few moments, and of the tree last year, lighted again in full colors by President Truman.

Miss Crump covered the Christ-

The sister of Mississippi Bar Executive Director, Alice Porter Nevels who was admitted in 1942, also became a member of the bar. Frances Porter Cunningham was admitted in 1947. She was among four women who passed the bar exam in 1947 – Mrs. Mildred W. Norris, Mrs. Helen D. White, Miss Nannie-Mayes Crump, and Miss Frances Porter.

Frances attended Woman's College in Hattiesburg and graduated from Jackson School of Law. She was a member of the National Association of Women Lawyers and practiced at Watkins & Eager.

Her parents were Mr. and Mrs. Benjamin F. Porter of Lexington. In 1949, she married Dr. Robert Edwin Cunningham, a well-known Jackson dentist.

In 1937, she was a Charter Member of the Jackson Pilot Club, along with these other women lawyers: Mrs. Elizabeth Hulen, Mrs. Alice Nevels, Mrs. Clara Sims, and Mrs. Marie Upton.

(Above): Frances, sister of long-time Mississippi Bar Executive Director Alice Porter Nevels.
(Right): A feature about Frances's involvement in the Pilot Club. (Below): A memorial resolution read in 1957 at the Pilot Club.

Miss Frances Porter

The first plans for the Pilot International District Council meeting to be held in Jackson on Saturday and Sunday of this week at the Heidelberg Hotel have been announced b ythe local Jackson Pilot club president Mrs. Mabel Batte Mullins, who is general chairman of the council meeting.

Registration of delegates will begin at 1:30 o'clock Saturday and the general business meeting at 2:30 o'clock in the Rose Room of the Heidelberg Hotel with Miss Frances Porter, of Jackson ,district president, presiding.

At 7:30 o'clock a reception will be held at the governor's mansion with the Jackson Pilot Club as host to the members and visitors. On account of the illness of the governor's mother, Mrs. Bailey will not be present.

On Sunday morning at 8:30 o'clock breakfast will be held in the Rose room of the hotel with district president presiding. Mrs. Etha G. Hall, president of Pilot International, from Greensboro, N. C., will bring greetings from Pilot International and discuss international program plans for the coming year.

A panel discussion on "Women in the world of Tomorrow" will be held and those participating in the panel discussion will be the presidents of the Pilot clubs: Miss Ione Boudreax, Greenville, Miss.; Mrs. Pearl Long, Alexandria., La., and year.

The election of a new district governor will take place and the selection for the next district council meet.

One of the highlights of the breakfast will be the installation of the new officers of the local Jackson Pilot club for the ensuing year with Miss Mable Dalzell, Biloxi, Miss.

A Memorial resolution was read at a Memorial Service held by the Pilot Club following her death in 1957.

WHEREAS, on the 10th day of February, 1957 our Heavenly Father gathered into His Immortal Kingdom the soul of one of our most loyal and beloved members, and

WHEREAS, it is fitting to pay tribute to the memory of our departed loved one, Frances Porter Cunningham, and express our appreciation and gratitude that we knew her as a friend, a guide, a solace, and an inspiration to the members of the Pilot Club of Jackson as well as to all whom she knew, and

WHEREAS, she was a person of high ideals and beautiful Christian character with a strong sense of obligation to her fellow-man and is deserving of perpetual recognition by us, and

WHEREAS, she accomplished any undertaking worthily and with honor, and at all times with the view of bettering the conditions of the needy, encouraging the education in cultural arts, inspiring the young people toward finer living, and spreading the beauty of the Christian life through each endeavor, and

WHEREAS, she did this ennoble everything she touched and gave an upward impetus toward the finer things in life, and

WHEREAS, we shall miss the association, the friendly smile, the acts of love and kindness, the sympathetic word and the loyalty of her, whose quality of goodness shall always remain with us,

Therefore BE IT RESOLVED by the Pilot Club of Jackson that we, her friends and contemporaries, regret her untimely passing and with her family and friends mourn our loss, and that we profit by her example and let the inspiration of the memories of her beautiful life help to guide the path of our future."

Virginia I. Ferguson ❖ 1948

Another graduate of the Jackson School of Law was Virginia I. Ferguson. She was born on June 18, 1921, in Missouri. Her mother died when Virginia was four years old. By the time she was nine years old, she was living in Harrison County in Mississippi. In 1942 at the age of 21, she was living in Columbus attending the Mississippi State College for Women. Her father died while she was in law school. She was admitted to the bar in 1948 by Chancellor V. J. Stricker in Jackson.

Virginia died at the age of 72 on December 9, 1993, and is buried in Gulfport.

Tillie Odom Nixon ❖ 1948

Clothilda "Tillie" Odom Nixon was born on May 14, 1925. She was a native of Petal, Mississippi. She was a graduate of Jackson School of Law and took the bar exam in February 1948. She was admitted to practice in Mississippi on May 1, 1948, by Judge V. J. Stricker in Jackson.

In 1949, she became the first president of the Desk and Derrick Club. The Jackson Club was the second in the nation to be formed. An article in the *Clarion Ledger* on October 17, 1951, stated, "Tillie herself sets a good example, having obtained a Degree in Law in night school while efficiently executing secretarial duties in the Land Department of Continental Oil Company. A tiny girl, with tremendous vitality, she switches with ease from the Little Theater to swimming, cooking or bridge. She also shoots a good game of golf."

In 1953, she began working for the Continental Oil Company. Three years later, Tillie practiced with Ginther, Warren, & Ginther in Houston, Texas. A year later, she moved to Lafayette, Louisiana, where she practiced until in 1961, when she declared an inactive status with The Mississippi Bar.

Tillie was married to James C. Nixon, Sr. She died on February 17, 2007, at the age of 81. She is buried in Lafayette, Louisiana.

Charter members Betsy Watson, Margaret Maxwell, Margaret Neff, Irline Hans, Tillie Nixon, Nina Pope

Desk, Derrick marks milestone

Rose Price May ❖ 1948

A native of Wynne, Arkansas, Rose Price May's family moved to Vicksburg when she was five years old. She was born on January 8, 1911. She attended Vicksburg public schools and All Saints Junior College. She received degrees from MSCW and the University of Mississippi Law School. She is the 22nd female graduate of the University of Mississippi Law School.

She was admitted to practice on May 24, 1948, by Chancellor Herbert Holmes of Lafayette County.

Rose was married to Walter Dent May. She was a resident of Jackson and active in many community affairs. Rose was an attorney and a school teacher.

Rose died on June 15, 1976, at the age of 65 and is buried in Mendenhall Cemetery.

(Left): Rose Price May from the 1948 *Ole Miss* yearbook.
(Above): A photo from the 1948 *Mississippi Lawyer*.
Rose Price May, the only woman in the photograph, is on the second row, just right of her husband, Walter Dent May.

Rosalind Dottery Sanders ❖ 1949

The 23rd female to graduate from the University of Mississippi Law School was Rosalind Dottery Sanders. She graduated in 1949 and was admitted to the bar on August 27, 1949.

A native of Okolona in Chickasaw County, Rosalind was born on October 16, 1926, to parents Samuel Baker Dottery and Viola Vandiver Dottery. She later lived in San Francisco, California. She married Elvin Monroe Sanders in 1956.

She was then a lawyer in New Orleans. She died on March 31, 1998, at the age of 71 and is buried in Elkton, Kentucky.

(Above): Rosalind Dottery from the 1949 *Ole Miss* yearbook.
(Raight): A list of the 1949 recipients of Bachelor of Laws from the University of Mississippi.

Bachelor of Laws — Paul Gilbert Alexander, James Arden Barnett, Joseph Lawrence Dunne, Ernest McClain Jones and Maurice Clifton Maxwell of Jackson, Robert Magee Bass Jr. of Moselle, Thomas DeVane Bourdeaux of Meridian, Reuben Whittle Boydstun Jr. of Louisville, James Edwin Brown of Starkville, James Manning Cain of Canton, Harvey Lee Corban of Fayette and Cleveland Davis of Itta Bena.

Overton Anderson Currie and Davis Turner Fortenberry of Hattiesburg, Arthur Burton Custy and Guy Morrison Walker II of Laurel, Lucius Bryan Dabney Jr. and Charles Delbert Hosemann of Vicksburg, Rosalind Dottery of Okolona, Jackson Dalton Doty and William Byron Long of Tupelo, Ellis W. Finch of Booneville, Kenneth Irvin Franks and Donald G. Soper of Philadelphia, Thomas Keenan Green Jr. of Natchez and Will A.

TRAILBLAZING
WOMEN LAWYERS

Women of Color
& Non-Bar Members

WOMAN IS FIGHTING FOR LIFE

Mrs. Celia Cook Davis, of Clarksdale, Badly Wound-

(Above): Marian Wright in Mississippi in the mid-1960s.
(Below): Marian Wright and presidential candidate Robert Kennedy visiting the Mississippi Delta in 1967.

TRAILBLAZING
WOMEN LAWYERS
Women of Color

Marian Wright Edelman

First African American female lawyer admitted to The Mississippi Bar in 1965

In 1959, Marian Wright Edelman became involved in the civil rights movement, inspiring her to drop her plans to enter the foreign service, and instead to study law. While studying law at Yale, she worked as a student on a project to register African American voters in Mississippi. After graduating from Yale in 1963, she worked for the NAACP Legal Defense and Education Fund in Mississippi. She became the first African American female lawyer admitted to The Mississippi Bar in 1965.

Marian was born on June 6, 1939, in Bennettsville, South Carolina. Her father was Arthur Jerome Wright, a Baptist minister, and her mother was Maggie Leola Bowen. In 1953, her father died of a heart attack when she was fourteen years old.

She went to Marlboro Training High School in Bennettsville, where she graduated in 1956 and went on to Spelman College in Atlanta, Georgia. Due to her academic achievement, she was awarded a Merrill scholarship which allowed her to travel and study abroad. In 1959, she returned to Spelman for her senior year and became involved in the Civil Rights Movement. In 1960, she was arrested along with 14 other students at one of the largest sit-ins at the Atlanta City Hall. She graduated from Spelman as valedictorian. She went on to study law at Yale

(Above): Marian Wright Edelman testifying before Congress.
(Below left): Marian at Yale Law School.
(Below Right): Edelman is often called "America's Mom" because of her work to make the lives of children better.

Law School where she was a John Hay Whitney Fellow.

She began practicing law in Mississippi working on racial justice issues connected with the civil rights movement and representing activists during the Mississippi Summer of 1965. She also helped establish the Head Start program.

Marian moved to Washington D. C. in 1968, where she continued her work and contributed to organizing the Poor People's Campaign of Martin Luther King Jr. and the Southern Christian Leadership Conference. She founded the Washington Research Project, a public interest law firm, and also became interested in issues related to childhood development.

In 1973, she founded the Children's Defense Fund as a voice for poor children, children of color and children with disabilities. She also became involved in several school desegregation cases and served on the board of the Child Development Group of Mississippi, which represented one of the largest Head Start programs of the country.

As leader and principal spokesperson for the CDF, Marian worked to persuade the United States Congress to overhaul foster care, support adoption, improve child care and protect children who are disabled, homeless, abused or neglected. She stated, "If you don't like the way the world is, you have an obligation to change it. Just do it one step at a time."

Marian Wright Edelman, called "America's Mom," in her Washington office. She is in Philadelphia today to receive the Lucretia Mott Award.

Children's crusader

By Lini S. Kadaba
INQUIRER STAFF WRITER

WASHINGTON — At exactly 1 p.m. on a recent Wednesday, Marian Wright Edelman, flanked by two young assistants, quick-steps through the sunny lobby of her Children's Defense Fund (CDF) building, only a short ride

Health care, welfare reform, urban violence — Marian Wright Edelman, of the Children's Defense

selling author, recipient today in Philadelphia of the Lucretia Mott Award from Women's Way, hasn't a minute to waste.

The woman known as "America's Mom" has much to do.

She's lobbying for universal health care. "I've just come from a wonderful ceremony at the White House that launched a new week of immunization," says Edelman, who is being honored today for a life's work dedicated to bettering the stature of families. "We've got only 65 percent

Constance Slaughter-Harvey

First African American woman to receive law degree from the University of Mississippi Law School
By Chris Gilmer, Jackson State University, Originally published in The Mississippi Encyclopedia

Born in Jackson on June 18, 1946, and reared in Forest, Constance Slaughter was one of six daughters of Willie L. Slaughter and Olivia Kelly Slaughter, both of whom were educators and civil rights pioneers. Constance graduated as valedictorian of the segregated E. T. Hawkins High School and enrolled in 1963 at Tougaloo College, where she met civil rights leader Medgar Evers. His June 1963 murder, along with the values instilled by her parents and the racial injustices she witnessed, inspired her to join the civil rights movement.

After serving as student body president and graduating from Tougaloo College with a degree in political science, she attended law school at the University of Mississippi. In 1970, amid death threats and constant prejudice, she became the first African American woman to receive a law degree from the school.

She subsequently worked for the Lawyers Committee for Civil Rights under Law as a staff attorney and represented the families of two students who were killed by highway patrolmen during the Jackson State University massacre. She filed the desegregation lawsuit against the Mississippi State Highway Patrol that resulted in the hiring of African American highway patrolmen.

Constance became the Executive Director of the Southern Legal Rights and later the Director of East Mississippi Legal Services, an

(Above): Constance as a law student at The University of Mississippi.
(Below left): Receiving the 2001 Public Service Award from the UM law school
(Opposite): Constance Slaughter-Harvey in action.

organization she founded to provide high-quality legal representation for minority and economically disenfranchised people. She joined Mississippi Governor William Winter's staff in 1980 as Director of Human Development and later served as Assistant Secretary of State for elections and public lands under Secretary of State Dick Molpus. She led the effort that resulted in the enactment of mail-in voter registration in 1991 and the movement to permit voter registration at the Department of Motor Vehicles, becoming the first African American and first woman to serve on the Motor Voter National Advisory Board. She had served as a member of the Board of Trustees of Tougaloo College and was an adjunct professor there from 1970 to 2005. The Constance Slaughter-Harvey Endowed Chair in Political Science was created in her honor. Through her work as President of the W. L. and O. K. Slaughter Memorial Foundation, named for her parents, Constance supervised an after-school tutorial and summer enhancement program for at-risk children and youth.

She has received numerous awards from such organizations as the National Association for the Advancement of Colored People, the Mississippi Women Lawyers Association and The Mississippi Bar Women in the Profession Committee. The American Bar Association honored her with the Margaret Brent Award for professional excellence in her area of specialty and for actively paving the way to success for other women lawyers. The Black Law Students Association at the University of Mississippi is named in her honor, and in 2001, she received the law school's Public Service Award.

Constance has served as President of the Magnolia Bar Association, was the first African American judge in Mississippi, and was the first African American and woman elected president of the National Association of Election Directors. She is also the founder and President of the Legacy Education and Community Empowerment Foundation, which works to provide youth and student enrichment, mentoring, enhancement services, intergenerational programs, and other educational and empowerment programs in Forest.

Lawyer honored for public service

■ Ole Miss law school recognizes Slaughter-Harvey

Special to The Clarion-Ledger

OXFORD — Forest attorney Constance Slaughter-Harvey, termed "a soldier for justice," has been honored with the University of Mississippi School of Law's 2001 Public Service Award.

Since 1970 when she became the first African-American female to graduate from the Ole Miss law school, Slaughter-Harvey's life has been marked by selfless service, friends and colleagues have observed.

Making the presentation at a recent dinner in her honor, Law School Dean Samuel M. Davis said: "Constance Slaughter-Harvey is a force. She is a force for change — change in the social order and change in our system of justice.

"And she is a soldier in the continuing struggle for justice and equality for all. ...

She is, in the truest sense, a public servant."

Slaughter-Harvey credited the upbringing by her parents for her success. She said of all her accomplishments, she is probably proudest of her daughter Constance Olivia Slaughter-Harvey, especially "seeing her adopt values in recognizing the needs of others.

"The award is one that I will cherish," Slaughter-Harvey said Tuesday. "It means a lot because my values that were instilled in me by my parents were first and foremost to help other people.

"For the university to recognize me for that is a tribute to my parents," she said. "They are not honoring me for being a good lawyer. They are honoring me for being an excellent public servant."

Like her mother, a cum laude graduate of Tougaloo College, Constance Olivia Slaughter-Harvey attends law school at Roger Williams See **LAWYER, 4B**

Constance Slaughter-Harvey was named the Mississippi Women Lawyers' Association's Outstanding Lawyer of the Year earlier this year.

Greg Jenson/The Clarion-Ledger

TRAILBLAZING
WOMEN LAWYERS
Women of Color

"All the News That's Fit to Print"

The New York Times

LATE CITY EDITION

Weather: Mostly sunny, mild today; fair tonight. Fair, mild tomorrow. Temp. range: today 83-55; Saturday 79-55. Temp.-Hum. Index yesterday 75. Full U.S. report on Page 81.

SECTION ONE

VOL. CXIX..No. 41,049 © 1970 The New York Times Company   NEW YORK, SUNDAY, JUNE 14, 1970   50 CENTS

FOE IN CAMBODIA ENTERS KEY TOWN ON ROUTE TO PORT

Troops South of Phnompenh Cut Highway, Imperiling Capital's Oil Supply

RAIGON, South Vietnam, Sunday, June 14—Enemy troops mounted fresh attacks on the key town of Kompong Speu, about 30 miles southwest of Phnompenh, the Cambodian capital, and had elements fought their way into the center of the town, a Cambodian military communiqué said today.

The enemy again cut Route 4, the only remaining road link...

HUSSEIN APPEALS TO RESTIVE ARMY FOR 'OBEDIENCE'

Guerrillas Report Attempt by Dissident Tank Crews to Advance on Capital

A GENERAL IS SHOT AT

Amman Quiet Despite Burst of Gunfire — More U.S. Citizens Are Evacuated

By ERIC PACE

AMMAN, Jordan, June 13—King Hussein called upon his...

Six black lawyers were graduated from the formerly all-white University of Mississippi Law School this year. Five went right to work for civil rights and related organizations, all of them in Mississippi and Louisiana.

Nausead Stewart, one of the graduates, joined the Jackson office of the Lawyers Constitutional Defense Committee, a legal organization that has been defending the rights of Southern Negroes since 1964, mainly with white lawyers.

Her first case involved herself. She and 52 other black students at the University of Mississippi were arrested earlier in the year during a black power demonstration for black teachers. All 53 were expelled or suspended from school.

Laird Said to Tighten Rein On the Joint Chiefs of Staff

Melvin R. Laird, Secretary of Defense, and Gen. Earle G. Wheeler, Chairman of Joint Chiefs of Staff. Their working relationship is expected to undergo some changes.

By WILLIAM BEECHER

WASHINGTON, June 13—After 10 months of giving military leaders their head at the Pentagon, Secretary of Defense Melvin R. Laird has reportedly decided to rein them in.

The decision, according to ranking Defense Department officials, came during the height of the decision-making on operations into Cambodia and just after heavy American casualties in North Vietnam. The ...

Black Lawyers Push Rights Drive in South

By ROY REED

...small but growing number of these attorneys of the more black lawyers are bringing about... a major change in the legal...years. From that number, it...

Humphrey in Senate Race; Leaves Door Ajar for '72

Today's Sections

Section 1	
Section 2	
Section 3	
Section 4	

Brazil to Free 40 To Obtain Release Of German Envoy

By JOSEPH NOVITSKI

Young Black Lawyers Are Emerging to Take Command of the Civil Rights Movement in the South

Continued From Page 1, Col. 2

the expulsions and suspensions overturned.

But the lawyers are going further. In the same lawsuit, they are charging that Mississippi still operates a dual system of higher education with only token integration in the still identifiable "white" schools. They are asking the court to order the desegregation of all state-supported institutions of higher learning.

More Complex Problems

"We were always trying to get someone out of jail," said Alvin J. Bronstein, a 41-year-old white civil rights lawyer who came South during the turbulent days of 1964. Mr.

...and Educational Fund is starting a scholarship and internship program aimed at placing 1,500 black students in law schools during the next five years. From that number, it hopes to put 200 to work as interns in Southern law offices. Magnolia jail represent only one some in the integrated law firms that have been formed in civil rights lawyers. Among a few of the South's major cities during the last year. The phone calls; unnecessary stops $500,000 and $600,000 by two major foundations to carry out the program.

The need for more black Southern lawyers is repeatedly stressed by older black and white lawyers who have carried the civil rights load for the last decade.

Most of these men and women have suffered physically, mentally and financially, and many it's there.

...of the whites have paid the added price of social and political estrangement from the sources of power in the South.

Under such pressure, some drink too much. Others suffer psychological re-entry problems when they try to return to "normal" law practices. A few have come to doubt that the system they have grappled with can be made to work.

A Case in Point

Richard B. Sobol was a member of the prestigious Washington law firm of Arnold & Porter when he took a leave in 1966 to work in civil rights litigation in the South.

"If I got in trouble, he's the lawyer I would want to represent me," said one recently. "You don't look over your lawyer..."You don't...

know who will get you, but you know somebody will."

...fought civil rights cases in the South for three years. Some of his time was spent trying fruitlessly to break the wall of segregation in Plaquemines Parish.

Mr. Sobol did not return to Arnold & Porter when he became too tired to continue fighting in the South. He tried teaching for a while at the University of Michigan Law School. Then he joined Marian Wright Edelman and Ruby Martin, acquaintances in civil rights law, in their Washington Research Project. His friends say that nothing seemed to interest him after his Southern experience. He is now reported to be cause he touched a white boy on the elbow by way of urging him not to fight. It happened in Plaquemines Parish.

An incident on March 25 in Homer, in northern Louisiana,

...Institute of Politics of the Kennedy School of Government at Harvard University. He is now associate director of the institute.

He and his wife sometimes talk of returning to the South where, as they see it, the issue is not the morality of the Reserve Officers Training Corps, but rather, the life and death of people.

He was in New Orleans last week filling in for Mr. Sobol on the women beaten by a nightstick—a four-year-old lawsuit that grew out of a Negro boy's being charged with battery be-

...seemed almost designed to prove Mr. Bronstein's point.

The police broke up a protest group of Negroes by taking into custody all the men and women then using high-pressure fire-serve hoses and nightsticks on women and children. An affidavit by a participant in the march said that one week women who were beaten seven-and-a-half months pregnant. Two of the women who were beaten were charged with attempted murder.

Protests were halted in Homer for a while. Then George Strickler, a white Texan, and Stanley A. Halpin, who are associated

...the Lawyers Constitutional Defense Committee, went to Federal Court and got an injunction to restore the right to protest in Homer.

The bruising and bloodying of the women and children at Homer amounted to little more than a momentary distraction in the long history of that town's litigation over integrating its schools.

But it served to remind Mr. Strickler and Mr. Halpin that civil rights law books in their New Orleans office are illusory in their peacefulness. There is still passion in the streets and there are hundreds of Homers across the South.

Nausead L. Stewart

First African American student to serve on the Mississippi Law Journal

Nausead Lyvelle was born on August 15, 1931, in Starkville to Tommy James Stewart and Rosa Rogers Stewart. Upon graduation from Oktibbeha County Training High School, she attended Tougaloo College where she graduated with honors in History and Home Economics. Afterwards, she taught high school for thirteen years in West Point, while acquiring her M.A. degree from Atlanta University.

Nausead entered the University of Mississippi School of Law in 1967 and graduated with honors in May 1970, where she was the first African American law student to serve on the law journal. In law school, she roomed with Constance Slaughter-Harvey, who graduated as the first African American female graduate.

Upon graduation, she was hired by the Lawyers Constitutional Defense Committee to assist with civil rights litigation. A year later, when LCDC closed its Mississippi office, Nausead was hired to work at Anderson, Banks, Nichols, and Leventhal to assist with the NAACP Legal Defense Fund civil rights litigation. That work consisted primarily of dealing with the post desegregation discriminatory practices in teacher and administrator hiring and retention. Additionally, Nausead worked on other successful employment class actions against large employers in our state.

In 1975, Nausead became a partner and the firm name was changed to Anderson, Banks, Nichols and Stewart. Three years later, she left the firm to assume the position as head of the Jackson office for the Lawyers Committee for Civil Rights Under Law. In the 1980s, the Lawyers Committee closed its Jackson office. Nausead joined the Walker and Walker firm in Jackson. She then assumed a position with Minact, Inc. where she engaged in grant writing and compliance until her retirement.

On July 8, 2000, and during her retirement, she served as a Jackson Civil Service Commissioner after having been appointed by Jackson Mayor Harvey Johnson and served until May 2, 2006.

Nausead Stewart died in Jackson on November 10, 2015.

(Above): Nausead circa 1970. (Below): Nausead in the 1980s. (Right): A newspaper clipping from her judicial campaign announcement. (Opposite): Nausead was featured on the front page of a June 14, 1970 story in the *New York Times*.

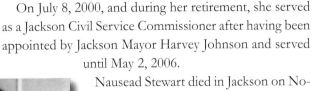

New candidate files for election of Post 1 judge

By MARTIN ZIMMERMAN
Clarion-Ledger Staff Writer

Nausead Stewart, chief counsel for the Lawyers' Committee for Civil Rights Under Law, filed Thursday as an independent candidate for Hinds County Court Judge Post 1 in the Nov. 2 general election.

Ms. Stewart will be running against incumbent Carl E. Guernsey, a Democrat, and his Republican challenger James Bell.

Ms. Stewart, a native of Starkville, said she hopes to make changes in the Hinds County Youth Court, which is administered by a County Court judge. Until January, Guernsey handled Youth Court cases.

MS. STEWART

He later exercised his authority as senior County Court judge and assigned the Youth Court duties to Judge Karen Gilfoy.

Guernsey has been criticized by police and others in the criminal justice system for being too liberal in sentencing juvenile offenders. Both Bell and the man he beat in the June primary, Charlie Head, made an issue of Guernsey's record as Youth Court judge.

Ms. Stewart said she also intends to concentrate on the Youth Court issue during her campaign. If elected, she said she hopes to work with juvenile offenders and said her experiences during 13 years of teaching "would allow me to deal with the Youth Court very effectively."

Ms. Stewart left her teaching career in West Point to earn a law degree at the University of Mississippi. For the past five years, she has been with the lawyers' committee, an activist group that was prominent in the redistricting fight in Hinds County three years ago and is involved in the current state congressional reapportionment battle.

Ms. Stewart, who is black, said she doesn't expect her race to hinder her campaign. Hinds County has one black judge, Circuit Judge Reuben V. Anderson, and one female judge, Ms. Gilfoy.

TRAILBLAZING WOMEN LAWYERS
Women of Color

Helen Rembert Carloss

Remarks by Hon. John C. Stennis in the United States Senate on July 7, 1949

Yazoo City native Helen Carloss, an Assistant U. S. District Attorney, has the distinction of being the second woman lawyer to argue a case before the U.S. Supreme Court. She was the first woman lawyer to argue cases before all the United States Courts of Appeal.

Helen Rembert Carloss died in December 1948. She was widely recognized throughout the legal profession as one of the outstanding tax authorities in the country. Few lawyers in any field have ever received such praise from Justices of the U.S. Supreme Court.

After graduating from Mississippi State College for Women, she taught for several years in the public schools in Mississippi. Ambitious to become a lawyer at a time when few members of her sex were active in the profession anywhere in the country, she went to the late Senator John Sharp Williams for advice. At his suggestion, she secured a position as a clerk with the Bureau of Internal Revenue during the first World War, and attended the law school of George Washington University at night.

Graduating from that institution in 1923 with a fine record, Miss Carloss became a member of the legal staff of the Department of Justice, and before many years was known as one of the outstanding attorneys in its Tax Division, where her special field was gift taxes.

By nature a quiet and unassuming person, Miss Carloss never sought fame or honors, but her abilities were widely recognized by all who came in contact with her work. She was given the George Washington University alumni award for distinguished attainments, and on one occasion was honored as the alumnae speaker at Mississippi State College for Women.

*Caption (below) and photo (opposite) from
International News Press Release, June, 15, 1934*

SOFT-SPOKEN SOUTHERN LASS IS SUCCESSFUL LAWYER

WASHINGTON, D.C. — Members of the sterner sex, who are also members of the bar and who have had occasion to pit their legal skill against that of Miss Helen R. Carloss, special assistant to the attorney general of the United States, will attest to Miss Carloss' proficiency in law, and legal practice. She's a typical daughter of the South; dark eyed, languorous and soft spoken, but she knows all the tricks of legal procedure, and she knows too how to present a case before the bar. She has the honor of being the first woman to argue cases before all of the U.S. Courts of Appeal; scattered from San Francisco to Boston and she spends much time dashing about from city to city, and from federal court to federal court presenting "the case for the government" for adjudication.

At her memorial service, Attorney General Tom Clark stated that, " Miss Carloss had argued 27 cases before the U. S. Supreme Court, a record for anyone in the Department." Judge James W. Morris of the United States District Court of the District of Columbia stated, "Helen R. Carloss is deserving of tribute. She was an outstanding lawyer and reflected great credit upon her profession. I have not the slightest hesitation in saying that, in her own field of tax law, she achieved an eminence shared by few and surpassed by none."

Justice Jackson of the U. S. Supreme Court was quoted as saying, "I had the highest regard for Miss Carloss. Her knowledge of the record was perfect; she mastered the facts. On the law, she not only had research, which many people have, but she had a balance of judgment as to what should be advanced. She had a candor that made you feel, when she had finished, that you had the entire story."

The final quote at her memorial service was a beautiful and appropriate expression from Justice Frankfurter: "One of my earliest experiences on the Court has remained one of the most vivid. It was the sight of a frail lady through whose countenance shone nobility of spirit. It seemed almost incongruous to have her open a tax case involving the most technical issues. I had never even heard of Helen Carloss. But at the end of less than 5 minutes of her argument, she left no doubt in my mind that I was listening to a lawyer of distinction. During the course of the years, no lawyer whom I heard often so consistently confirmed that first impression. In her, reason and art and character were fused; advocacy at its best resulted. Our profession should cherish the memory of one who adorned it."

Helen Rembert Carloss from the 1913 Industrial Institute and College (now Mississippi University for Women) yearbook.

Celia Cook Davis

Progressive in politics, Cook shattered glass ceilings — but her secret personal affairs ended in tragedy

Celia Cook Davis's professional life was, at the time, unparalleled when it came to breaking barriers for women. Celia was the product of attorneys. Her father, John Henry Cook, was a U.S. District Attorney; her paternal uncle, Sam C. Cook, was a justice of the Mississippi Supreme Court; and her maternal uncle, Virgil Griffith, was chief justice of the Mississippi Supreme Court. Celia's sister, Vivian Cook (see 1920s), graduated from the University of Mississippi law school with fellow female classmate Lucy Somerville Howorth.

In 1924, as Celia celebrated her 20th birthday, she was appointed deputy clerk of U.S. Court for the Northern District of Mississippi. The same year, Celia was appointed a U.S. Commissioner for the Mississippi Delta. She heard cases ranging from prohibition violations to peonage law violations in the Delta. Celia was one of the few women in the country that held positions at the federal level.

Five years after those appointments, in 1929, Celia passed The Mississippi bar exam.

In addition to her federal role as clerk and commissioner, Celia was a leader in the republican party in Mississippi. In the summer of 1932, she was a delegate at the republican national convention in Chicago. Celia was a part of the progressive "black and tan" faction that maintained the republican party should be biracial — and sought to include most African American voters.

Vivian Cook (above) was Celia Cook's older sister (see 1920s Section). Vivian graduated from Ole Miss in 1922; Celia passed the bar in 1929.

Despite her public, professional successes, details about her private life were about to unravel.

On December 23, 1932, Celia and her husband, R. B. "Happy" Davis, held a holiday bridge party at their home in Clarksdale. At midnight that evening, Mr. Davis phoned the Clarksdale Police Department and informed officers that there had been "a shooting scrape" at their home. Officers arrived and discovered that Celia had been shot four times in the abdomen.

Mr. Davis surrendered to officers without incident. Celia was rushed to the hospital where doctors discovered that bullets had pierced her lungs, liver, and intestines.

At no time during the night did Celia lose consciousness. In fact, she insisted on giving instructions to her office in the federal courthouse, conversed with friends, and declared, with emphasis, that she intended to survive. She also stated that the shooting was a result of excessive alcohol consumption by her husband.

The next day, officers began to research Mr. Davis's past. He was a Tate County native and formerly in the lumber business. Most recently, Davis held a desk position with the Clarksdale Police Department. The officers were also tipped off by a school teacher, who knew the accused as a child, that Davis wasn't his real name. They also discovered two wedding records. The first ceremony was between Celia Cook and R. B. "Happy" Davis performed on March 14, 1926. The second wedding, held eleven days later in Dallas, Texas, was between Celia Cook and L.A. Martin (apparently the birth name of "Happy" Davis).

Despite the best efforts of physicians, Celia Cook Davis died on Christmas Day, 1932. The following Spring, her husband was sentenced to life in prison. A newspaper report from later in 1933 described Lorenzo Martin a.k.a. Happy Davis as a "model prisoner."

TRAILBLAZING WOMEN LAWYERS
Non-Bar Members

WOMAN DEPUTY CLERK SHOT BY HUSBAND

Mrs. Davis Of Clarksdale, Miss., In Critical Condition In Hospital—Shooting Followed Argument

CLARKSDALE, Miss., Dec. 22. ▬ ▬ R. B. Davis, deputy

WOMAN IS FIGHTING FOR LIFE

Mrs. Celia Cook Davis, of Clarksdale, Badly Wounded by Husband

QUARREL IS BLAMED FOR DELTA SHOOTING

Celia Cook Davis Was Twice Married To "Happy" Davis

MEMPHIS, Tenn. (AP) — A d'spatch to the Evening Appeal from Clarksdale, Miss., today, said R. H. (Happy) Davis was twice married to Mrs. Celia Cook Davis, former deputy federal court clerk, for whose slaying h▬

EX-OFFICER MAKING A MODEL PRISONER

CLARKSDALE, March 24.—Lonzena Martin, known in Clarksdale as R. B. (Happy) Davis, sentenced to life imprisonment in the state penitentiary, is making a model prisoner, according to prison officials. Martin was removed to the penitentiary from the Coahoma county jail two days ago.

He slew his wife, Mrs. Celia Cook Davis, United States deputy court

Burnita Shelton Matthews

By Kate Greene, Professor at the University of Southern Mississippi

reprinted from The Mississippi Lawyer magazine, March-April 2000, Vol. XLVI, pages 32-34

When Burnita Shelton Matthews left Mississippi following her marriage to Percy Matthews in 1917, she never looked back. Percy Matthews had joined the Army as a pilot and had left to fight in World War I shortly after the wedding. Burnita Shelton Matthews moved to a small town in Georgia to teach music. Like many talented, creative Mississippians before and since, she had left her family and would soon leave the Deep South in pursuit of a calling. She would find a first career as a lawyer and a second career as the first woman appointed to a U.S. District Court judgeship.

Born December 28, 1894, in Copiah County to Burnell Shelton and Lora Barlow Shelton, Burnita became a member of an educated, civic-minded family. Her mother was a graduate of Whitworth College, a local boarding school for young women, and her father was a planter/cattleman and elected official. Her father served at various times as sheriff, tax collector and as the Clerk of the Chancery Court.

Although she was the only daughter among five sons, Burnita was not excluded from her father's political life. He often took her along on the campaign trail and brought her to the courthouse when he worked. At the age of 11, she won an oratory contest and overheard a friend of her father, a criminal attorney, tell him, "You ought to make a lawyer out of that little girl." From that point on, she decided that she wanted to be a lawyer.

Burnita never waivered from her desire to attend college and law school, but her father preferred that she pursue a more lady-like profession – music. After the early death of her mother, her father sent her to the Cincinnati Conservatory of Music. After receiving her teaching certificate, she taught music and piano in Texas for one year and for two years at a high school in Fayette, Mississippi.

In 1916, her high school friend Percy Matthews returned from Chicago where he had just received his law

A young Burnita Shelton Matthews

degree at Chicago-Kent School of Law. In 1917, they married. Percy went to fight in World War I. Upon arriving in Georgia, Burnita saw an advertisement for jobs with the federal government during the war. She took the exam and when she received word that she had passed the exam

and should report to Washington, D.C., she jumped on a train. She reported to the Veteran's Administration where she was given a job as a clerk.

Burnita enrolled in the National University Law School's night program. When she wrote her father to tell him that she had enrolled in the night program, he continued to express his opposition to her studying law. While attending law school, she joined the National Woman's Party (NWP). The NWP was a militant suffrage organization that had broken away from the National American Woman's Suffrage Association (NAWSA). The NWP engaged in parades and picketing of the White House for a national suffrage amendment. Burnita worked at the Veteran's Administration during the day, attended law school at night, and picketed the White House with the NWP on the weekends. She earned her LL.B. in 1919 and her LL.M. and Master in Patent Law in 1920.

She continued with the NWP after passage of the Nineteenth Amendment and her graduation from law school. Throughout the 1920s, while establishing a small legal practice, she headed up the Legal Research Department of the NWP. This department engaged in a decade-long project of identifying the legal discriminations against women in state laws. She drafted several laws securing equal rights for women which were passed by state legislatures, including a law removing the disqualification of women as jurors in the District of Columbia, laws eliminating the preference for men over women in inheritance in Arkansas, the District of Columbia and New York, laws in Maryland and New Jersey giving women teachers equal pay with men teachers for equal work, and a law in South Carolina allowing married women to sue and be sued without rejoinder of their husband. During this time, she also became actively engaged in the Party's effort to secure the Equal Rights Amendment and assisted in finalizing the draft of the original version of the Equal Rights Amendment.

Throughout the 1920s and 1930s, she was the legal expert for the NWP when testifying before Congress in support of the Equal Rights Amendment. Her job was to use the data from the state digests to counter the opposition's arguments that there was no need for an Equal Rights Amendment because most states had eliminated the discriminations against women. As legal counsel for the NWP, she also secured the largest government condemnation award ever granted at the time when the United States acquired the Woman's Party house and land to build the Supreme Court building. Her success against the government in that case cemented her reputation as one of the best lawyers in Washington, D.C. and her private practice grew. She joined two other women lawyers with NWP ties, Rebekah Greathouse and Laura Berrien, in the firm Matthews, Berrien and Greathouse. Burnita's activities gravitated toward work with legal and professional organizations such as the D.C. Bar Association, the Woman's Bar Association, the American Bar Association and the National Association of Women Lawyers. She also taught at the Washington College of Law, now a part of American University.

(Above): Burnita Shelton Matthews in law school; (Opposite): Matthews in 1947.

In 1949, President Truman appointed Burnita to the United States District Court for the District of Columbia, and she became the first woman ever appointed to a federal trial court and only the second woman ever appointed to a federal constitutional court. Upon her arrival, she experienced some distrust and resentment on the part of other judges, but her hard work and wit overcame those problems eventually. While on the bench, she only hired women law clerks. Her main justification for the practice was that since she was the only woman judge, this would probably be the only opportunity women lawyers would have to clerk for a federal judge.

During her 28-year tenure on the bench, Burnita presided over several major trials. In 1957, she presided over the Jimmy Hoffa bribery trial in which he was acquitted. In 1962, in *Fulwood v. Clemmer*, 206 F. Supp. 370 (D.D.C. 1962), Judge Matthews upheld the right of Black Muslims in the local prison to conduct religious services. She took senior status in 1969 and heard cases at both the District Court and Court of Appeals until her retirement in 1977.

Burnita proved to be quite conservative as a judge, usually siding with the government. But this conservatism came from her belief in judicial self-restraint. In her private life, she supported civil rights for blacks and equal rights for women, but she felt that these should be achieved through the legislative rather than the judicial process.

In 1988, she died of a stroke and was buried in the Shelton family cemetery in Copiah County. Her headstone records the things for which she wished most to be remembered: as the author of laws advancing the status of women and the first woman in the nation to serve as a Federal District Judge.

Women Crusaders Build Fire Around White House

They want woman appointed federal judge

By Robert Riggs
Courier-Journal Washington Bureau

WASHINGTON, July 22.—If you think you know something about pressure groups, you should see the one which has dedicated itself to obtaining from President Truman the appointment of a Washington woman to a federal judgeship in the District of Columbia.

Washington Merry-Go-Round

Jimmy Hoffa Hired Close Friend Of Federal Judge's Brother As His Attorney; Arkansas State Senator Hired By Hoffa Is Boyhood Friend Of A. D. Shelton, Brother Of Judge Burnita Shelton Matthews

By DREW PEARSON

WASHINGTON — The public doesn't yet know the half of what Jimmy Hoffa and teamster cohorts did to make sure he was acquitted in his recent bribery trial.

This column can now reveal that Hoffa's Michigan attorney, George S. Fitzgerald, Democratic politician and former candidate for lieutenant governor of Michigan, reached all the way to Hot Springs, Ark., to hire Q. Byrum Hurst, an Arkansas state Senator, as one of the battery of Hoffa defense attorneys. This was in addi-

Hamil, who is from Colorado, has been in office less than a year but has been far too liberal for the private utility boys who now swing such powerful influence in Washington. Hamil has been strong for the rural electric co-ops. He publicly opposed hiking of interest rates just as President Eisenhower was getting ready to ask Congress to authorize such increases. As a result, Hamil will get the ax.

The new REA Administrator

explained reason. No matter what the conversation, Eisenhower eventually steers it around to commenting on how wonderful it will be when the new merchant ship is actually sailing the high seas. . . . The White House has ordered the FHA not to reduce the rates on FHA-insured mortgages—despite a law passed by Congress lowering down-payment rates. President Eisenhower himself signed the bill. But the White House now claims the l

More Firsts
For Mississippi Women Lawyers

FELICIA ADAMS
■ 1st female African American United States Attorney in Northern District

JUDGE ALLAN ALEXANDER
■ 1st female United States Magistrate Judge on Federal Bench
■ 1st female law clerk, Northern District Court

AMANDA ALEXANDER
■ 1st President from Mississippi of the National Conference of Women's Bar Association

JUDGE LINDA ANDERSON
■ 1st female African American U.S. Magistrate Judge

JUDGE SHARION AYCOCK
■ 1st female Federal District Court Judge
■ 1st female Mississippi Bar Foundation President

JUDGE DONNA BARNES
■ 1st female to serve as the Chief Judge of the Mississippi Court of Appeals

CATHERINE BASS
■ 1st female to teach an upper level, doctrinal course at the UM Law School

CORINNE BASS
■ 1st female to hold a full-time faculty position at the UM School of Law

DEBBIE BELL
■ 1st female Director of Clinical Education at the University of Mississippi Law School

FELICIA ADAMS

AMANDA ALEXANDER

JUDGE LINDA ANDERSON

JUDGE SHARION AYCOCK

JUDGE DONNA BARNES

PATRICIA BENNETT

JUDGE DEBRA M. BROWN

MARTHA BERGMARK

MARY ANN CONNELL

MARIAN WRIGHT EDELMAN

PATRICIA (PAT) BENNETT
◼ 1st female African American Mississippi Bar President

JUDGE DEBRA M. BROWN
◼ 1st female African American appointed as a Judge of the United States District Court for the Northern District of Mississippi

SARAH LOU BUCHANAN
◼ 1st female lawyer to argue before the Mississippi Supreme Court

SUSIE BLUE BUCHANAN
◼ 1st female lawyer licensed to practice before the Mississippi Supreme Court

MARTHA BERGMARK
◼ Founder of the Mississippi Center for Justice

RUTH CAMPBELL
◼ 1st Mississippi woman lawyer to spend her entire career in private practice

KATHERINE BRIGGS COLLIER
◼ 1st female attorney Executive Director of the Public Service Commission

MARY ANN CONNELL
◼ 1st female Counselor for University of Mississippi
◼ 1st female President of National Association of College and University Attorneys from Mississippi

LOUISA DIXON
◼ 1st female Commissioner of Public Safety for the State of Mississippi

EUPLE DOZIER
◼ 1st female lawyer in Mississippi to be appointed as an Assistant United States Attorney
◼ 1st female lawyer to be elected attorney for a Board of Supervisors in Mississippi
◼ 1st female lawyer to be elected a county prosecuting attorney

MARIAN WRIGHT EDELMAN

- 1st female African American lawyer admitted to The Mississippi Bar

LA'VERNE EDNEY

- 1st female African American member of Mississippi Chapter of ABOTA
- 1st female African American President of the Mississippi Bar Foundation

MARGARET ELLIS

- 1st female President of Mississippi Association of Justice

CAMILLE HENICK EVANS

- 1st female Outstanding Young Lawyer of The Mississippi Bar's Young Lawyers Division recipient
- 1st female lawyer to serve as Chair of the Litigation Section of The Mississippi Bar

SARAH A. O'REILLY-EVANS

- 1st female African American city attorney for the City of Jackson
- 1st female African American city attorney for the City of Yazoo City

ATTORNEY GENERAL LYNN FITCH

- 1st female Attorney General in Mississippi
- 1st Mississippi Bar Women in the Profession Committee Chair

JUDGE DEBORAH GAMBRELL

- 1st female African American Justice Court Judge in Forrest County

EVELYN GANDY

- 1st female lawyer elected State Representative from Forrest County
- 1st female lawyer elected State Treasurer
- 1st female lawyer elected Commissioner of Public Welfare
- 1st female lawyer elected Commissioner of Insurance
- 1st female lawyer appointed as Assistant Attorney General of Mississippi
- 1st female lawyer elected Lieutenant Governor
- 1st Mississippi recipient of the ABA Margaret Brent Award
- 1st female elected President of Ole Miss Law School Student Body
- 1st female to serve as Editor of Mississippi Law Journal

LA'VERNE EDNEY

CAMILLE HENICK EVANS

SARAH A. O'REILLY-EVANS

LYNN FITCH

JUDGE DEBORAH GAMBRELL

EVELYN GANDY

PATTI GANDY

TIFFANY GRAVES

PELICIA HALL

CLARE SEKUL HORNSBY

PATTI GANDY
■ 1st female Mission First Executive Director

MARTHA WILSON GERALD
■ 1st female President of Hinds County Bar Association
■ 1st female President of Mississippi Women Lawyers Association

TIFFANY GRAVES
■ 1st full-time female African American in-house law firm pro bono counsel in Mississippi

ELIZABETH WATKINS HULEN GRAYSON
■ 1st female lawyer to argue before the United States Supreme Court

LUCY HARRISON GREAVES
■ 1st female member of The Mississippi Bar

MARTHA GRIFFIN
■ 1st female Mississippi Worker's Compensation Commission Judge

PELICIA HALL
■ 1st female Commissioner of the Mississippi Department of Corrections

MICHELE PURVIS HARRIS
■ 1st female African American to serve as the Chief City Prosecutor for the City of Jackson

VIOLA JAMES HILBERT
■ 1st female law clerk, Southern District Court

JEAN MAGEE HOGAN
■ 1st female Mississippi Bar Young Lawyers Division President

CLARE SEKUL HORNSBY
■ 1st female Local Bar Association President (Harrison County Bar)
■ 1st Susie Blue Buchanan Award recipient

LUCY SOMERVILLE HOWORTH

■ 1st female member to formally address The Mississippi Bar Annual Meeting
■ 1st female legislator from Hinds County
■ 1st woman appointed to Board of Bar Examiners
■ 1st woman official delegate from Mississippi to the American Bar Association Annual Meeting

NELL WILKINSON HUNT

■ 1st female Notary Public in Mississippi

KATHY KING JACKSON

■ 1st female to serve as an Assistant District Attorney in Mississippi

LEOTA ANGELINA TAYLOR KIRKPATRICK

■ 1st female law student at Millsaps College School of Law

ZELDA SIEGEL LABOVITZ

■ 1st female lawyer to serve on the Junior Bar's Executive Committee

HELEN PATRICIA MALTBY

■ 1st full-time female senior staff member at the UM Law School (Law Librarian) and 1st woman to lead a law school classroom (legal bibliography lab)

PEARL MARIE MCLELLAN

■ 1st female lawyer President of Mississippi Court Reporters Association

JEAN MUIRHEAD

■ 1st female lawyer to be elected to the state senate from Hinds County

ALICE PORTER NEVELS

■ 1st female Executive Director of The Mississippi Bar

SHIRLEY NORWOOD

■ Mississippi College School of Law's first chaired professor

LUCY SOMERVILLE HOWORTH

LEOTA TAYLOR KIRKPATRICK

ZELDA SIEGEL LABOVITZ

PEARL MARIE MCLELLAN

MARY LIBBY PAYNE

FAYE PETERSON

JOY LAMBERT PHILLIPS

JUSTICE LENORE PRATHER

JUDGE ERMEA RUSSELL

CONSTANCE SLAUGHTER-HARVEY

MARY LIBBY PAYNE
- 1st female Mississippi College Law School Dean
- 1st female Mississippi Court of Appeals Judge

FAYE PETERSON
- 1st female African American to serve as the District Attorney for Hinds County

JOY LAMBERT PHILLIPS
- 1st female Mississippi Bar President

CLAIRE PORTER
- 1st Commissioner of Workers' Compensation Commission

JUSTICE LENORE PRATHER
- 1st female Mississippi Supreme Court Chief Justice
- 1st female Chancery Court Judge

JUDGE ZELMA WELLS PRICE
- 1st female Judge in Mississippi

ZELMA PRICE & ZELMA WELLS PRICE SCHUETTA
- 1st mother-daughter law partnership in Mississippi

JUDGE ERMEA RUSSELL
- 1st female African American Judge on the Mississippi Court of Appeals

KATHERINE MALLEY SAMSON
- 1st female to serve as a Bankruptcy Court Judge in Mississippi

LYDA GORDON SHIVERS
- 1st female on Editorial Staff of Mississippi Law Journal

CONSTANCE SLAUGHTER HARVEY
- 1st female African American Judge in Mississippi
- 1st female African American graduate of the University of Mississippi Law School

CAROLYN ELLIS STATON

■ 1st Mississippi Women Lawyers Association Outstanding Woman Award recipient
■ 1st female Interim Dean of the University of Mississippi School of Law
■ 1st female Provost of the University of Mississippi

NAUSEAD STEWART

■ 1st female African American on the Mississippi Law Journal

CAROL STONE

■ 1st female Curtis Coker Access to Justice Award recipient

JUDGE BETTY BARTEE TUCKER

■ 1st female lawyer to become Hinds County Judge

ZENORE WILLIAMS

■ 1st female Editor of the Mississippi Bar's *Mississippi Lawyer* magazine

JUDGE PATRICIA WISE

■ 1st female African American President of the Magnolia Bar Association

BESSIE YOUNG

■ 1st female University of Mississippi Law School graduate
■ 1st female attorney to open a solo practice

LENA CAROLINA ZAMA

■ 1st female President of Copiah County Bar Association
■ 1st female Mississippi Bar Commissioner representing the 14th District

CAROLYN ELLIS STATON

NAUSEAD STEWART

JUDGE BETTY BARTEE TUCKER

JUDGE PATRICIA WISE

LENA CAROLINA ZAMA

APPENDIX: Women Lawyers in The Mississippi Bar

As of August 1, 2020

A

LeAnne L. Abbott
Lindsey B. Abdalla
Mary C. Abdalla
Kendra M. Abfalter
Wanda X. Abioto
Jennifer M. Abraham
Katherine Abraham
Heather M. Aby
Nikki J. Acord
Marla F. Adair
Tammy R. Adair
Alberta L. Adams
Anita B. Adams
Cynthia M. Adams
Felicia C. Adams
Kasey M. Adams
Sylvia R. Adams
Terri L. Adams
Whitney M. Adams
Jennifer Adams-Williams
Jennifer L. Adcock
Julie H. Addison
Myrtle M. Addison
Rebecca Adelman
Meredith B. Aden
Arin C. Adkins
Eseosa G. Agho
Corey A. Aiken
Adrienne H. Aikens
Alicia M. Ainsworth
Rebecca J. Ainsworth
Gail S. Akin
Nancy H. Akin
Jenny M. Albritton
Jessica J. Aldison
Meredith M. Aldridge
Amanda G. Alexander
Christa L. Alexander
Earnestine Alexander
Judge S. A. Alexander
Katherine B. Alexander
Marian S. Alexander
M.J. Alexander
Patricia R. Alexander
Sara E. Alexander
Judge Margaret Alfonso
Helen J. Alford
Assma A. Ali
Wendy L. Allard
Brandie Alldredge
Ashley R. Allen
Courtney A. Allen
Debra L. Allen
Monica D. Allen
Michele Allen-Hart
Nancy F. Alley
Alissa J. Allison
Katherine H. Allison
Valerie Allison-Ring
Anastasia M. Allmon
Ellen M. Allred
Rhonda K. Allred
Brooke W. Altazan
Christine C. Althoff
Margaret H. Alves
Chelye P. Amis
Rhonda M. Amis
Liat Amsily
Cassie B. Anderson
Christi G. Anderson
Judge Linda R. Anderson

Katherine M. Anderson
Katherine M. Anderson
Lula M. Anderson
Michelle H. Anderson
Renia A. Anderson
Victoria M. Anderson
Jhasmine E. Andrews
Sharon L. Andrews
Valerie M. Andrews
Krista S. Andy
Brittney B. Ankersen
Anna M. Arceneaux
Elizabeth F. Archer
Cydney J. Archie
Paula G. Ardelean
Julie A. Ardoin
Erin E. Argo
Betty B. Arinder
Alissa H. Armstrong
Cali Armstrong
Caroline Armstrong
Torri T. Armstrong
Cecelia Arnold
Janet G. Arnold
Michele C. Arnold
Amy B. Arrington
Melinda B. Arrington
Mary R. Arthur
Danielle E. Ashley
Mary B. Ashley
Patricia F. Aston
Hilary P. Atkins, BA JD
Jay M. Atkins
Marisa C. Atkinson
Sally A. Atkinson
Elizabeth F. Ausbern
Moira R. Ausems
Judge Sharion Aycock
Jessica N. Ayers

B

Pamela G. Bach
Kaitlyn N. Badgley
Laureen F. Bagley
P A. Bailey
Carshena L. Bailey
Chynee A. Bailey
Jenna L. Bailey
Julianne K. Bailey
Kacey G. Bailey
Lacey L. Bailey
Lisa C. Bailey
Mary M. Bailey
Rachel L. Bailey
Elizabeth L. Baine
Lori C. Baird
Stephanie H. Baird
Tommie A. Baird
Alison B. Baker
Anna E. Baker
Jennifer T. Baker
Katherine S. Baker
Lesa H. Baker
Margaret B. Baker
Suzanna Baker
Tammy L. Baker
Vicki V. Baker
Sarah A. Baker
Alicia C. Baladi
Courtney V. Baldwin
Shirlee F. Baldwin
Shunda L. Baldwin

Annette E. Ball
Carmelita V. Ball
Mary D. Ballard
Greta R. Ballard
Jamie R. Ballard
Caroline C. Ballentine
Mary M. Baltz
Vidhi Bamzai
Tabitha Bandi
Alexis D. Banks
Jamie M. Banks
Kimberly C. Banks
Nickita S. Banks
Taunya M. Banks
Ahsaki E. Baptist
Gwendolyn Baptist-Rucker
Brittany E. Barbee
Melanie M. Barber
Tara D. Barber
Amanda B. Barbour
Laura K. Barbour
Tammy L. Barham
Marcie F. Baria
Claire Barker
Dorothy A. Barker
Ann Regan B. Barlow
Leslie A. Barlow
Sarah C. Barlow
Mary E. Barnard
Andrea' R. Barnes
Judge Donna M. Barnes
Judge Vicki R. Barnes
Martha E. Barnes
Stephanie D. Barnes
Mandie M. Barnes
Gail S. Barnett
Mary J. Barnett
Emily G. Barr
Amy C. Barrett
Fay N. Barrett
Mary E. Barrett
Pshon Barrett
Lisa E. Barrett
Barbara J. Barron
Sarah F. Barron
Leslie P. Barry
Gail B. Barton
Laura C. Barton
Ja'Nekia W. Barton
Lori N. Basham
Kathryn J. Bass
Lilli A. Bass
Patricia A. Bass
Shelly M. Bass
Deidra J. Bassi
Wendy L. Bateman
Jessica L. Bates
Brittney E. Batton
Tabatha A. Baum
Margaret L. Baxley
Jeanne W. Baxter
Kay B. Baxter
Mary E. Baxter
Patricia L. Beale
Dawn H. Beam
Amanda S. Beard
Lisa G. Beard
Amanda M. Beard
Katharine A. Beatty
Stephanie G. Beaver
Amanda M. Beckett
Melanie N. Beckham

Sheila A. Bedi
Cathy M. Beeding
Jonell B. Beeler
Valena E. Beety
Steffanie G. Beissel
Catherine B. Bell
Deborah H. Bell
Lori M. Bell
Laura S. Beltran
Kristin G. Belvin
Shakti Belway
Crystal J. Bender
Christine K. Benefield
Deborah L. Benner
Ashley S. Bennett
Heather F. Bennett
Kristy L. Bennett
Megan M. Bennett
Patricia W. Bennett
Tameika L. Bennett
Mary T. Benoist
Stephanie J. Bentley
Betty M. Benton
Cameron L. Benton
Michelle L. Benton
Sally B. Berger
Jacque L. Bergman
Martha J. Bergmark
Lynn M. Bergwerk
Diana T. Berman
Ashlee D. Berry
Katie C. Berry
Leigh K. Berry
Maggie E. Berry
Renee H. Berry
Sarah E. Berry
Jean C. Bertas
Jackye C. Bertucci
Brenda B. Bethany
Lesley E. Bettenhausen
Judge Staci S. Bevill
Sheryl Bey
Michele D. Biegel
Shaniqua S. Biggins
Paige H. Biglane
Mellie M. Billingsley
Heidi E. Billington
Lisa P. Binder
Teresa B. Birmingham
Christine C. Bischoff
Christa R. Bishop
Katherine D. Bishop
Monti C. Bishop
Shannon B. Bishop
Pamela J. Bittick
Maria N. Bjornerud
Ellen A. Black
Mary K. Black
Shanah F. Black
Barbara M. Blackmon
Janessa E. Blackmon
Lydia R. Blackmon
Lyndsey B. Blackston
Angela B. Blackwell
Judge Debra W. Blackwell
Margaret H. Blackwell
Staci Y. Blackwell
Kelly R. Blackwood
Jennifer L. Blair
Rachel A. Blair
Robin B. Blair
Tonya M. Blair

Candace C. Blalock
Mary L. Blalock
Hillary M. Blalock
Martha Jane E. Blanche
Alexandria W. Blanchette
Rebekah J. Bland
Jennifer H. Bland
Mallory K. Bland
Heather D. Blansett
Meredith K. Blasingame
Hannah E. Bleavins
Katherine M. Blount
Lisa L. Blount
Je'Nell B. Blum
Mary D. Blumentritt
Rebecca S. Blunden
Barbara A. Bluntson
Doris T. Bobadilla
Leslie J. Bobo
Maggie K. Bobo
Semmes H. Bobo
Vicki K. Bobo
Cynthia H. Bockman
Katherine M. Boerner
Jasmine T. Bogard
Mary K. Bogard
Angela D. Boisseau
Cecilia A. Boland
Nicki M. Boland
Mary Elizabeth S. Bolen
Christina M. Bolin
Elizabeth S. Bolin
Mary Allie E. Boller
Beverly A. Bolton
Susan D. Bomar
Emily S. Bonds
Whitney W. Bondurant
Eric D. Bonner
Grace L. Bonner
Laci M. Bonner
Ellen C. Bonner-Guidry
Patricia A. Booker
Elizabeth M. Boone
Emily C. Boone
Linda B. Boozer
Catherine A. Boozman
Jana D. Bormann
Barbara A. Boschert
Sheila M. Bossier
Robin R. Boswell
Emily A. Bosworth
Kathy S. Boteler
Leslie Bounds
Elizabeth A. Bounds
Jessica N. Bourne
Kathryn M. Bourne
Katherine M. Bousquet
Evelyn A. Bowden
Tracy A. Bowen
Mary M. Bowers
Judge Karen J. Bowes
Courtney A. Bowie
Tamarra A. Bowie
Tracy K. Bowles
Kimberly B. Bowling
Terra H. Bowling
Frances E. Bowman
Donna L. Boyce
Kathryn C. Boyd
Andrea N. Boyd
Kristen E. Boyden
Jennifer L. Boydston

Diane Boyette
Lorraine W. Boykin
Elizabeth M. Boyle
Andrea J. Boyles
Alison C. Brackins
April B. Braddock
Amanda D. Bradley
Antoinette Bradley
Deborah L. Bradley
Emily C. Bradley
Judge Jaye A. Bradley
Susan S. Bradley
Katie A. Bradshaw
Sandra C. Bradshaw
Victoria R. Bradshaw
Angela L. Bradwell
LeAnne F. Brady
Melissa G. Brady
Theresa L. Brady
Olivia C. Brame
Debra P. Branan
Mary C. Brand
Marilyn R. Brand
Ashlea R. Brandon
Jenifer B. Branning
Chelsea H. Brannon
Emmylou R. Branscome
Meredith P. Brasfield
Kasie M. Braswell
Toni J. Braxton
Autumn T. Breeden
Suzette F. Breland
Margaret A. Bretz
Allison M. Brewer
Judge Cynthia Lee E. Brewer
Laurie A. Bridewell
Bethany K. Bridges
Hallie G. Bridges
Sharon F. Bridges
Charity R. Bridgewater
Kelly P. Bridgforth
Erin E. Briggs
Laurel B. Brinkley
Kim T. Britt
Meagan C. Brittain
Katie E. Britton
Allyson L. Brock
Angela S. Brooks
Kenya D. Brooks
Shannon G. Brooks
Shawnassey H. Brooks
Haley N. Broom
Paula H. Broome
Emilee L. Broussard
Amy H. Brown
Brandi L. Brown
Brittany W. Brown
Cynthia A. Brown
Dawn S. Brown
Haley M. Brown
Jacqueline F. Brown
Judge Debra M. Brown
Julie W. Brown
Katrina S. Brown
Kristi R. Brown
Laura S. Brown
Le R. Brown
Leslie R. Brown
Lindsey C. Brown
Lindy D. Brown
Lisa M. Brown
Mary A. Brown
Mary L. Brown
Natalie K. Brown
Pernila S. Brown
Robin L. Brown
Shandreka S. Brown
Sherrye J. Brown
Stephanie A. Brown
Susan F. Brown
Tamaca L. Brown

Tammye C. Brown
Terri S. Brown
Tina D. Brown
Whitney R. Brown
Monique Brown-Barrett
Kimberly A. Brown-Gibbs
Leneatra C. Brownlee
Mary L. Brubaker
Susan F E. Bruhnke
Nancy S. Brumbeloe
Abby W. Brumley
Jennifer H. Brunetti
Casey Brunson
Faison C. Brunson
Celeste Brustowicz
Kacy N. Bryan
Manya C. Bryan
Michelle T. Bryan
Nicole W. Bryan
Susan R. Bryan
Amy G. Bryant
April T. Bryant
Bethany C. Bryant
Mary H. Bryant
Misti L. Bryant
Tchanavia C. Bryant
Kerry M. Bryson
Sandra D. Buchanan
Stacey M. Buchanan
Rachel C. Buck
Zahra T. Buck
Kate E. Buckley
Kimberly A. Buckley
Irene M. Buckley
Sara E. Budslick
Mary B. Buffington
S A. Bufkin
Elizabeth T. Bufkin
Brandi T. Bukvich
Patricia W. Bullard
Tina M. Bullock
Vanessa A. Bullock
Dana L. Bumgardner
Stacy E. Bunch
Sally B. Buntin
Amanda L. Burch
Emily H. Burch
Patricia A. Burchell
Caitlyn S. Burchfield
Jennifer C. Burford
Jennifer D. Burgar
Julie N. Burke
Annie M. Burke
Felicia D. Burkes
Jennifer P. Burkes
Danielle L. Burks
Brandy N. Burnette
Candy Burnette
Suzanne M. Burnette
Cynthia D. Burney
Kasey C. Burney
Mary K. Burnham
Shelly G. Burns
Judy L. Burnthorn
Lori T. Burson
Elizabeth W. Burton
Cheryl L. Burton
Rebecca G. Burton
Joanna E. Busby
Candice R. Bush
Patsy A. Bush
Rebecca G. Bush
Paige C. Bush-Scruggs
Carol A. Bustin
Ayanna B. Butler
Deborah A. Butler
Sarah M. Butler
Zakia H. Butler
Shani M. Butler Anderson
Jayne L. Buttross
Casey L. Butts

Courtney C. Buxner
Whitney B. Byars
Robbie A. Byers
Shirley C. Byers
Allyson C. Byrd
Elisabeth W. Byrd
Barbara H. Byrd
Julie D. Byrd Ashworth

C

Andrea J. Cabrera
Cleo D. Cacoulidis
Leigh Anne K. Cade
J R. Cain
Jane L. Calamusa
Katherine J. Caldwell
Ashley E. Calhoun
Chandra D. Calhoun
Kristy K. Callahan
Baylea B. Callicutt
Alison D. Callison
Jennifer Ann C. Calvillo
Bernadette K. Camille
Tonya K. Cammon
Carol R. Camp
Heather J. Camp
Alma C. Campbell
Anna F. Campbell
Kena T. Campbell
Kimalon S. Campbell
Kimberly L. Campbell
Leah K. Campbell
Cynthia J. Camuel
Ashley E. Cannady
Amy H. Cannon
Marta V. Canossa Ortega
Laura A. Cantral
Lauren G. Cantrell
Lauren R. Cappaert
Kimberly L. Cappleman
Jeanine M. Carafello
Leslie H. Carbo
Barbara H. Carboni
Tia K. Cardwell
Tiffany N. Carey
Judge Margaret Carey-McCray
Tanya N. Carl
Melissa Carleton
Valerie L. Carlisle
Lois L. Carlson
Judge Virginia C. Carlton
Neely C. Carlton
Elizabeth U. Carlyle
Carly J. Carman
Allyson N. Carmody
Rose H. Carney
Susan O. Carnley
Angela T. Carpenter
Haley C. Carpenter
Gayla L. Carpenter-Sanders
Ann B. Carr
Caroline R. Carr
Debra R. Carr
Emily Carr
Elizabeth R. Carr
Laurel A. Carrier Feilmeier
Christina L. Carroll
Elizabeth B. Carroll
Keri H. Carroll
Vanessa J. Carroll
Christine A. Carson
Dawn D. Carson
Martha G. Carson
Adrienne C. Carter
Amelia S. Carter
Laura H. Carter
Lynda C. Carter
Shronda T. Carter
Stacy A. Carter
Tangi Carter
Tammra O. Cascio

Jennifer L. Case
Roxanne P. Case
Trisha L. Casey
Kelly L. Cash
Regina F. Cash
Kathryn E. Cassady
Tami R. Cassaro
Betty C. Castigliola
Carmen G. Castilla
Traci M. Castille
Pamela L. Castle
Lesley G. Casto
Caroline H. Catchings
Jessica E. Catchings
Patricia A. Catchings
Kimberly G. Causey
Lauren E. Cavalier
Stephanie B. Cavender
Lila E. Caves
Rhonda R. Caviedes
Shari Cavin
Suzanne W. Cervantes
Julie E. Chaffin
Erin O. Chalk
Victoria M. Chamberlain
Brandy L. Chamblee
Amy L. Champagne
Patricia C. Champagne
Ann R. Chandler
Anna M. Chandler
Lisa J. Chandler
Cynthia A. Chandler-Snell
Diala H. Chaney
Tracy A. Chapman
Yvonne K. Chapman
Jeanna D. Chappell
Nita L. Chase
Patricia D. Chatelain
Geraldine J. Chayer
LaToya Cherry
Sloan N. Chesney
Sandra R. Chesnut
Elizabeth H. Chesser
Donna M. Chesteen
Chelsea H. Chicosky
Suzanne L. Childress
Joyce I. Chiles
Laura S. Chism
Elizabeth A. Chisolm
Kristy L. Christen
Dana R. Christensen
Jamie L. Christian
Jessa K. Christian
Amy V. Christina
Lynne Christopher
Demeka Church
Lisa E. Circeo
Elizabeth A. Citrin
Barbara W. Clark
Bethany P. Clark
Carla J. Clark
Elizabeth L. Clark
Geneva J. Clark
Mary Kathryn R. Clark
Peyton B. Clark
Shannon F. Clark
Tara S. Clark
Linda F. Clausen
Beth C. Clay
Shallanda J. Clay
Karen G. Clay
Kathryn D. Clay
Monica J. Clay
Bridgett M. Clayton
Rebekah S. Clayton
Anna C. Clemmer
Lindsay K. Clemons
Rachelle R. Cleveland
Tara S. Clifford
Latisha N. Clinkscales
Anita C. Clinton

Stacy H. Clinton
Kay B. Cobb
Madison E. Coburn
Clara Cochran
Margaret E. Cocke
Angela Y. Cockerham
Corrie W. Cockrell
Courtney E. Cockrell
Susan E. Coco
Kimberly S. Coggin
Revia N. Cohen
Cynthia D. Cohly
Kathryn H. Colbert
Ashlee E. Cole
Megan A. Cole
Royce M. Cole
Shundral H. Cole
Alice W. Coleman
Kassie A. Coleman
Linda F. Coleman
Ikeecia L. Colenberg
Katharine R. Colletta
Katherine B. Collier
Betty T. Collins
Beverly D. Collins
Condrea M. Collins
Deborah L. Collins
Freida G. Collins
Gena N. Collins
Jennifer H. Collins
Kandi K. Collins
Laura E. Collins
Shameca S. Collins
Shannon B. Collins
Suzanne M. Collipp
Lisa D. Collums
Judge Dorothy W. Colom
Allison R. Colon
Deidre L. Colson
Jamee E. Comans
Gwen G. Combs
Su-Lyn Combs
Jean A. Comley
Caroline C. Commer
Christine A. Commiskey
Priscilla C. Conerly
Mary Ann Connell
Mary Ann S. Connell
Megan B. Conner
Mary M. Conville
Kathleen A. Conway
Ashley H. Cook
Cecelia R. Cook
Jamie E. Cook
Kathleen S. Cook
Margaret M. Cook
Nancy M. Cook
Sarah L. Cook
Joseph M. Cook
Suzanne H. Cooke
Lucy R. Coolidge
Elissa M. Coombs
Judge LaRita M. Cooper-Stokes
Linda F. Cooper
Rhonda C. Cooper
Subrina S. Cooper
Marie S. Cope
Charles P. Copeland
Meta S. Copeland
Susan S. Copeland
Megan N. Copley
Theresa H. Cordell
Jayne D. Corley
Mary H. Cosby
Laura C. Cosgray
Mary C. Cossar
Lauren A. Costa
Marilyn L. Costa
Judge Mary B. Cotton
Cathy C. Coughlin
Mackenzie A. Coulter

Sharon A. Counts
Emily K. Courteau
Polly J. Covington
Rebecca B. Cowan
Meryl L. Cowan
Ashley N. Cox
Colleen A. Cox
Janet T. Cox
Melanie H. Cox
Jessica L. Cox
LeeAnne M. Cox
Rachel A. Coxwell
Cathrine A. Craig
Loretta Crane
Lyn P. Crawford
Meredith D. Crawford
Michelle S. Crawford
Brittany L. Crawford
Linda H. Crawley
Casey A. Creasey
Ellen M. Creel
Kelly H. Creely
Jami L. Crews
Laura J. Crissey
Chelsea C. Crittenden
Dorothy L. Crocker
Frances P. Croft
Marcy B. Croft
Julie E. Cropp
Dawn R. Crosby
Wanda W. Cross
Alona R. Croteau
Lynda M. Crouse
Gail A. Crowell
Jennifer R. Crowson
Jessica C. Culpepper
Susan W. Culpepper
Alexis D. Culver
Michelle P. Cumberland
Sarah E. Cummings
Theresa L. Cummings
Susan O. Cumpton
Hazel K. Cunningham
Merritt E. Cunningham
Margaret O. Cupples
Kathrine C. Curren
Gaye N. Currie

D

Melissa G. Dabar
Emily C. Dabney
Lisa J. Dale
Sarah R. Daley
Shawna D. Dalrymple
Mary L. Damare
Amanda T. Daniels
Judge Vicki B. Daniels
Meta C. Danzey
Leigh A. Darby
Tracee O. Darby
Alison A. Darsey
Elizabeth Rhae R. Darsey
Christina F. Daugherty
Marilyn H. David
Deborah Davidson
P T. Davidson
Courtney T. Davis
Cynthia D. Davis
Dareth C. Davis
Deborah S. Davis
Jasmine J. Davis
Kimberly C. Davis
Larissa A. Davis
Linda C. Davis
Mary L. Davis
K E. Davis
Lyonnette M. Davis
Madeline K. Davis
Margaret N. Davis
Marjorie P. Davis, BS, JD
Mary B. Davis

Rhonda L. Davis
Teyona M. Davis
Zaritta J. Davis
Nakimuli O. Davis-Primer
Kashonda L. Day
Maria E. de Gracia
Elizabeth R. de Gruy
Brittany H. Dean
Shuntal S. Dean
Elise E. Deano
Dana G. Dearman
Stacy C. Deas
Heather S. Deaton
Julianne F. Decker
Elizabeth L. Decoux
Candace M. Deer
Deborah S. Dees
June L. DeHart
Lyn M. Del Caro
Linda S. DeLancey
Mignon A. DeLashmet
Virginia Y. Deliman
Kimberly C. Delk
Sara E. DeLoach
Jonathan R. DeLuca
Katina S. Demoran
Rebecca P. Denham
Susan D. Denley
Darrian A. Denman
Mary M. Dennis
Mono M. Dennis
Padrick D. Dennis
Sara F. Dent
Sandra F. DePriest
Betty S. DeRossette
Navketan K. Desai
Holly M. Descant
Kimberly S. DeShazo
Susan F. Desmond
Jill A. Deutchman
Melanie B. Devlin
Kimberly M. DeVries
Sherrie W. Dewease
Sherrie L. DeWolf
Martha A. Diaz
Patricia A. Dicke
Kelly C. Dicken
Janet W. Dickens
Tiffany N. Dickenson
Becca U. Dickerson
Claire T. Dickerson
Robin L. Dickerson
Sarah L. Dickey
Shirley W. DiConcilio
Melissa B. DiFatta
Cassandra G. Dillon
Jessica L. Dilmore
Marielle E. Dirkx
Kelsey L. Dismukes
Laura H. Dixon
Linda M. Dixon
Louisa O. Dixon
Melba L. Dixon
Rebecca V. Dixon
Rebecca Shantel Dixon
Teresa A. Dixon
Melanie T. Dobbs
S Kay F. Dodge
Judge Lisa P. Dodson
Olivia L. Dodson
Lyn B. Dodson
Barbara C. Dogan
Kristin M. Doherty
Carolyn Dohn
Barbara M. Dollarhide
Emily C. Donaldson
Allyson H. Doran
Bailey H. Dorsey
Vallrie L. Dorsey
Sally B. Doty
Shelly Doucet

Jennifer A. Doughty
Stephanie Dovalina
Ruth A. Dover
Stephenie J. Dowdle
Lindsay T. Dowdle
Kelli M. Dowell
Chesney B. Doyle
Ursula T. Doyle
Carmen B. Drake
Paige F. Draper
Brooke N. Driskell
Lindsey T. Druhan
Beverly F. Druitt
Merideth J. Drummond
Judge Paula E. Drungole
Carrie H. Dry
Cynthia C. Dubrow
Ashley H. Duck
Kimberly Dudenbostel
Kimberly S. Duffy
Marian F. Dulaney
Sue E. Dulin
Kelly K. Dunbar
Wylene W. Dunbar
Nicole B. Dunlap
Patricia F. Dunmore
Linda J. Dunn
Caylan D. Dunnells
Jessica M. Dupont
Adrienne I. Dupre
Lynn P. Dupree
Maryellen Duprel
Keyla M. Duran
Aimee E. Durel
Rosemary G. Durfey
Lisa M. Durlacher
Cheli K. Durr
Lacey M. Duskin
Kathleen F. Duthu
Margaret N L. Dutton

E

Melody H. Eagan
Brittney S. Eakins
Kabah S. Ealy
Stacey E. Earnest
Mary J. Easley
Michelle D. Easterling
Connie M. Easterly
Susan A. Eaton
Virginia B. Eaton
Maudine G. Eckford
Marian W. Edelman
Stephanie Edgar
Macey L. Edmondson
Tabitha P. Edmonson
La'Verne Edney
Annie M. Edwards
Cecile C. Edwards
Jabrina C. Edwards
Jamie N. Edwards
Jennifer C. Edwards
Susan E. Egeland
Jennie A. Eichelberger
Kate S. Eidt
Kathleen H. Eiler
Hadley G. Eisenberger
Amy K. Elder
Cynthia L. Eldridge
Dimitra L. Eleopoulos
Wendy H. Ellard
NeShondria D. Ellerby
Toni J. Ellington
Briley M. Elliott
Katherine H. Elliott
Martha A. Elliott
Michelle L. Elliott
Shannon S. Elliott
Dianne H. Ellis
Rhonda H. Ellis
Sarah A. Ellis

Tanya D. Ellis
Tara P. Ellis
Susan L. Ellner
Sarah K. Embry
Elizabeth H. Emmett
Mary F. England
Deirdre M. Enright
Sarah L. Entrekin
Julie A. Epps
Barbara B. Erickson
Abigail P. Ersin
Katherine D. Ervin
Margaret Eschbach
Christie L. Estes
S L. Etheridge
Barbara N. Ethredge
Cecily L. Ethridge
Cynthia T. Eubank
Anitra L. Eubanks
Loni N. Eustace-McMillan
Camille Henick Evans
Carole W. Evans
Dana H. Evans
Stephanie J. Evans
Rhonda S. Evans
Kim E. Evers
Wendy G. Evinger
Eden C. Ezell

F

Laura E. Fahy
Bailey R. Fair
Sue H. Fairbank
Victoria A. Fairman
Kendall L. Fann
Katherine K. Farese
Paula S. Farese
Alexis L. Farmer
Casey B. Farmer
Tanza C. Farr
Alyssa D. Farrell
Becky A. Farrell
Abigayle C. Farris
Zora E. Farris
Judge Catherine L. Farris-Carter
Michele B. Fassbender
Patricia J. Faver
Shannon F. Favre
Adrienne B. Fazio
D E. Featherston
Celeste E. Feder
Amy C. Felder
Margaret A. Ferguson
Molly E. Fergusson
Faye E. Fernandes
Sherry S. Fernandez
Jessica F. Ferrante
Stacy Ferraro
Kenoaha Ferrell
Tina H. Ferrell
Pamela A. Ferrington
Emily K. Ferris
Emily S. Fertig
Kathleen R. Fewel
Nancy S. Field
Cameron L. Fields
Jill K. Fields
Karen D. Fineran
Kelly E. Firing
Robert A. Fischer
Robin V. Fiser
Amy K. Fisher
Angelita E. Fisher
Elizabeth A. Fisher
Robbie D. Fisher
Trudy D. Fisher
Valerie F. Fisher
Aleita S. Fitch
Lynn Fitch
Kimberly H. Fleitz

Kristen M. Fletcher
Alison L. Flint
Charlinda M. Florence
Serena R. Flowers
Evelyn Floyd
Michele H. Floyd
Rebecca A. Floyd
Susan M. Floyd
Patty S. Flynn
Kendra R. Fokakis
Lean Y. Follett
Jean M. Folsom
Carnelia P. Fondren
Meltory D. Fondren
Shana D. Fondren
Amanda P. Fontenot
Kathryn G. Ford
Mary K. Ford
Caroline K. Forks
Ashley T. Fortenberry
Memrie M. Fortenberry
Rachelle L. Fortenberry
Sheila R. Fortenberry
Sayward E. Fortner
Allyson B. Foster
Amy C. Foster
Kiana L. Foster
Betty R. Fox
Sara M. Fox
Jennifer M. Frank
Brittany B. Frankel
Judge Beverley M. Franklin
Shirlethia V. Franklin
Tonya P. Franklin
Lisa N. Frascogna
Dianne B. Fraser
Joanna M. Frederick
Zelma M. Frederick
Joyce M. Freeland
April R. Freeman
Genara D. Freeman-Morris
Kristina L. Freese
Katie W. Freiberger
Megan D. French
Elizabeth L. Friary
Meredith S. Friday
Renetha L. Frieson
Margo R. Friloux
Amanda Fritz
Mary K. Frost
Sharla J. Frost
Elizabeth M. Fruge
Allison P. Fry
Jenna K. Fugarino
Dawn E. Fulce
Katy E. Fulghum
Mary B. Fuller
Mary J. Fuller
Joyce Funches
Teselyn M. Funches
Glenda F. Funchess
Anna C. Furr
Karen E. Futch
Elizabeth J. Futrell

G

P E. Gable
Jan F. Gadow
Chareka M. Gadson
Amanda L. Galle
Elizabeth D. Gamble
Amelia B. Gamble
Judge Deborah J. Gambrell
Clair M. Gammill
Patricia C. Gandy
Stephanie L. Ganucheau
Janis L. Garcia
Stephanie D. Garcia
Gloria M. Gardner
Melissa L. Gardner
Sarah E. Gardner

Marianne C. Garner
Rebecca B. Garner
Sharon M. Garner
John S. Garner
Mary Beebe S. Garrard
Bernetta M. Garrett
Wesley H. Garrett
Jan D. Garrick
Nancy E. Garrison
Megan E. Garrott
Christy R. Garth
Melissa S. Gaskin
Beverly S. Gates
Elizabeth Gates
Tanisha M. Gates
Brandi D. Gatewood
Cheri T. Gatlin
Leslie M. Gattas
Eileen A. Gault
Virginia S. Gautier
Rachael L. Gautier
Mary M. Gay
Kaeley N. Gemmill
Gretchen L. Gentry
Mitzi L. George
Tena S. George
Katy T. Gerber
Pamela S. Gerity
Mary L. Gervin
Ellen K. Giarratana
Laura L. Gibbes
Ariana N. Gibbs
Debra H. Gibbs
Katrina M. Gibbs
Mary J. Gibson
Ginger E. Gibson
Kandis C. Gibson
Robin G. Gibson
Natalie J. Gideon
Lindsey J. Gilbert
Kathryn R. Gilchrist
Judge Debra M. Giles
Lara E. Gill
Lisa J. Gill
Jessica L. Gillentine
Jamita Q. Gilleylen
Carole C. Gilliam
Meghan A. Gilliam
Vicki L. Gilliam
Jane C. Gillis
Jennifer L. Gillis
Lana E. Gillon
RaToya J. Gilmer
Meta P. Ginn
Lora S. Gipson
Sharon D. Gipson
Laura W. Givens
Whitney W. Gladden
Stacey L. Gladding
Laura M. Glaze
Teri D. Gleason
Stephanie C. Gobert
Patty N. Godfrey
Teresa M. Goetsch
Breanna F. Goff
Kathryn P. Goff
Corby M. Goforth
Trena N. Goggans
Patti C. Golden
Carolyn E. Golding
Tamekia R. Goliday
Stacey W. Golmon
Heather N. Goodlett
Alison K. Goodman
Laura D. Goodson
Aubrey D. Goodwin
Nancy J. Goodwin
Charisse C. Gordon
Kathleen S. Gordon
Meri B. Gordon
Ta'Shia S. Gordon

Kimberly G. Gore
Judge Janace H. Goree
Joy H. Goundas
Amy C. Gowan
Meredith Gowan-Le Goff
Pamela N. Grady
Allison J. Graham
Billie J. Graham
Judge Veldore Y. Graham
Lori J. Graham
Mona P. Graham
Bonnie P. Granger
Bridgette N. Grant
Meredith D. Grant
Priscilla Grantham
Margaret S. Gratz
Deanna L. Graves
Joy W. Graves
Tiffany M. Graves
DeVoyce S. Gray
Lucy B. Gray
Rosalind D. Gray
Sally G. Gray
Angela J. Grayson
Phyllis M. Grayson
Lori S. Grayson
Cheri D. Green
Donna P. Green
Gloria J. Green
Jennifer L. Green
Jennifer B. Green
Judge Tomie T. Green
Karen O. Green
Lynne K. Green
Angela D. Greene
Stacy N. Greene
Chimeaka L. Greenwood
Haley F. Gregory
Rebekah B. Gregory
Sarah E. Gregory
Candace W. Gregory-Mayberry
Julie J. Gresham
Ann L. Griffin
Ashley P. Griffin
Martha R. Griffin
Piper D. Griffin
Ravonda L. Griffin
Roslyn N. Griffin
Whitney J. Griffin
Beverly P. Griffith
Mary M. Griffith
Laura A. Grifka
Barbara G. Grimes
Kellie D. Grizzell
Judge Tiffany P. Grove
Alexandra S. Gruber
Lori D. Gruver
Jennifer R. Guckert
Susan M. Guerieri
Cristina Guerrero
Judy M. Guice
Elena L. Guida
Alison L. Guider
Aubrey B. Gulledge
Laura H. Gullett
Anne B. Gullick
Amanda C. Gunasekara
Ashley W. Gunn
Pamela E. Gunter
Donna L. Gurley
Frances S. Gustafson
Raynetra L. Gustavis
Kimberly L. Guthrie
Latuesday P. Guy
Erin D. Guyton

H

Karen N. Haarala
Caroline E. Haas
Psonya C. Hackett
Elizabeth R. Hadley

Erina H. Hagy
Adrienne Haines
Jennifer D. Hale
Polly M. Haley
Judge Debbra K. Halford
Alicia S. Hall
Anna J. Hall
Candace L. Hall
Heather L. Hall
Jacinta A. Hall
Jamie M. Hall
Diana J. Hall
Jennifer G. Hall
Joyce Hall
Mary E. Hall
Linnea K. Hall
Melanie G. Hall
Pamela L. Hall
Pelicia E. Hall
Robin A. Hall
Cara E. Hall
Marie W. Halvatzis
Jessica M. Hamadeh
Brandy B. Hambright
Nancy C. Hamby
Kelly E. Hamill
Brandi R. Hamilton
Jerlyn C. Hamilton
Lydia H. Hamlet
Jacqueline K. Hammack
Mary H. Hammett
Jan W. Hammond
Sarah L. Hammons
Kimberly M. Hampton
Christian W. Hancock
Christina A. Hancock
Helen Hancock
Pamela L. Hancock
Patricia A. Hancock
Valarie B. Hancock
Leslie M. Hand
Kye C. Handy
Carole J. Haney
Diane P. Haney
Kim M. Haney
Sloane J. Hankins
Shannon D. Hanley
Patricia M. Hanrahan
Macy D. Hanson
Kathleen P. Harbour
Frances Hardage
Katina M. Hardee
Natalie H. Harden
Rebecca L. Harden
Ka'Leya Q. Hardin
June Hardwick
Dawn C. Hardy
Kimberly P. Hardy
Sarah F. Hardy
Lynn E. Hare
Allyson D. Hargett
Candice C. Hargett
Kaci J. Hargett
Jane C. Harkins
Waverly A. Harkins
Bonnie K. Harkness
C J. Harkness
Nicole M. Harlan
Lauren B. Harless
Sage E. Harless
Kimberly T. Harlin
Brander C. Harper
Melissa M. Harper
Shelby S. Harper
Jamie V. Harrell
Louise Harrell
Sarah K. Harrell
Shelley M. Harrigill
Amethyst Harris
Amy S. Harris
Ashley N. Harris

Bridget K. Harris
Clarissa N. Harris
Greta M. Harris
Hartwell V. Harris
Jennifer S. Harris
Jennifer A. Harris
Laurel L. Harris
Lindsey B. Harris
Lisa Harris
Michele P. Harris
Peggy Y. Harris
Christe R. Harris-Leech
Janet M. Harrison
Jennifer S. Harrison
Melissa A. Harrison
Sarah L. Harrison
Lori K. Harris-Ransom
Kaylin L. Hart
Carrie M. Hartfield
Tammy G. Harthcock
Allison K. Hartman
Amanda M. Hartman
Barbara E. Harvey
Lady M S. Harvey
Teresa E. Harvey
Victoria M. Harvey
Judge Tanya L. Hasbrouck
Laura S. Hash
Katie H. Hassell
Glynis H. Hatcher
Roberta L. Haughton
Agnieszka M. Haupt
Julie A. Hawkins
Rebecca W. Hawkins
Jennifer L. Hawks
Emily W. Haxton
Marcia L. Hayden
Leyser Q. Hayes
Ylani A. Hayes
Chandley Hayes-Crawford
Erica S. Haymer
Glenda R. Haynes
Natasha N. Hazlett
Katherine Headley
Angela B. Healy
Amanda B. Heard
Cheryl M. Hearn
Diana D. Heather
Taylor A. Heck
Barbara F. Hederman
Hannah R. Heffernan
Melissa R. Heidelberg
Ann M. Heidke
Kasee S. Heisterhagen
Emiko F. Hemleben
Sara J. Hemphill
Carol L. Henderson
Diane H. Henderson
Flordia M. Henderson
Heidi M. Henderson
Jeanne P. Henderson
Jocelyn V. Henderson
Katherine W. Henderson
Sharon D. Henderson
Tammy M. Henderson
Tiffanee W. Henderson
Laura Henderson-Courtney
Vera G. Hendon
Ashley H. Hendren
Casey L. Hendricks
Christy C. Hendrix
Dawn R. Hendrix
Mary C. Henkel
Ida C. Henley
Keri Henley
Rebecca E. Henley
Vivian C. Henley
Judy N. Henry
Kimberly M. Henry
Mackenzie E. Henry
Camille M. Hensley

Desiree C. Hensley
Cassie S. Henson
Deborah S. Henton
Jessica L. Hept
Jennifer W. Herbert
Alison B. Herlihy
Julie S. Herlihy
Patricia Herlihy
Katherine A. Herndon Barton
Lindsey U. Herr
Hannah K. Herrin
Shari K. Herring
Tracie D. Herring
Victoria B. Herring
Tina L. Herron
Bethany N. Hesser
Jennifer R. Hesser
Catherine A. Hester
Deborah K. Hester
Kathryn H. Hester
Laura D. Heusel
Susan L. Hewitt
Deetric M. Hicks
Jenessa J. Hicks
Judge Carlyn M. Hicks
Malea A. Higdon
Michelle T. High
Kristie M. Hightower
Barbara A. Hilburn
Caitlin J. Hill
Cassi G. Hill
Faith R. Hill
Sandra J. Hill
Kathryn G. Hill
Suprena L. Hill
Tina L. Hill
Lauren R. Hillery
Erica R. Hilliard
Bertha M. Hillman
Charmaine S. Hilton
Amy J. Hinton
Victoria L. Hinton
Pamela M. Hitchcock
Deborah Ho
Shannon D. Hoagland
Elizabeth C. Hocker
Sheila J. Hode
Sharon H. Hodge
Donna J. Hodges
Melissa K. Hodges
Peggy M. Hodges
Tametrice E. Hodges
Rachel L. Hodges
Jennifer A. Hoffman
Victoria J. Hoggatt
Christina H. Holcomb
N V. Holladay
LaDonna C. Holland
Wendy C. Hollingsworth
Lacy A. Hollins
Andreka P. Hollins
Kerissa S. Hollis
Tangala L. Hollis
Annette M. Hollowell
Jenna D. Holmes
Margaret W. Holmes
Mary L. Holmes
Ursula Y. Holmes
Sadarie C. Holston
Dannah C. Holtzclaw
Sarah D. Holz
Caroline S. Hommell
Katherine H. Hood
Kendra C S. Hood
Elizabeth G. Hooper
Paige M. Hooper
Judge Adrienne Hooper-Wooten
Jena J. Hoover
Leigh A. Hoover
Jessica S. Hoppe

Melanie H. Hopper
Deanisha F. Hopson
Dorothy G. Horecky
Shireen Hormozdi
Debora L. Horn
Leigh Horn
Allison E. Horne
Glenda B. Horne
I K. Horne-Murry
Gay Horne-Nelson
Elizabeth A. Horton
Kristen A. Horton
Tiffany Horton-Williams
Diandra Hosey
Catherine M. Houlahan
Maria S. House
Heather M. Houston
Iyona H. Houston
Katherine Hovas
Cinnamon M. Howard
Minnie P. Howard
Claire I. Howard
Cynthia C. Howell
S.J. Howell
Judge Lisa J. Howell
Karen E. Howell
Sabrina D. Howell
Susan E. Howell
Katherine L. Howie
Kimberly N. Howland
Angela M. Huck
Amelia K. Huckins
Linda W. Huddleston
Aa'Keela L. Hudnall
Amy L. Hudson
Carolle R. Hudson
Carrie G. Hudson
Collen L. Hudson
Josie M. Hudson
Johnnie R. Hudson
Shalanda R. Hudson
Shannah T. Hudson
Suzanne C. Hudson
Nicole C. Huffman
Jordan L. Hughes
Sandra J. Hughes
Eleanordawn R. Hughes
Rivers H. Humber
Caroline F. Hunsicker
Courtney C. Hunt
Catherine O. Hunter
Kelly P. Hunter
Lora E. Hunter
Stella M. Hurtt
Emily H. Huseth
Julie L. Hussey
Penelope C. Hutcherson
Laurie J. Hutchings
Rebecca H. Hutchins
Lauren J. Hutchins
Natalie S. Hutto
Robbin W. Hutton
Elizabeth E. Hyde
Julie D. Hynum

I

Lois P. Ice
Sarah E. Iiams
Francis D. Ingram
Kathleen E. Ingram
Stephanie J. Ingram
Danielle D. Ireland
Judge Tomika H. Irving
Lyndsy L. Irwin
LaKeysha G. Isaac
Caroline K. Ivanov
William C. Ivison
Naomi A. Ivker

J

Jamie F. Jacks

Amy L. Jackson
L A. Jackson
Ava N. Jackson
Brenda G. Jackson
Deborah A. Jackson
Janice T. Jackson
Jessica M. Jackson
Joy R. Jackson
Mary E. Jackson
Molly M. Jackson
Morgan K. Jackson
Patti A. Jackson
LaShundra B. Jackson-Winters
Catherine H. Jacobs
Donna B. Jacobs
Gina M. Jacobs
Kimberly S. Jacobs
Shruti Jaishankar
Ceola James
Faye James
Trudy F. James
Imogene M. Jamison
Ollie F. Jamison
Nancy Leigh T. Janous
Debbie L. Jared
M C. Jarman
Lauren A. Jee
Carolyn W. Jefferson
Connie S. Jelliffe
Forrest A. Jenkins
Sonja A. Jenkins
Emily A. Jennings
Mary B. Jensen
LaToya T. Jeter
Adria H. Jetton
Enghry K. Jewell
Yvonne W. Jicka
Julia B. Jimenez
Gwendolyn D. Jimison
Cynthia S. Joachim
Mara M. Joffe
Scherry L. Joffe
Lisa S. Johns
Amanda N. Johnson
Ashley A. Johnson
Bethany B. Johnson
Bettie R. Johnson
Camila A. Johnson
Candace D. Johnson
Cara M. Johnson
Jane C. Johnson
Carrie E. Johnson
Elissa F. Johnson
Jacqueline M. Johnson
Jennifer I. Johnson
Jennifer H. Johnson
Judge Vernita K. Johnson
Judith J. Johnson
Kanesha A. Johnson
Karen G. Johnson
Keia M. Johnson
Kimberly M. Johnson
Kathryn W. Johnson
Kristina M. Johnson
Kristi H. Johnson
Letitia S. Johnson
Lori M. Johnson
Lucy R. Johnson
Margarett A. Johnson
Melinda O. Johnson
Mitzi C. Johnson
Nancy P. Johnson
Richerish D. Johnson
Sabrina L. Johnson
Shakeba Johnson
Sheryl S. Johnson
Teresa P. Johnson
Tiffany G. Johnson
Tressa V. Johnson
Elta L. Johnston
Lori A. Johnston

Zenora Joiner
Rebecca M. Jolly
Alyson B. Jones
Anastasia G. Jones
Andrea C. Jones
Andreanna D. Jones
Angela Jones
Ashley D. Jones
Brenda C. Jones
Christi G. Jones
Christy D. Jones
Danielle B. Jones
Devin M. Jones
Diane Y. Jones
Drew D. Jones
Elizabeth F. Jones
Kimberly S. Jones
Lindsay K. Jones
Mattye Ann G. Jones
Nicole R. Jones
Paige C. Jones
Pearlene Jones
Peggy A. Jones
Sarah E. Jones
Scarlett A. Jones
Shannon R. Jones
Sheila A. Jones
Sheneka A. Jones
Shirley N. Jones
Stephanie R. Jones
Susan S. Jones
Valorri C. Jones
Vanessa J. Jones
Victoria R. Jones
Virginia T. Jones
Melissa L. Jones
Shannon M. Jones
Lindsay A. Jones
Andrea C. Jones Rogers
Amy D. Jordan
Constance Q. Jordan
Lou S. Jordan
Margaret K. Jordan
Rosalind H. Jordan
Carrie A. Jourdan
Juliet Jowett
Evangeline E. Joy
Helen F. Joyce
Ginger J. Joyner
Heather B. Joyner
Mary C. Joyner
Sarah C. Jubb
Rebecca K. Jude
Patricia B. Judice
Stephanie C. Jue
Kanika Juneja
Poonam Juneja
Chelsi P. Junkin
Blair H. Jussely

K

Cecily L. Kaffer
Jennifer H. Kahn
Johanna Kalb
Cassandra H. Kalupa
Jane H. Kany
Sampada Kapoor
Paula N. Kasul
Nan T. Katsaboulas
Laura H. Katzenmeyer
Elizabeth A. Kaufman
Christen E. Kazery
Briana S. Keeler
Christine S. Keenan
Rebecca A. Keith
Patricia E. Keith
Victoria O. Keith
Tara L. Kellar
Catherine H. Keller
Lauren E. Kelley
Maria K. Kelley

Alison O. Kelly
Ann H. Kelly
Elizabeth B. Kelly
Helen B. Kelly
Kimberly B. Kelly
Christina J. Kelsey
Katherine V. Kemp
Brittani C. Kendrick
Cynthia L. Kendrick
Linda B. Keng
Blair L. Kennedy
Bree R. Kennedy
Deborah D. Kennedy
Gwendolyn M. Kennedy
Kristi D. Kennedy
Shirley T. Kennedy
Amanda B. Kennerly
Elizabeth R. Kenwright
Helen H. Kenwright
Katherine S. Kerby
Carolyn C. Kessinger
Claire W. Ketner
Morgan M. Keup
Leigh A. Key
Suzanne G. Keys
Tamara P. Kidd
Rebecca L. Kidder
Jennifer S. Kiesewetter
Jennifer H. Kilburn
Catherine V. Kilgore
Allison W. Killebrew
Emily C. Killion
Tiffany L. Kilpatrick
Sungshil Kim
Denise S. Kimble
Gretchen W. Kimble
Jennifer B. Kimble
Mable S. Kimbrough
Elyse M. Kinder
Bobbie L. King
Erin N. King
Gidget H. King
Kimberly C. King
Janice L. King
Melissa A. King
Natalie R. King
Pamela B. King
Katherine A. Kingren
Karen L. King-Vanek
Ronna D. Kinsella
Wendy C. Kinsey
Amber L. Kipfmiller
Martha A. Kirby
Revonda A. Kirby
Leslie Kiriakos
Myra E. Kirkland
Amanda G. Kisner
Kimberly K. Kitchens
Kendra L. Kite
Judge Allison P. Kizer
Mary P. Kleinman
Mari E. Kleven
Parker S. Kline
Amy M. Klotz
Brace L. Knox
Kellie W. Koenig
Jeanne M. Koger
Heather A. Kolasinsky
Lisa A. Koon
Sarah K. Koon
Abbie E. Koonce
Judith E. Koons
Nancy P. Kossman
Helen V. Kramer
Nancy Krecker
Patricia A. Krueger
Emily W. Kruger
Robin C. Kruger
Deborah D. Kuchler
Mary M. Kuhlmann
Joanna B. Kuhn

Juanita P. Kuhner
Eileen Kuo
Angela M. Kupenda
Candace H. Kyle
Dawn B. Kyle

L

Sarah D. Labosier
Lucy C. Lacey
Kathryn A. Lachowsky-Khan
Meredith M. Lackey
Kathy O. Ladipo
April C. Ladner
Lynn P. Ladner
Linda S. Laher
Judge Ann H. Lamar
Mary M. Lambert
Dana L. Lammers
Anastasia L. Lampton
Sidney E. Lampton
Daphne M. Lancaster
Rhonda M. Landrum
Amanda B. Landry
Ashley N. Lane
Erin P. Lane
Margaret M. Lane
Sherra H. Lane
Karen M. Laneaux
Stephanie R. Lang
Tara L. Lang
Mary E. Langenbacker
Amanda S. Langford
Walterine Langford
Elizabeth Y. Langley
Katherine B. Langston
Rebecca M. Langston
Eleanor G. LaPorte
Margie C. Largent
Rachel M. Lary
Anne H. Latino
Cynthia L. Law
Lauren O. Lawhorn
Sara K. Lawrence
Taylor M. Lawrence
Chari-Elyse Lawrence
Ky'sha K. Lawson
Penny B. Lawson
Maxine Lawson-Conway
Marsha L. Lay
Lindsey E. Lazinsky
Ann C. Lazzara
Michelle C. Le
Caroline Q. Leary
Mary W. Leary
Alexandra LeBron
Denise M. Ledet
Leah N. Ledford
Ann C. Lee
Avery M. Lee
Catherine W. Lee
Chandra T. Lee
Cynthia A. Lee
Cynthia T. Lee
Davetta C. Lee
V D. Lee
Heather A. Lee
Judy D. Lee
Jennifer S. Lee
Jenny C. Lee
Leslie S. Lee
Raina A. Lee
Stephanie S. Lee
McCann E. LeFeve
Vicki R. Leggett
Mary J. Lemon
Angela K. Lenderman
Jessica M. Lennard
Julie E. Lennon
Rachael A. Lenoir
Kimberly R. Lentz
Anna M. Lenz

Ina B. Leonard
Mildred J. LeSure
Sandra K. Levick
Kristen M. Levins
Laura Mae S. Levitt
Claudia V. Levy
Nicole T. Lewellyn
Katherine E. Lewey Carr
Ashura S. Lewis
Audra P. Lewis
Carina Y. Lewis
Carolyn A. Lewis
Chelsea C. Lewis
Judge Jannie M. Lewis
Marilyn Kay Lewis
LaShundra M. Lewis
Laura Leigh Lewis
Patricia R. Lewis
Pauline S. Lewis
Shanda L. Lewis
Brandi B. Lewis
Courtney L. Leyes
Leigh C. Liao
Gloria J. Liddell
Nancy Liddell
Sarah J. Liddy
Stacie B. Lieberman
Cynthia P. Liebling
Melody L. Light
Kara L. Lincoln
Kaara L. Lind
Lisa Lindley
Meda B. Lindley
Emily K. Lindsay
Mary Catherine E. Lindsay
Jennifer S. Lindsey
Keli Q. Lindsey
Linda B. Lipe
Victoria L. Lippincott
Whitney H. Lipscomb
Linda D. Litke
Nicole G. Litton
Wendi D. Litton
Kathryn A. Littrell
Maria Liu
Anna M. Livingston
Karen Livingston-Wilson
Erica J. Lloyd
Brenda C. Locke
Leighanne E. Lockett
Sharon G. Locklear
Virginia L. LoCoco
Gladys H. Lofton
Laura A. Logan
Blythe K. Lollar
Lauren C. Lomax
Sarah R. Lomenick
Jessica T. London-Roundtree
Betty J. Long
Brenda G. Long
Jessica L. Long
Cheryl P. Long
Amy E. Lott
Deneise T. Lott
Deborah E. Love
Julie L. Love
Kristen N. Love
Caroline C. Loveless
Chloe M. Lowe
Sandra Lowe
Sherry L. Lowe
Christine Elise H. Lowery
Gail W. Lowery
Victoria A. Lowery
Clare A. Lowman
Janelle M. Lowrey
Jolene M. Lowry
Joan L. Lucas
Lisa D. Luke
Judge Richelle Lumpkin
Mary A. Lumpkin

Joan E. Lund
Ann E. Lundy
Carolan D. Luning
Susan E. Lusher
Sarah K. Lusk
Amber E. Luttrell
Maria L. Lyles
Theressia A. Lyons
Kathleen S. Lyons

M

Meagan L. MacBean
Jara C. MacDermott
Janet L. MacDonell
Stephanie B. Macvaugh
Anna K. Maddan
Nancy M. Maddox
Selene D. Maddox
Magnolia Madsen
Jasmine D. Magee
Jean S. Magee
Natasha R. Magee-Woods
Jerrie G. Magruder
Eileen M. Maher
Rachel E. Mahoney
Debjani G. Maken
Christy V. Malatesta
Jennifer P. Malik
Betty A. Mallett
Stephanie L. Mallette
Akillie L. Malone
Jessica S. Malone
Leigha L. Malone
Maureen G. Malone
Melissa A. Malouf
Mallory J. Mangold
Kimberly P. Mangum
Sharon M. Mangum
Jana N. Manlove
Christy T. Mann
Sarah W. Mann
Rebecca Mansell
Patricia L. Manson
Cynthia B. Mansour
Lyndsay D. Mapp
Jane L. Mapp
Abigail M. Marbury
Alicia K. Margolis
Brittany T. Marigliano
Kathy L. Marine
Angela L. Marino
Jennifer A. Mark
Robin B. Mark
Ashley J. Markham
Alexandra F. Markov
Ruth F. Maron
Terri L. Marroquin
Sarah E. Mars
Carpenter S. Marsalis
McGehee V. Marsh
Angela G. Marshall
Patricia B. Marshall
Sandra D. Marshall
Alice Howze A. Martin
Brooke T. Martin
Catherine M. Martin
Jacqueline D. Martin
Georgia A. Martin
Greta K. Martin
Haley S. Martin
Heather W. Martin
Jamie P. Martin
Judge Crystal W. Martin
Judy T. Martin
Kathryn S. Martin
Kristen E. Martin
Elizabeth D. Martin
Catoria P. Martin
Vaterria M. Martin
Wendy W. Martin
LaTeshya L. Martin

Desire'e C. Martinelli
Maria Martinez
Heather R. Martin-Herron
Judge Jacqueline E. Mask
Jordan M. Mason
Marsha C. Mason
Mary E. Mason
Venecca G. Mason
Kathy Mason
Jessica L. Massey
Lisa S. Massey
Susan V. Massey
Patricia L. Masters
Karen K. Maston
Valerie T. Matherne
Annette B. Mathis
Ava C. Mathis
Haley B. Mathis
Linda M. Mathis
Katie S. Matison
Marjorie T. Matlock
Rita F. Mattera
Ashlyn B. Matthews
Chrystal M. Matthews
R E. Matthews
Johnell M. Matthews
Maurine B. Mattson
Charlene Mauk-Williams
Patria F. Maulden
Sady E. Mauldin
Emily Lucy A. Maw
Megan F. Mawhorter
Karen A. Maxcy
Miranda L. Maxwell
Ashley M. May
Eloise H. May
Meredith A. Mayberry
Velia A. Mayer
Urura W. Mayers
Leontra M. Mayes
Dennie B. Mayhone
Betty W. Maynard
Mercedes C. Maynor
Chelsey M. Maywalt
Sandra M. McAdams
Courtney E. McAlexander
Carolyn A. McAlister
Mary E. McAlister
Melody McAnally
Margaret P. McArthur
Yvonne S. McCabe
L M. McCain
Tiffany H. McCaleb
Kelly A. McCall
Tara E. McCallum
Brooke L. McCarthy
Aphrodite K. McCarthy
Kelly E. McCarthy
Lauren A. McCarty
Kaylyn H. McClinton
Kelli C. McCloskey
Kimberly D. McCormack
Carrie R. McCormick
Elizabeth S. McCormick
Sarah A. McCormick
Christi R. McCoy
Kalleigh McCoy
Kristian A. McCray
Jessica L. McCreedy
Lauren R. McCrory
Cheryl R. McCullough
Rhonda L. McCullough
Tammie M. McCullough
Sandra M. McDaniel
Sarah A. McDavid
Meredith F. McDermott
April L. McDonald
Judge Ysleta W. McDonald
Judge Deborah A. McDonald
Kathryn C. McDonald
Helen M. McDonald

Shellye V. McDonald
Susan McDonald
Yawanna N. McDonald
Maloree G. McDonough
Leah D. McDowell
Molly F. McEacharn
Cheryl D. McElfish
Anna T. McElroy
Laura C. McElroy
Mary E. McFadyen
Saundra T. McFarland
Shannon S. McFarland
Kristin M. McGee
Tujuana S. McGee
Rhonda A. McGinnis
Lisa B. McGloflin
Lisa C. McGovern
Amelia S. McGowan
Anna E. McGowan
Sarah M. McGrew
Laurin E. McGuffee
Kristi C. McHale
Erica R. McHard
Angel M. McIlrath
Jennifer M. McInerney
Lorraine P. McInnis
Treva L. McInnis
Lisa W. McKay
Mindy McKay
Oona C. McKenzie
Shequeena McKenzie
Erica T. McKinley
Melissa R. McKinney
Tammie L. McKinney-Sledge
Andrea M. McKinnon
Tamara B. McKinnon
Beverly E. McKittrick
Frances L. McLaney
Amy R. McLaughlin
Crystal L. McLaughlin
Maura D. McLaughlin
Nicole H. McLaughlin
Jessica R. McLaurin
Mary C. McLaurin
Julie S. McLemore
Gia N. McLeod
Jo Anne M. McLeod
Katherine R. McLeod
Kelly M. McLeod
Marcia C. McMahan
Kaitlyn J. McMellon
Jordan L. McMichael
Nikita S. McMillian
Joseph R. McMillin
Mollie M. McMillin
Sarah C. McMillin
Alison O. McMinn
Johanna M. McMullan
Regina M. McMullan
Linda McMullen
Stacy A. McMullen
Janet D. McMurtray
Michelle R. McMurtray
Cambri A. McNair
Jaime E. McNair
Kathryn R. McNair
Molly H. McNair
Susan D. McNamara
Shannon D. McNeal
Jessica B. McNeel
Deborah L. McNeely
Monica M. McNeely
Andrea D. McNeil
Keely R. McNulty
Beth B. McNutt
Mary S. McPherson
Nora F S. McRae
Sheena C. McShan
Marcia D. McShane
Natalie K. McSwain
Kimberly S. McSwain

Sidney K. McWilliams
Malenda H. Meacham
Sheri A. Meador
Amanda H. Meadows
Donna M. Meehan
Jacqueline G. Meek
Barbara J. Meeks
Margarette L. Meeks
Lisa L. Meggs
Susan S. Mellen
Patricia F. Melvin
Bonnie H. Menapace
Caroline M. Meng
Kimberly J. Merchant
Susanne A. Merchant
Merritt J. Mercier
Hannalore B. Merritt
LaToya F. Merritt
Ouida L. Meruvia
Kristie L. Metcalfe
Sarah Lane M. Metz
Erin M. Meyer
Margaret A. Meyer
Jane W. Meynardie
Carol P. Michel
Rachel W. Michel
Judge Robin A. Midcalf
Keesha D. Middleton
Margaret O. Middleton
Morgan A. Middleton
Rebecca B. Mighton
Tiffany S. Mikkelson
Heidi S. Milam
Mary E. Milek
Anglenetta Miller
Anna S. Miller
Anna T. Miller
Beverly M. Miller
Ginger M. Miller
Hollie M. Miller
Jane S. Miller
Jennifer L. Miller
Jill R. Miller
Katrina D. Miller
Leanna H. Miller
Lesley G. Miller
Margaret M. Miller
Mary E. Miller
Mary L. Miller
Molly M. Miller
Nancy G. Miller
Tammy N. Miller
Summerann S. Miller
Alysson L. Mills
Katherine Mills
Martha A. Mills
Rebecca S. Mills
Adrian W. Mills
Caryn A. Milner
Michelle B. Mims
Kristen A. Minch
Mary E. Minchew
Chelsea J. Minton
Scanlon F. Minton
Adelyn B. Mintz
May Lipe Z. Mintz
Robin A. Minyard
Morgan G. Miranda
Kimberly-Joy Miri
Amy D. Mitchell
Brenda F. Mitchell
Cynthia I. Mitchell
Julie B. Mitchell
Marissa D. Mitchell
Mary C. Mitchell
Patrice M. Mitchell
Rachel H. Mitchell
Ursula K. Mitchell
Vickie R. Mitchell
Victoria N. Mitchell
Kiana A. Mitchell

Grace W. Mitts
Anna C. Moak
Linda B. Moak
Ann C. Mockbee
Margaret L. Mockbee
Anita K. Modak-Truran
Barbara W. Moffitt
Sandra S. Mohler
Susanna M. Moldoveanu
Jenny J. Moman
Sondra O. Moncure
Mary Emily V. Monroe
Misty W. Monroe
Mary A. Monteith
Shella M. Montgomery
Natalie L. Montgomery
Allison K. Moody
Kathryn K. Moody
Molly J. Moody
Adrienne L. Moore
Amery E. Moore
William H. Moore
Caroline R. Moore
Hollie R. Moore
Jamie L. Moore
Larrissa C. Moore
Laura M. Moore
Pamela A. Moore
Samantha R. Moore
Sherrie L. Moore
Sherry E. Moore
Shirley M. Moore
Tanecka Y. Moore
Madeline T. Morcelle
Micholle W. Mordock
Cynthia P. Moreland
Lauren R. Moreland
Maurcie L. Moren
Christle D. Moreno
Margaret L. Morey
Angela L. Morgan
Bridgette M. Morgan
Brynn P. Morgan
Chase F. Morgan
Hannah B. Morgan
Jade O. Morgan
Jennifer L. Morgan
Kathryn H. Morgan
Kathleen P. Morgan
Christian M. Morgan
Mary C. Morgan
Roechelle R. Morgan
Ruth R. Morgan
Jane B. Morgan
Alexis E. Morris
Angela D. Morris
Lindley A. Morris
Helen Morris
Jessica I. Morris
Juliane D. Morris
Mildred M. Morris
Shari V. Morris
Stephanie N. Morris
Tracy L. Morris
Emily M. Morrison
Jennifer M. Morrison
Monica R. Morrison
Constance L. Morrow
Deanne M. Mosley
Rajita I. Moss
Katie N. Moulds
Muriel O. Mounger
Virginia W. Mounger
Rebecca S. Moutoux
Janel B. Mudry
Angela W. Mueller
Randi P. Mueller
Gertrude L. Muench
Katherine D. Muldoon
Jennifer D. Mullins
Peggy G. Mullins

Rebecca W. Mullins
Wendy R. Mullins
Kamesha B. Mumford
Virginia T. Munford
Elise B. Munn
Samarria Y. Munnerlyn
Tami L. Munsch
Angela M. Munson
Margaret E. Murdock
Andrea L. Murff
Carole E. Murphey
Ginger Murphree
Heather E. Murphy
Heather E. Murray
Jessica E. Murray
Shawna A. Murrell
Gina M. Mushmeche
Jennifer L. Musselwhite
Margaret D. Myatt
Joan E. Myers
Joann T. Myers
Natosha E. Myers

N

Eleanor B. Nabors
Kimberly R. Nailor
A E. Namanny
Sherri Narro
Mary Anne S. Narron
Holly Nash
Katrell Nash
Margaret M. Nasif
Denita W. Neal
LeAnn W. Nealey
Stacy L. Neames
Natica C. Neely
Donna S. Negrotto
Pamela L. Nelson
Kathryn N. Nester
Alicia N. Netterville
Laura C. Nettles
Cheryn L. Netz
Teri D. Newcomb
Mallory L. Newlon
Amanda S. Newman
Charlene V. Newman
Crystal A. Newman
Dinetia H. Newman
Kathryn W. Newman
Ammie T. Nguyen
Jennifer F. Nicaud
Caren B. Nichol
Heather B. Nicholas
Heidi M. Nichols
Jennifer A. Nichols
Mary A. Nichols
Sara R. Nichols
Susan Nichols
Gail D. Nicholson
Tina L. Nicholson
Shantrell H. Nicks
Darnell L. Nicovich
Retha E. Niedecken
Emily K. Niezer
Amy D. Nisbett
Emily S. Nobile
Krissy C. Nobile
Carol S. Noblitt
Madeline L. Nolan
Julie S. Noone
Merrill K. Nordstrom
Lisa S. Nored
Nora M. Norman
Lisa A. Norris
Susan K. Norton
Angela Norwood

O

M E. Oakes
Kathleen S. O'Beirne
Alaine A. Obert

Sarah W. O'Callaghan
Elizabeth A. Odom
Katrina M H. Odom
Jennifer H. O'Donnell
Sally J. O'Flynn
Christie E. Ogden
Celestial R. Oglesby
Alexandra H. Oglesby
Lauren W. Ojha
Celeste G. O'Keeffe
Demetrica T. Olabintan
Colette Oldmixon
Lana A. Olson
Nancy A. Olson
Ellen D. O'Neal
Judge Staci A. O'Neal
Susan N. O'Neal
Amelia M. O'Neil
Briana A. O'Neil
Mary E. O'Neill
Harriett F. Oppenheim
Judi L. Oram
Sarah A. O'Reilly-Evans
Beth L. Orlansky
Amanda L. Orr
Amorya M. Orr
Laura I. Osborn
Tracy M. O'Steen
Patricia H. Oster
Laura C. Ostrem
Stephanie E. Otts, JD
Deborah H. Outlaw
Anna M. Outzen
Lisa T. Ouzts
Judith W. Overall
Lisa A. Overall
Sylvia S. Owen
Elizabeth J. Owens
Brittany D. Owens
Delia Y. Owens
Jerrolyn M. Owens
Joi L. Owens
Judge Denise Owens
Cecelia C. Oyola
Genevieve A. Ozark
Shannon L. Ozerden

P

Margaret L. Pace
Niki L. Pace
Jeannene T. Pacific
Geraldine H. Page
Mitzi D. Paige
Tiffany R. Paige
Catherine C. Paine-Snider
Jane V. Pak
Darla M. Palmer
Morgan J. Palmer
Rhoda H. Palmer
Lisa A. Papale
Kimberly M. Papania
Nicolette Parisi
Adrienne P. Parker
Anne M. Parker
Barbara B. Parker
Emily M. Parker
Kathy B. Parker
Rosemary P. Parker
Toni C. Parker
Nancy M. Parkes
Mary A. Parks
Melinda J. Parks
Dorothy C. Parr
Elizabeth H. Parrott
Erica L. Parsons
Janice H. Parsons
Kristin T. Parsons
Michelle C. Partridge
Songil Maxene S. Paschal
Ann Marie M. Pate
Robin E. Pate

Mital D. Patel
Megan M. Patrick
Hayley E. Patterson
Kate H. Patterson
Leigh H. Patterson
Lindsay C. Patterson
Melissa C. Patterson
Nancy A. Patterson
Stacy S. Patterson
Trhesa B. Patterson
Stephanie J. Patton
Laura F. Paulk
LaSheka T. Payne
Mary L. Payne
Ormonde L. Payne
Rachel R. Payne
Sasha L. Payne
Shirley Payne
Sandra F. Peaches
Lauren L. Peacock
Karen T. Peairs
Hermine M. Peel
Melinda L. Peevy
Anna R. Pegram
Tiffany R. Pendleton
Elizabeth R. Penn
Mary C. Pentecost
MaryAnna Penton
E F. Percy
Lisa B. Percy
Felecia Perkins
Martha L. Perkins
Takiyah H. Perkins
Jessica L. Perri
Francine J. Perry
Jane H. Perry
Mary J. Perry
Sue M. Perry
Tameka T. Perry
Kaye J. Persons
Caren M. Peters
Ceejaye S. Peters
Larkin H. Peters
Abigail M. Peterson
Judge Eleanor J. Peterson
Megan S. Peterson
Ellen L. Pfister
Tiffany K. Pharr
Kimberly D. Phifer
Donna R. Philip
Adrienne C. Phillips
Joy L. Phillips
Loraleigh C. Phillips
Sarah B. Phillips
Sonya D. Phillips
Tanya L. Phillips
Rebecca C. Phipps
Elizabeth M. Phipps
Laura B. Pickens
Marlena P. Pickering
Kaytie M. Pickett
Mary A. Pickett
Charlene R. Pierce
Cheryl K. Pierce
Jacqueline S. Pierce
Karla J. Pierce
Anna S. Pieschel
Amy K. Pietrowski
Susan G. Pinkston
Kellye R. Piro
Cynthia G. Pitesa
Leanna B. Pittard
Alison P. Pittman
Ashley W. Pittman
Mona T. Pittman
Rahmana Pittman
Anne E. Pitts
Sarah Ellen T. Pitts
Ashley J. Platt
Kathryn B. Platt
Jennifer B. Plummer

Janika D. Polk
Judge Gay Polk-Payton
Lilly J. Ponce
Dixie M. Pond
Justin R. Ponds
Beverly D. Poole
Katherine E. Poor
Morgan H. Poore
Laurie H. Porciello
Natalia V. Porsche
Claire M. Porter
Elizabeth L. Porter
Nebra E. Porter
Renee M. Porter
Samantha A. Porter
Evelyn T. Portie
Katherine M. Portner
Rosamond H. Posey
Linda O. Posner
Joan P. Potter
Christyn B. Potts
Courtney O. Powell
Dorothy A. Powell
Elizabeth M. Powell
Holly S. Powell
Alice E. Powers
Sara A. Powers
Anne D. Powers
Amanda L. Powers
Melissa A. Poynter-Powell
Ashley Pradel
Lauri H. Prather
Pamela Prather
Loren H. Pratt
Nancy L. Presley
Debra S. Press
Ana M. Price
Brandy F. Price
Cassandra P. Price
Cathleen I. Price
Elizabeth C. Price
Laura J. Price
Norma N. Price
Teri C. Price
Vanessa W. Price
Elizabeth C. Priester
Scherrie L. Prince
Elizabeth H. Pritchard
Karen D. Pritchard
Constance K. Pritchett
Amanda J. Proctor
Anna C. Puckett
Jessica T. Pulliam
Diane P. Pumphrey
Kimberly T. Purdie
Jacqueline L. Purnell
Tameko M. Purnell
Mary L. Purvis
Kimberly D. Putnam
Rachael E. Putnam
Susan S. Pylate

Q

Lydia M. Quarles
Amy J. Quezon
Caryn S. Quilter
Ashleigh L. Quinn
Michelle L. Quinn
Regina R. Quinn
Holli A. Quiroz

R

Tianna H. Raby
Kenya K. Rachal
Rosemary E. Ragsdale
Erin D. Rahaim
Amanda T. Rainey
Julie H. Ralph
Nora H. Rasco
Robin H. Rasmussen
Holly R. Ratcliff

Julie P. Ratliff
Pamela S. Ratliff
Emily S. Ratliff
Valerie H. Raupp
Liza L. Rawls
Beverly A. Ray
Jacqueline H. Ray
Cynthia A. Re
Apryl L. Ready
Kelsey R. Reckart
Kay S. Rector
LaToya M. Redd
Jennifer W. Redditt
Mona G. Reddy
Brenda T. Redfern
Shayla M. Reed
Simine B. Reed
Alecia Reed-Owens
Sarah C. Reese
Abbey A. Reeves
Kimberly B. Reeves
Lauren F. Reeves
Meghann D. Reeves
Glenda M. Regnart
Brittany E. Reid
Margaret A. Reid
Stephanie C. Reifers
Mary S. Reinhardt
Monica R. Rejaei
Amber S. Rembert
Kathryn A. Renik
Sheila V. Rennison
Ashley M. Rentz
Lisa A. Reppeto
Sarah M. Resavy
Melissa N. Reso
Adreain J. Reynolds
Leanna Reynolds
Adrianne C. Rhoads
Jessica L. Rice
Romaine L. Richards
LuJaclyn T. Richardson
Rachelle S. Richardson
Rhea A. Richardson
Patricia J. Richardson
Madeline Richmond
Melody J. Rickels
Candance L. Rickman
Lorrie K. Ridder
Karen W. Riddle
Kelly A. Riddle
Shauncey H. Ridgeway
Brittany B. Ridinger
Nina Rifkind
Lee W. Rikard
Katelyn A. Riley
Katherine B. Riley
Elizabeth L. Riley
Jennifer Riley-Collins
Sarah D. Rimes
Stephanie M. Rippee
Kathy A. Rito
Patricia A. Rives
Ellen P. Robb
Anna K. Robbins
Courtney L. Robbins
Debra M. Robbins
Carolyn F. Roberts
Holly R. Roberts
Leigh A. Roberts
Lindsay K. Roberts
Sara H. Roberts
Susan L. Roberts
Dianne L. Roberts
Aimee W. Robertson
Amy L. Robertson
April D. Robertson
Dana F. Robertson
Hawley R. Robertson
Ginger M. Robey
Lisa F. Robin

Claire K. Robinett
Abby G. Robinson
Bridget H. Robinson
Brittan W. Robinson
Charity S. Robinson
Helen K. Robinson
Lacy K. Robinson
Lindia P. Robinson
Amanda B. Robinson
Paheadra B. Robinson
Sylvie D. Robinson
Amber M. Robinson
Chanda L. Roby
Kyra D. Roby
Martha D. Roby
Elizabeth A. Roche
Elizabeth F. Rocquin
Catherine R. Rodgers
Erin S. Rodgers
Laura L. Rodgers
Patricia A. Rodgers
Sarah S. Rodriguez
Charliene Roemer
Donna N. Rogers
Jennifer A. Rogers
Jennifer M. Rogers
Stephanie V. Rogers
Charity J. Rohlfs
Danette C. Roland
Ora C. Roney
Marie E. Roper
Laura F. Rose
Kimberly W. Rosenberg
Lauren E. Rosenblatt
Kimberly S. Rosetti
DeShandra L. Ross
Fritzie T. Ross
Lisa M. Ross
Megan B. Ross
Jennifer S. Rossi
Sara M. Rossmanith
Sara L. Rosson
Kimber R. Roten
Celena D. Rouse
Sheri T. Rouse
Valerie M. Roussalis
Lanie R. Roussel
Victoria S. Rowe
Ann W. Rowland
Sherry Rowlett
Lakeita F. Rox-Love
Ann G. Roy
Diane B. Roy
Ellen V. Royal
Jackie L. Rozier
Lindsey E. Rubenstein
Candice L. Rucker
Norma C. Ruff
Brooke L. Ruffin
Sabrina B. Ruffin
Victoria H. Rundlett
Jodi B. Runger
Susan L. Runnels
Anna K. Rush
Jennifer G. Rush
H D. Rushing
Stevie F. Rushing
Terryl C. Rushing
Yumeka B. Rushing
Adrian O. Russell
Claudia C. Russell
Judge Carol J. Russell
Katherine K. Russell
Kathy S. Russell
Kristi A. Russell
Pepper A. Russell
Sara B. Russo
Erin E. Rutherford
Leigh A. Rutherford
Victoria P. Ryals
Alison T. Ryan

Amy F. Ryan

S

Mildred L. Sabbatini
Leslie R. Sadler
Latasha T. Sago
Regina S. Saint Jour
Lamanda C. Sakalarios
Janeah R. Sakalaukus
Corina E. Salazar
Erin D. Saltaformaggio
Deanne B. Saltzman
Stacy D. Saltzman
Jennifer E. Salvo
Angela L. Sampson
Joanne S. Samson
Judge Katharine M. Samson
M T. Sandahl
Aisha A. Sanders
Andrea A. Sanders
Anne C. Sanders
Judge Betty W. Sanders
Judge Lillie B. Sanders
Judge Watosa M. Sanders
Lyndsay F. Sanders
Melinda L. Sanders
Neysha Sanders
Shelia L. Sanders
Jennifer E. Sanford
Gabriella Sang
Susan Sanich
Emmagene Sansing
Jeannie H. Sansing
Cynthia M. Sarthou
Rebecca B. Sartor
Carolyn C. Satcher
Ryanne D. Saucier
Lucy E. Savorgnan
Natalya T. Savransky
Elizabeth I. Sawyer
Karen K. Sawyer
Dana G. Sbravati
Susan M. Scaggs
Elizabeth B. Schaffenburg
Cynthia L. Schemel
Ana B. Schepens
Ashley B. Schepens
Lauren P. Schick
Judge Jennifer T. Schloegel
Karen B. Schneller
Sara M. Schock
Shelly W. Schools
Amanda M. Schwartz
Berkley E. Schwarz
Jennifer H. Scott
Leslie Scott
Linda A. Scott
Melissa S. Scott
Tina Scott
Laura G. Scruggs
Tara B. Scruggs
Ramona Seabron-Williams
Jaleesa R. Seals
Christina M. Seanor
Charli C. Searcy
Crystal U. Secoy
Lynn J. Segars
Tracey B. Seghini
Jennifer L. Selby
Janet R. Self
Marjorie S. Self
Della B. Sellers
Madora M. Sellers
Melinda E. Sellers
Sebie G. Sellers
Cristina M. Sequeira
Jeanette Seraile-Riggins
Barbara R. Serlin
Catherine C. Servati
Shelly R. Sessions
Courtney W. Severino

Amanda B. Seymour
Jennifer L. Shackelford
Brandi S. Shafer
Eileen N. Shaffer
Delilah A. Shandy
Avery C. Shannon
Nichon Shannon
Susan M. Shanor
Brinkley D. Shappley-Spillers
Miranda B. Shaughnessy
Amber G. Shaw
Lori W. Shaw
Mary B. Shaw
Tammy L. Shaw
Jane Shaw-Jackson
Alethea M. Shaw-Milton
Haidee L O. Sheffield
Judge S. Rhea H. Sheldon
Sandra M. Shelson
Emily V. Shelton
Wendy M. Shelton
Elaine Sheng
JoAnne N. Shepherd
Amber C. Sheppard
Felisha A. Sheppard
Dorinda J. Shiel
Frances R. Shields
Katherine W. Shireman
Elizabeth B. Shirley
Hannah Shirley
Kathryn B. Shoalmire
Tracy A. Shoemaker
Lillous A. Shoemaker
Daniella M. Shorter
Kaylyn B. Shoultz
Susan A. Shubert
Angelique A. Shupe
Sonia L. Shurden
Traci B. Shuttz
Judge Sharon W. Sigalas
Jennifer W. Signs
Kimberly R. Silas
Alyssa W. Silberman
Rita N. Silin
Pamela R. Sills
Daphne L. Silverman
Jenna K. Simmons
Lindsey T. Simmons
Winnie Sue H. Simmons
Kimberly A. Simoes
Angela F. Simpkins
Allison C. Simpson
Bobbie M. Simpson
Kristine L. Simpson
Patricia M. Simpson
Sondra L. Simpson
Dana P. Sims
Denise T. Sims
Janet L. Sims
Jennifer D. Sims
Lanesha L. Sims
Patricia B. Sims
Stacey L. Sims
Tina G. Singletary
Carole-Anne E. Sistrunk
Pamela J. Skelton
Grace H. Skertich
Dara A. Skinner
Jennifer J. Skipper
Pamela D. Slate
Vicki R. Slater
Constance Slaughter-Harvey
Lindsay E. Slawson
La'Toyia J. Slay
Alida L. Slipher
G R. Sloan
Allison J. Slusher
Mary M. Smalley
Judge Sheila H. Smallwood
Kathleen L. Smiley
Allison W. Smith

Amanda W. Smith
Amelia Y. Smith
Amelia G. Smith
Amy G. Smith
Angela C. Smith
Dorothy H. Smith
Bonnie B. Smith
Caitlin M. Smith
Caroline B. Smith
Chaka D. Smith
Christa C. Smith
Christina J. Smith
Connie M. Smith
Courtney A. Smith
Dawn Smith
Dellwyn K. Smith
Denita N. Smith
Diane M. Smith
Donna S. Smith
Dorissa S. Smith
Evelyn R. Smith
Felicia Smith
Gina K. Smith
Jacqueline L. Smith
Jamie H. Smith
Jenna B. Smith
Jennifer L. Smith
Jovaunda L. Smith
Karen Z. Smith
Kathy K. Smith
Kelly H. Smith
Kendall S. Smith
Kimberly E. Smith
Lacey D. Smith
Lea Ann Smith
Leah R. Smith
Lindsay J. Smith
Lindsey M. Smith
Lori M. Smith
Magdalene L. Smith
Margaret Z. Smith
Meaghan J. Smith
Melanie A. Smith
Michelle M. Smith
Nikki L. Smith
Paige B. Smith
Margaret D. Smith
Patricia P. Smith
Susan C. Smith
Tammy Smith
Tiffany B. Smith
Tiffany H. Smith
Latisha C. Smith
Bethany C. Smith
Heather L. Smith
Wendy G. Smith
Elizabeth M. Smitherman
Laura E. Smittick
Mary M. Smythe
Katherine B. Snell
Courtney M. Snodgrass
Evelyn E. Snow
Sarah L. Snow
Angela N. Snyder
Mary F. Snyder
Lindsey M. Soboul
Lori M. Solinger
Kathy D. Sones
Lauren Sonnier
Brandi E. Soper
Nancy J. Sorensen
Lynn H. Sorey
Jennifer Dianne N. Soto
Nichole E. Soule
Anna M. South
Judge Marcie T. Southerland
Jessica B. Spade
Catherine S. Spann
Christy M. Sparks
Judith B. Sparling
Barbara F. Spayde

Kathryn D. Spear
Reagan J. Spears
Stacey G. Spears
Lea H. Speed
Tiffany E. Speegle
Cynthia H. Speetjens
Amarette H. Speights
Elizabeth J. Spell
Amanda L. Spencer
Jessica D. Spencer
Karen H. Spencer
Olivia Spencer
Sharon A. Spencer
Maureen B. Speyerer
Amy P. Spicer
Frances L. Spinelli
Angela Spivey
Angela S. Spragins
LuAnn B. Springer
Sarah P. Springer
India M. Sprinkle
Rachel A. Sprinkle
Patricia W. Sproat
Lynn Spruill
Amy L. St Pe
Marsha W. Stacey
Dawn E. Stacy
Casey C. Stafford
Marie K. Stagg
Lane W. Staines
Claire F. Stamm
Alice T. Stamps
Anita M. Stamps
Robin D. Stanard
Lisa N. Stanley
Amanda L. Stansberry
Amy H. Stanton
Kelly L. Staples
Sarah S. Starns
Sandra Stasher
Barbara J. Steadman
Susan K. Steadman
Anna C. Steel
Tere R. Steel
Patta A. Steele
Suzanne B. Steele
Nancy E. Steen
Tracy J. Steen
Susan L. Steffey
Martha Stegall
Amelia K. Steindorff
Alison R. Steiner
Kate C. Steiner
Yvette L. Stelly
Abigail A. Stephens
Carole W. Stephens
Rebekah J. Stephens
William M. Stephens
Frances S. Stephenson
Tabatha M. Stern
Belinda J. Stevens
Lisa J. Stevens
Mary E. Stevens
Sarah C. Stevens
Robin L. Steward
Amber L. Stewart
Cynthia A. Stewart
Denise Stewart
Kaila G. Stewart
Kandace C. Stewart
Margaret A. Stewart
Melanie M. Stewart
Melinda J. Stewart
Lauran G. Stimac
Kelly D. Stimpson
Nance F. Stokes
Marcia Stokes Johnson
Keisha L. Stokes-Hough
Carol C. Stone
Emmy H. Stone
Whitney M. Stone

Dawn L. Stough
Stacey P. Stracener
Stacey L. Strain
Eleni V. Stratigeas
Frances M. Strayham
Cynthia L. Street
Jennifer L. Street
Mallory M. Street
Amy E. Strickland
Otisa C. Strickland
Edna J. Stringer
Kelly H. Stringer
Lindsey H. Stringer
Mariah K. Stringer
Leoghain A. Strnad
Anna G. Stroble
Saundra B. Strong
Nancy H. Stuart
Ashley N. Stubbs
Jennifer M. Studebaker
Dawn E. Stuntz
Syria Sturdivant
Margaret E. Stutts
Christiana S. Sugg
Anna W. Sukmann
Amber D. Sullivan
Beth A. Sullivan
Carla C. Sullivan
Catherine C. Sullivan
Cheryl C. Sullivan
Keleigh R. Sullivan
Lauren R. Sullivan
Lindsey M. Sullivan
Nicole W. Sullivan
Wesla A. Sullivan
Ashley L. Sulser
Michelle M. Sultan
Amanda D. Summerlin
Jennifer M. Summers
Emily R. Sumrall
Katherine B. Sumrall
Katharine M. Surkin
Lindsey E. Surratt
Kari L. Sutherland
Kimberly A. Sutherland
Theresa S. Sutherland
Neva E. Swan
Debra L. Swank
Helen E. Swartzfager
Kristin J. Swearengen
Kimberly S. Sweeney
Susanna L. Sweeney-Gates
Angela D. Swilley
Hannah E. Swoope

T

Leigh-Ann Tabor
Sarah M. Tadlock
Amanda P. Tailyour
Kiara A. Taite
Pamela D. Taplin-Williams
Patti S. Tarkington
Bethany A. Tarpley
G G. Tart
Grace H I. Tate
Laura E. Tate
Michelle Tate
Christine B. Tatum
Gwennetta L. Tatum
Jimmie J. Tatum
Alva P. Taylor
Amy K. Taylor
Ann C. Taylor
Bevin W. Taylor
Brittany S. Taylor
Carolyn B. Taylor
Kathryn S. Taylor
Linda B. Taylor
Michele E. Taylor
Rebecca G. Taylor
Rebecca C. Taylor

Robin B. Taylor
Shakita L. Taylor
Shirley A. Taylor
Stephanie A. Taylor
Susan D. Taylor
Vikki J. Taylor
Semoune L. Taylor
Robyn K. Teague
Laura H. Tedder
Kathy B. Tennison
Judge Toni W. Terrett
Jennifer C. Terry
Julia H. Terry
Katharine D. Terry
Jacqueline E. Thach
Sammye S. Tharp
Carolyn A. Thayer
Sharon P. Thibodeaux
Lee A. Thigpen
Aileen S. Thomas
Alison F. Thomas
Ashley B. Thomas
Bridgette T. Thomas
Aelicia L. Thomas
Elizabeth E. Thomas
Elizabeth C. Thomas
Eugenia S. Thomas
Hon. Gwendolyn J. Thomas
Jessica M. Thomas
Martha R. Thomas
Melanie K. Thomas
Nancy D. Thomas
Rhonda J. Thomas
Rina R. Thomas
Sumeka C. Thomas
Ashley B. Thompson
Flora L. Thompson
Gail P. Thompson
Linda A. Thompson
Luanne S. Thompson
Lynn P. Thompson
Lynn W. Thompson
Ranie T. Thompson
Rebecca S. Thompson
Tasha B. Thompson
Wendy K. Thompson
Brittney P. Thompson
Brett B. Thompson-May
Rebecca A. Thornhill
Megan S. Thornton
Peggy L. Thornton
Tracey T. Thrash
Whitney M. Thrasher
Carol F. Thweatt
Teresa B. Tiller
Regina E. Tillman
Megan E. Timbs
Linda T. Timpson
Carole L. Tingle
Leigh A. Tingle
Stephanie R. Tippit
Senith C. Tipton
Moneshia N. Tisdale
Latricia S. Tisdale
Betty R. Todd
Bridget R. Todd
Karen Todd
Cynthia L. Tolbert
Amanda J. Tollison
Nina S. Tollison
Amy S. Tolliver
Stephanie C. Tomlinson
Gina B. Tompkins
Heather M. Toney
Kenitta F. Toole
Amy L. Topik
Lindsey A. Topp
Vivian B. Toussaint
E C. Towles
Christinia C. Townsend
Patricia L. Trantham

G Kay L. Trapp
Amy L. Travis
Angela L. Trawick
Amanda P. Traxler
Elizabeth B. Treadway
Kathleen F. Treadwell
Angela K. Trehan
Karen E. Trevathan
Regina Triplett
Deborah R. Trotter
DeeAnn R. Truelove
Ethel Truly
Katherine L. Trundt
Olivia Y. Truong
Brooke M. Trusty
Susan R. Tsimortos
Jane E. Tucker
Marisol F. Tucker
Melinda M. Tucker
Sherrie G. Tucker
Lucy E. Tufts
Lindsey M. Turk
Ellie F. Turnage
Amanda S. Turner
Anne L. Turner
Anne M. Turner
Barbara J. Turner
Carol B. Turner
Dorian E. Turner
Emily W. Turner
Freda M. Turner
Kay F. Turner
Kimberly P. Turner
Lee A. Turner
Marissa S. Turner
Mary J. Turner
Paulette M. Turner
Angela Turner Ford
Angela D. Turner-Kimbrough
Tiffany L. Tyler
Vicki R. Tyler
Leilani L. Tynes
Treasure R. Tyson

U

Kirsten K. Ullman
Dorothy J. Ulmer
Catherine A. Umberger
Catherine W. Underwood
Caroline M. Upchurch
Jennifer A. Urban
Amanda M. Urbanek
Brooke Usher
Lisa M. Usry
Honey B. Ussery

V

Rebecca M. Valentine
Kathlyn R. Van Buskirk
Katie R. Van Camp
Clara L. Van Horn
Kathryn K. Van Namen
Michelle W. Van Norman
Mary W. Van Slyke
Kathy B. van Zutphen
Alison T. Vance
Bobby T. Vance
Margaret M. VanHook
Melanie T. Vardaman
Terre M. Vardaman
Michelle R. Varnado
Lindsay E. Varnadoe
Jean A S. Vaughan
Allyson L. Vaughn
Dixie L. Vaughn
Jessica B. Vaughn
Anne P. Veazey
Sabrina C. Vickers
Marta E. Villanea
Rebecca S. Vinocur
Margie C. Virden

Judge Jane M. Virden
Jamila Virgil
Tana N. Vollendorf
Valera J. Vollor

W

Marni L. von Wilpert
Carolyn Y. Voyles
Tammy M. Voynik
Amanda C. Waddell
Emma N. Waddell
Cherie R. Wade
Elizabeth H. Wade
Rose Marie Wade
Vangela M. Wade
Heather P. Wagner
Mary L. Wagner
Rachel P. Waide
Michelle C. Waits
Cheryl G. Waldron
Locke H. Waldrop
Betty L M. Walker
Carol A. Walker
Caroline D. Walker
Gale L. Walker
Kelly C. Walker
Kimberly C. Walker
Krystal D. Walker
Liem A. Walker
Madeline R. Walker
Melissa C. Walker
Molly M. Walker
Stephanie W. Walker
Tara B. Walker
Khiedrae M. Walker
Lynn C. Wall
Mary H. Wall
Barbara C. Wallace
Brie D. Wallace
Caroline F. Wallace
Cynthia J. Wallace
Katie L. Wallace
Patricia A. Wallace
Deborah W. Waller
Consuelo W. Walley
Maretta M. Walley
Tracy A. Walley
Sandra D. Wallis
Alma Walls
Tracy B. Walsh
Cassandra B. Walter
Lesley C. Walters
Megan C. Walters
Tracey S. Walters
Brantley E. Walton
Marita P. Walton
Rebecca C. Wanee
Shalon L. Wansley
Betty L. Ward
Lauren E. Ward
Heather S. Ware
Kayla F. Ware
Zandrea K. Ware
Iesha L. Warmack
Anne S. Warren
Carol Ann S. Warren
Jane B. Warren
Lavone R. Warren
Leanne S. Warren
Lora G. Warren
Lydia C. Warren
Vera S. Warthen
Emily A. Warwick
Christy F. Washington
Edwina T. Washington
Kimberly J. Washington
Lorin R. Washington
Shaunte D. Washington
Victoria V. Washington
Jane E. Wasson
Twyla J. Waters

Julie K. Waterstone
Nakesha M. Watkins
Virginia L. Watkins
Anna H. Watson
Camilla E. Watson
Shellee D. Watson
Lindsey O. Watson
Dunbar D. Watt
Lindsay G. Watts
Jane S. Waugh
Samantha D. Weathersbee
Judge Jane R. Weathersby
Virginia T. Weaver
Lisa M. Weaver
Abigail J. Webb
Rachael H. Webb
Tanya E. Webber
Wilma F. Webber-Colbert
Cheryl A. Webster
Emily C. Webster
Keishunna R. Webster
Elizabeth A. Weeks
Christie R. Weidemann
Hannah C. Weiland
Colleen S. Welch
Crystal L. Welch
Elizabeth M. Welch
Jayne M. Welch
Laura Welikson
Amanda S. Wells
Julie J. Wells
Porter H. Wells
Ophelia R. Wells
Jennifer L. Welsh
Ginger T. Wentz
Helen C. Werby
Sue A. Werre
Pamela Wescovich Dill
Denise C. Wesley
Vicki Wesson
Christina D. West
Pamela M. West
Plezetta M. West
Tanya S. West
Judge Latrice Westbrooks
Ginger Weston
Helen Wetherbee
T. M. Whalen
Candace C. Wheeler

LaTrish C. Wheeler
Julia T. Whisenant
Tara L. Whitaker
Angelique C. White
M Christine C. White
Frankie W. White
Jillian L. White
Judith L. White
Kira Z. White
Leigh T. White
Madeline R. White
Maurie L. White
Ruby White
Sara H. White
Taylor O. White
Ashlea M. White
Patricia B. Whiteaker
Emilie F. Whitehead
Kenosha K. Whitehead
Judge Carol L. White-Richard
Mary M. Whitfield
Ruth B. Whitfield
Onetta S. Whitley
Christine B. Whitman
Allie T. Whitten
Amy D. Whitten
Ashley N. Wicks
Felice D. Wicks
Marie E. Wicks
Judith M. Wiener
Bridgette W. Wiggins
Holly B. Wiggs
Rebecca L. Wiggs
Jane M. Wilbourn
Caitlin E. Wilcox
Cheryl L. Wild-Don de'Ville
Tameka L. Wilder
Kendall H. Wiley
Shannon L. Wiley
Kay L. Wilkerson
Heather J. Wilkins
Jennifer P. Wilkins
Dian B. Willhoite
Angela D. Williams
Angela C. Williams
Annette Williams
Azande W. Williams
Becky Jo H. Williams
Christin B. Williams

Claire D. Williams
Courtney M. Williams
Deborah M. Williams
Elise V. Williams
Ingrid D. Williams
Joyce S. Williams
Joyce H. Williams
Julia G. Williams
Kelly G. Williams
Kelly M. Williams
Kristen W. Williams
Lauren V. Williams
Lauren C. Williams
Laurie R. Williams
Lyneille C. Williams
Margaret H. Williams
Mary C. Williams
Melissa D. Williams
Peggy H. Williams
Elizabeth P. Williams
Patricia R. Williams
Princess Williams
Priscilla K. Williams
Seirra S. Williams
Shannon H. Williams
Catherine M. Williams
Suneisha L. Williams
Susan B. Williams
Tori E. Williams
Trena M. Williams
Louwlynn V. Williams
Vicky F. Williams
Wanda A. Williams
Angela G. Williams
LaJuanda S. Williams-Griffin
Ann A. Williamson
Ann B. Williamson
Candace L. Williamson
Elizabeth W. Williamson
Mary K. Williamson
Sarah A. Williamson
Demetrice Williams-Wells
Miranda L. Williford
Amelia S. Willis
Patricia H. Willis
Robbie E. Willis
Megan C. Willoughby
Elizabeth B. Wilsner
Cindy P. Wilson

Courtney P. Wilson
Erica J. Wilson
Feleica L. Wilson
Jillian H. Wilson
Sherry J. Wilson
Judge Marie Wilson
Judge Celeste E. Wilson
Juliette V. Wilson
Kathi C. Wilson
Malissa Wilson
Rebecca T. Wilson
Sarah E. Wilson
Virginia B. Wilson
Wendi K. Wilson
Wendy S. Wilson
Jennings C. Wilson
Jennifer Wilson-Harvey
Tiffany A. Winchester
Sarah B. Windham
Deana P. Windham
Marion R. Windham
Tori L. Winfield
Tess Winkler
Allyson L. Winter
Anne V. Winter
Sidra P. Winter
Susan O. Winters
Mary A. Winzerling
Judge Patricia D. Wisc
Michelle M. Wise
Suzanne S. Wise
Lindsey S. Wiseman
Chereka L. Witherspoon White
Candace P. Witt
Sharon A. Witty
Lori A. Wolff
Rebecca L. Woltjer
Andrea B. Womack
Kristina A. Woo
Stephanie B. Wood
Vicki S. Wood
Laina D. Woodard
Stephanie S. Woodard
Cynthia C. Woodington
Ann S. Woodliff
Amanda M. Woodruff
Elizabeth K. Woodruff
Laura M. Woodruff
Amy M. Woods

Mary J. Woods
Martha W. Woodward
Ellie B. Word
Allison A. Worley
Diana L. Worthy-Nash
Carmen Wright
Donna H. Wright
Lydia A. Wright
Rachel H. Wright
Rebecca T. Wright
Jaklyn Wrigley
Sunrui Wu
Paloma Wu
Adolyn C. Wyatt
Camala C. Wyatt
Katherine L. Wyly
Terese T. Wyly
Elizabeth L. Wynn

Y

Emily M. Yancey
Miranda D. Yancey
Paula S. Yancey
Jennifer W. Yarborough
Rachel P. Yarborough
Shanda M. Yates
Tiffany A. Yates
Frances P. Yeatts
Reca R. Youell
Jennifer M. Young
Karen J. Young
Lora F. Young
Tobi M. Young
Rebecca A. Younger

Z

Susan G. Zachos
Andrea S. Zanca
Haley L. Zelenka
Patricia A. Zielke
Gretchen L. Zmitrovich
Brenda V. Znachko
Stacie E. Zorn
Rebecca A. Zotti
Laura M. Zouein